Mentoring Children and Adolescents

A Guide to the Issues

Maureen A. Buckley and Sandra Hundley Zimmermann

Contemporary Youth Issues
Richard M. Lerner, Series Editor

Westport, Connecticut
London

Library of Congress Cataloging-in-Publication Data

Buckley, Maureen A., 1964–
    Mentoring children and adolescents : a guide to the issues / Maureen A. Buckley and Sandra Hundley Zimmermann.
       p. cm. — (Contemporary youth issues)
    Includes bibliographical references and index.
    ISBN 0-275-97975-X (alk. paper)
    1. Children—Counseling of. 2. Teenagers—Counseling of. 3. Mentoring. I. Zimmermann, Sandra H., 1944– II. Title. III. Series.
    BF637.C6B8 2003
    371.102—dc21   2002044997

British Library Cataloguing in Publication Data is available.

Library of Congress Catalog Card Number: 2002044997

ISBN: 0-275-97975–X

First published in 2003

Praeger Publishers, 88 Post Road West, Westport, CT 06881
An imprint of Greenwood Publishing Group, Inc.
www.praeger.com

Printed in the United States of America

The paper used in this book complies with the Permanent Paper Standard issued by the National Information Standards Organization (Z39.48–1984).

10 9 8 7 6 5 4 3 2 1

Mentoring Children and Adolescents

Contents

vi   **Contents**

Series Foreword

Contemporary Youth Issues is a series of volumes that provides new and important educational materials for middle schools, high schools, public libraries, and the youth and adults involved in these institutions. Volumes in the series offer accessible information about the nature of the issues facing contemporary youth (children in the first two decades of life), parents, and youth-serving professionals—for example, teachers, practitioners, and governmental and nongovernmental organization personnel.

Both the challenges to healthy development confronting contemporary youth and the assets or strengths of adolescents and of the communities that contribute to their positive development are represented. Each book in the series reviews current knowledge about these challenges and/or assets, directs youth and adults to current community resources available to address challenges or enhance assets, and discusses key issues of policy and program design pertinent to improving the lives of the diverse youth of the United States and the world.

THE CONCEPT OF THE SERIES

Childhood and adolescence are periods within the life span when most of a person's biological, cognitive, psychological, and social characteristics are changing from what is present at birth to what is considered adult-like. For children and adolescents, and for the parents, friends, and teachers who support and nurture them, the first two decades of life are a time of dramatic challenge requiring adjustment to changes in the self, in the family, and in the peer group. In contemporary Western society, youth experience institutional changes as well. Infants and young children leave the home for preschool and then elementary school. Among young adolescents, there is a change in school setting, typically involving a transition from elementary school to either junior high school or middle school; and in late adolescence, there is a transition from high school to the worlds of work, university, or childrearing.

Given the changes and challenges of the first two decades—especially now when issues of youth population growth; insufficient economic, energy, educational, and employment resources; inequalities of opportunity; and violence and war affect hundreds of millions of young people a year—childhood and adolescence are periods replete with the possibilities of developmental problems. Indeed, because of the strong connection (correlation) that exists among the various problems of youth, and as a consequence of the high rates of these problems, the combined challenge to healthy child and adolescent development exists today at historically unprecedented levels.

As well, however, childhood and adolescence are periods wherein there is a great potential for positive and healthy behavior and development. Children and adolescents may possess considerable physical, psychological, and interpersonal abilities. These strengths may be coupled with the assets provided by friends supporting healthy choices, by parents providing authoritative guidance, and by caregivers, teachers, and communities creating opportunities for positive contributions and leadership. When the individual and ecological strengths, or assets, of youth align, developmental thriving can result. The possession of developmental assets can result in youth who, instead of possessing a set of problem behaviors (associated with unsafe sex, substance use, crime, violence, educational failure, poor health, and poverty), are marked by competence, confidence, character, connection, and caring/compassion.

Accordingly, this series is aimed at issues pertinent both to the challenges to and the opportunities for healthy development among contemporary youth, and will present both the problems and positive potential of youth. In each volume in this series, young people and the adults charged with promoting their healthy development are provided with:

1. the key concepts and substantive issues pertinent to each issue of concern in a given volume in the series;

2. the important events in the development of the issue, of knowledge about it, and of policies and programs pertinent to it;

3. short biographical sketches of key people who have worked
   and/or are working to address the issue;

4. contemporary data pertinent to the incidence, impact, or developmental course of the issue;

5. the key organizations, associations, and national and international governmental and nongovernmental organizations
   addressing the issue;

6. key annotated print references pertinent to the issue;

7. key annotated nonprint resources (e.g., CD ROMs, training
   programs) pertinent to the issue; and

8. a glossary of key terms pertinent to the issue.

Each book in the series also includes a name and subject index.

Across the volumes in the series, the scholarship that is presented
focuses on the advances of the last several decades in the medical, biological, and social scientific study of childhood and adolescence, and in
the corresponding advances made by youth-serving professionals and
practitioners in the design, delivery, and evaluation of programs that are
effective not only in preventing youth problems but, in turn, in promoting the positive development of young people. In short, each volume in
the series integratively presents the best "basic" and "applied" information currently available about the physical, psychological, behavioral,
social, and cultural dimensions of a key contemporary issue pertinent to
the adolescent period.

All volumes inform youth and their adult caregivers about the rich-
ness, challenges, and positive potentials of this dynamic developmental
period. The volumes illustrate the diversity of child and adolescent life
found across different physical, behavioral, racial, ethnic, religious,
national, and cultural characteristics; emphasize the numerous (diverse)
life paths that may result in positive, healthy development; present the
key social relationships (e.g., involving peer groups, siblings, parents,
members of the extended family, teachers, or mentors) and institutional
contexts (e.g., schools, community organizations, faith institutions, and
the workplace) that influence the development of today's youth; and discuss and evaluate the policies and programs useful for alleviating problems, for preventing problems, and for promoting positive and healthy
development among contemporary youth.

Preface

While a variety of literature has been devoted to mentoring in general and to adult-adult workplace mentoring in particular, this book is concerned exclusively with the mentoring of children and youth. *Mentoring Children and Adolescents: A Guide to the Issues* presents comprehensive information regarding youth mentoring and highlights how the formation of a caring relationship between a young person (referred to alternately in this volume as a mentee or protégé) and an adult (referred to as a mentor) fosters positive development and resilience for the mentee.

PURPOSE

The purpose of this book is to offer individuals interested in youth mentoring with useful information regarding:

- The definition of mentoring
- The impact of mentoring on the development of youth
- Variations in mentoring relationships
- Types of mentoring programs
- What mentoring can do
- Limitations of mentoring
- Characteristics of effective programs
- Implementation of mentor programs

- Developing and maintaining mentoring relationships
- Biographical sketches of key individuals associated with mentoring
- Key mentoring initiatives, foundations, and organizations
- Key print resources for mentoring
- Key nonprint mentoring resources
- Glossary of key mentoring terms

The information in this volume is particularly useful for:

- Directors of volunteer programs
- Established mentoring programs
- Foundations seeking funding avenues
- Founding organizations seeking new funding outlets
- Individuals who care about youth and youth issues
- Leaders of youth groups
- New mentoring programs
- School personnel
- Students and adults researching the topic of mentoring

ORGANIZATION OF THIS VOLUME

The first part (chapters 1 through 4) provides an overview of mentoring, as well as practical information on mentoring programs. Chapter 1 explores the concept of mentoring and places mentoring in its historical and social context. It also is a source for concise information, including: a description of mentoring, mentoring and youth development, variations in mentoring relationships, and types of mentoring programs. Chapter 2 provides information relevant to mentoring program development and maintenance. Chapter 3 offers a glimpse of key figures in the mentoring movement, as well as information on model mentoring programs. Chapter 4 presents mentoring-related data, including information on the benefits and limitations of mentoring.

The second part (remaining chapters) serves as a resource guide for the mentor, as well as for the protégé and for the mentor program innovator/manager. Chapter 5 covers national, international, and state mentoring-related agencies and organizations. Chapter 6 offers a variety of print and nonprint resources. Chapter 7 consists of a timeline of key dates in the mentoring movement. The appendixes offer mentoring resources.

1

A Window on Mentoring

Mentors not only touch someone's life.... they have the potential to touch and change the life of the nation.

(*Newsweek*, 1999)

The concept of youth mentoring embraces ideals that serve the development of all youth, but particularly those growing up in challenging circumstances. The term "mentoring" is alleged to have its origin in Homer's *Odyssey*, when an older friend named Mentor cared for King Odysseus' son, Telemachus, while the king fought in the Trojan Wars. In leaving Telemachus in the care of Mentor, the king not only entrusted his child's safety to Mentor, but also his son's physical, emotional, and educational development.

This concept of enlisting a wise, trusted, nonfamilial adult to contribute to the education and nurturance of a young person continues to this day. Over the past several decades, mentoring has experienced a resurgence of interest as a vehicle for promoting healthy development in young people. For example, America's Promise (established in 1997), an initiative focused on making youth a national priority, calls for the mobilization of caring adults as critical tools in the effort to promote the building of character and competence in the nation's young people. As a result, mentoring programs have emerged in corporations, government agencies, and school districts, as well as in higher education. Many community organizations, businesses, and municipalities are developing and/or operating mentoring programs, either as stand-alone projects or as extensions of existing child and youth services. According to the Harvard Mentoring Project, 2.5 million young people in the United States currently engage in mentoring relationships.

When mentoring targets young people, the objective is typically to prepare them for effective adult living. Most children and adolescents would benefit from positive mentoring relationships, but young people labeled as "at-risk" or "vulnerable" are especially appropriate candidates for mentoring-related interventions. Mentoring also offers benefits to talented, motivated, and gifted youth, an often-overlooked group of students in need of support.

MENTORING DEFINED

Throughout history, mentoring has been variously defined and implemented. The classical model of a mentoring relationship emphasizes:

- achievement, such as in the encouragement and facilitation of the development of a career or vocation,
- nurturance, which typically conveys caring and support while imparting elements of positive character development, and
- generativity, which reflects the concept of intergenerational responsibility and the idea that elders/mentors transmit knowledge, values, and culture to the younger generation (Freedman, 1993).

Typically, any definition of mentoring includes the concept of a committed relationship between two people, one young or inexperienced (mentee or protégé) and the other possessing knowledge or experience (mentor). As the differences in knowledge and experience suggest, the mentor, by definition, possesses something that the protégé lacks. Thus, teaching, socializing, and role modeling are central aspects of the mentoring relationship. However, mentoring extends beyond the imparting of knowledge or skills. Unlike teaching or role modeling, which may occur without direct contact or emotional engagement, mentoring requires an *emotional connection*. Mentors and mentees possess a unique bond, created largely on the basis of the mentor's willingness to listen, to empathize, and to validate the young person's experience. The support, guidance, and friendship of the mentor widen the worldview of the mentee, potentially expanding the young person's sense of life roles and opportunities.

This is not to imply that the relationship is always without complication but, rather, to suggest that the mentor-mentee relationship requires an emotional investment by both parties in order to be effective. Mentor-mentee relationships lacking in emotional intensity prohibit the development of the attachment and support that are typically essential to the mentoring process. Indeed, it is likely that the benefits associated with mentoring depend on the creation of an emotional connection (Rhodes, 2002).

While the act of mentoring possesses many important affective elements common to a friendship, the mentor-protégé relationship is not merely about companionship or camaraderie as is commonly the case between friends. Mentoring differs from the traditional concept of friendship because a mentor relationship has a prestated purpose and because the relationship between the mentor and his or her protégé focuses on goals and challenges. Among the crucial differences is the expectation that, through the mentoring process, the protégé or mentee will master certain individual goals. Correspondingly, in order to assist the protégé in this process, the mentor must simultaneously provide both support and challenge. Often the security and encouragement offered by the mentor allow the protégé to take risks and explore new territory, thus enabling him or her to reach those preset mentoring goals.

While some mentoring relationships span decades, most mentoring is time-limited. The relationship may last a semester, a year, or five years, but eventually the relationship must change form if the goals of mentoring are being effectively pursued. With mentoring's emphasis on the transmission of knowledge, experience, and judgment, the mentoring process includes an understanding that the relationship is temporary, because, ultimately, it is anticipated that the protégé will achieve mastery, independence, and autonomy. That is, inherent in the notion of mentoring is the idea that the protégé will one day outgrow or develop beyond the initial goals of the mentoring relationship.

It is possible that the mentoring relationship will eventually grow into a friendship as the mentee reaches adult developmental stages in his or her life. At the very least, it is desirable that, when the mentoring relationship is finished, memories will endure of the special and helpful times spent together.

MENTORING PROMOTES YOUTH DEVELOPMENT

The specific reasons an individual child or youth would be a good candidate for a mentoring relationship may be as varied as the personality of the child himself or herself. Youth mentoring is typically undertaken to maximize youth development, helping children and adolescents to become healthy adults with a variety of productive options in their future. Typical mentoring goals might involve promoting life skills and/or improving the developmental outcomes of the protégé or mentee. The desired improvement or the healthy development for the mentee/protégé may be an immediate gain (i.e., improved academics or behavior), or the desired improvement may be a life-span enhancement such as career guidance, the development of social skills, or the improvement of decision-making abilities.

Overall, the value of mentoring resides in the central role that positive adult-child relationships play in healthy development. Human development occurs through social experiences. Research on fostering resiliency in at-risk children and adolescents consistently highlights the importance of adult-child relationships, including the important role of nonparent adults and extrafamilial sources of support. Our relationships with people who are important to us help determine our understanding of what we can expect from the world. As children interact with adults, they experience the sharing of knowledge, values, and culture. Children raised with responsive caregiving develop a sense of the world as a safe place in which they are acknowledged and their needs are met. As they mature, children and adolescents need the adults in their lives to provide care and protection. Children who, for a variety of reasons, do not experience responsive caregiving may come to believe that they are not valued and that they cannot count on others. When young people lack the protection that comes from relationships with supportive, nurturing adults who give them clear expectations regarding behavior, they may rely more heavily on other sources of influence, such as peers or the media.

Even with the solid foundation offered by nurturing adult-child relationships, young people in this country currently face a variety of challenges that make access to positive adult resources invaluable. Formidable hazards such as poverty, physical and sexual abuse, drug and alcohol abuse, family and community violence, inadequate health care, teenage parenthood, and failure to complete school pose significant barriers to positive youth development. How well a particular young person fares may depend on the unique combination of risk and protective influences encountered.

Compensatory relationships with people who care about them allow children to create a new, more positive understanding of their social world, and provide them with resources to draw on to combat developmental challenges. Research indicates that children who encounter and successfully overcome adversity possess the skills to make use of positive relationships, while maintaining an abiding belief that they are loved (Garbarino, 1999; Mrazek & Mrazek, 1987; Rutter, 1987; Werner & Smith, 1992). A young person's ability to engage in effective adult-child relationships as well as effective peer relationships is a crucial aspect of his or her overall well-being.

Despite convincing evidence that significant relationships with adults help youth overcome obstacles to healthy development, today's youth have access to far fewer adult resources than ever before. This means many youth may lack the emotional and physical support they need to develop in positive, healthy ways. Barriers to such relationships include age segregation, school budget crises, and the changing structure of family and community.

Historically, older adults fulfilled roles related to the nurturing and teaching of their own grandchildren and of other children as well. Unfortunately, age segregation in American society frequently isolates the elderly and denies children this important source of support. Similarly, numerous factors hinder children's access to their own parents. Many children live in families headed by a single parent. This may mean not only decreased contact with the noncustodial parent, but also more stress and strain on the custodial parent. For some young people, one or both parents are away from the home at work for 10 or more hours a day. In other situations in which children and adolescents have parents or guardians actually present at home, the life choices of these adults may not provide healthy role modeling. Some youth may be faced with gaps in their relationships with their parents due to differences of generation and culture. Others, though they come from homes in which the parents are working hard to provide a healthy environment, may still need that boost of someone "extra" in their lives to make them feel connected, capable, and cared about.

Another barrier to the development of adult-youth relationships and to formal mentoring programs pertains to declining financial resources in the schools. As schools struggle with budget cuts, the student-to-teacher and student-to-counselor ratio has increased. For example, in California schools in the year 2001, the school counselor-to-student ratio was one counselor to 945 students; in some California counties the student-to-counselor ratio was more than 3,000 students to one school counselor. In that same year, the ratio of school social workers to students was an alarming one social worker per 27,134 students. It is likely that this decrease in opportunities for supportive relationships in school relates to the state's serious drop-out issue, since a primary reason youth give for dropping out of school is the lack of connection to the school community and the feeling that nobody cares about them (Dondero, 1997; Smink, 1990).

Many young people, especially those living in communities where economic and interpersonal resources are scarce, have been deprived of a network of role models, support persons, and advocates that, in yester-year, helped them to make good decisions and develop healthy plans for the future. In neighborhoods plagued with significant community violence, social isolation often functions as a protective strategy against the dangers of the world outside the family home. Parents who are concerned with the safety of their children may take steps to keep them close to home, restricting their movement in the neighborhood. While this may protect youth from the dangers of neighborhood violence, it also limits their opportunities to interact with adults outside the family. School desegregation and the movement of middle-class families out of inner-city communities create a situation in which ethnically marginalized youth may experience diminished exposure to positive role models of the same ethnicity.

MENTORS PROVIDE IMPORTANT SUPPORT TO CHILDREN AND YOUTH

Mentors provide numerous important support structures and strategies for their mentees. These include:

• *Spiritual, Psychological, and Social Support:* Environmental protective factors that help at-risk youth overcome adversity include a secure emotional connection with a caregiver and social support from individuals in the wider community and extended family systems. These supplemental support persons provide nurturing and confirm the child's efforts to succeed. As such, strong mentoring bonds may provide youth with much-needed spiritual, psychological, and social anchors (Garbarino, 1999). For example, in the face of prior developmental challenges regarding relationships with adults, foster children are often able to form relationships with mentors and derive some benefit from these relationships (Rhodes, Haight, & Briggs, 1999). Good mentors naturally engage in many actions that go a long way toward helping mentees feel better about themselves, including listening, offering friendship and support, and engaging in a trusting relationship.

• *Supportive Connections with the Adult World:* The path by which youth in the United States become autonomous adults may be more difficult now than ever before. In our current society, there is a notable discontinuity between youth and adult roles. Youth still seek role models but may confuse a celebrity's status with that of a role model. Also, the so-called role models of today's youth, such as sports figures, may not provide meaningful examples of the roles young people will play in the adult world (Larson, 2000). Lack of relevant role models, along with isolation from relationships with adults in their communities, means that young people may reach adulthood with deficits in relationship skills and a lack of knowledge regarding adult occupations. For at-risk youth in particular, early learning in social relationships may limit their sense of potential adult roles. Minority youth, who grow up with an acute awareness of societal barriers to opportunities, may come to view certain life pathways as blocked. Traumatized youth often show a lack of future orientation, which limits their motivation to engage in activities that require delayed gratification and promote advancement toward long-term goals (Garbarino, 1999).

Mentoring relationships that include an interpersonal bond strong enough to allow the mentee or protégé to identify with the mentor may help fill the void created by a lack of positive role models. The presence of long-range goals helps determine life success, and mentors assist youth in exploring such goals (Lee & Cramond, 1999). The presence of meaningful adult relationships, particularly relationships with mentors, provides young people with credible role models that may significantly alter their beliefs about available opportunities (Rhodes & Davis, 1996). These adults also serve as models for how difficulties may be overcome (Werner, 1990). In fact, many individuals who faced a difficult or challenging childhood report that a mentor played a significant role in their ultimate success.

• *Transitional Support:* Mentors also play a role in helping young people make the sometimes difficult transition to adulthood. In adolescence, young people are charged with developing a sense of themselves apart from their families. While increasing their autonomy, they simultaneously examine where they fit in the larger world. This task involves revisiting prior developmental issues, including establishing trust and autonomy, taking initiative, and accepting responsibility for their goals and behavior. This transition is eased when adult mentors provide incremental advances that socialize youth into the roles and responsibilities of adulthood (Larson, 2000), as well as provide structure and supervision (Soucy & Larose, 2000). These activities include offering instruction on concrete career skills such as how to apply for a job, as well as general life skills such as budgeting. While encouraging a mentee's positive behavior, by attending a school concert or sporting event, for example, mentors provide positive reinforcement for participation and achievement.

A connection with a caring adult helps youth transition to adulthood by providing emotional support, motivation, and encouragement that includes high expectations, standards, and assistance with decision making and planning, along with access to resources (Roth, Brooks-Gunn, Murray, & Foster, 1998). Adolescence, in particular, is a time when youth are finding out where they fit into the world. As a significant adult who exists outside the youth's family, a mentor allows a young person to explore his or her identity as independent from the family (Roth et al., 1998).

Transitional life-skills mentoring, outlined by Mech and colleagues (Mech, Pryde, & Rycraft, 1995), also involves adult mentors aiding older adolescents in foster care (or other out-of-home placements) transition to independent living. For these youth, mentors serve as role models who provide support, guidance, and fellowship while facilitating the acquisition of independent living skills.

MENTORING HELPS A WIDE VARIETY OF YOUTH

Although every young person needs caring and supportive adults in his or her life, not every child will need a mentor. Those children and adolescents who do need that extra support come to the mentoring relationship through a variety of channels. A young person may seek out a mentoring relationship on his or her own, although typically adults— such as parents, school personnel, or representatives of a social service agency—will refer the young person. Most formal mentor programs require parental permission. However, young people frequently seek out and establish informal mentoring relationships, with or without their parents' knowledge or consent.

In a global sense, mentoring can benefit any young person *needing and seeking* extra support and guidance, as social support is key to human development. Young people whose support systems are particularly limited are excellent candidates for mentoring, especially those youth who do not have significant adults in their lives. Yet, the benefits of mentoring are not necessarily limited to improving outcomes for at-risk youth or young people in crisis. Mentoring also plays a preventative role in keeping children and adolescents who are not acutely at risk on a positive developmental path.

According to a 1998 survey conducted by the Commonwealth Fund, 8 out of 10 mentored youth had experienced one or more significant problems prior to being mentored (McLearn, Colasanto, & Schoen, 1998). Respondents to this survey indicated that the five most common difficulties experienced by mentored youth are (1) negative feelings about themselves, (2) poor relationships with family members, (3) poor grades, (4) associating with friends who are a negative influence, and (5) getting into trouble at school. Other common problem areas identified by the survey include substance abuse, skipping school, and getting into trouble outside of school. Many young mentees were described as coping with significant family issues. For example, almost half belonged to families struggling with financial problems. A similar number of young mentees belonged to single-parent families.

Mentoring programs exist for children coping with a myriad of obstacles, including poverty, parental substance abuse, exposure to violence, and teenage parenthood. While some programs broadly address these needs, other programs specialize in youth with one particular type of adversity, situation, or problem. The Big Brothers Big Sisters of America, for example, targets and provides services largely for youth in single-parent households. Additionally, a variety of mentoring programs focus on young people at risk for certain problematic developmental outcomes, such as dropping out of school, school failure, substance abuse, delinquency, pregnancy, or violence. Other mentoring programs identify and serve young people already on a course for success, such as gifted youth, helping them continue their momentum toward college or the world of work.

Although many young people may benefit from mentoring relationships, it is important to be aware of who is *not* the best candidate for mentoring. In order to successfully engage in the mentoring relationship, a child or adolescent needs some openness to the relationship and to the possibility of engaging in new experiences. Youth who do not want a mentor generally tend to have difficulty in the mentoring relationship. It is important not to force mentoring on youth indiscriminately. While some young people reach out to others for help, some prefer the route of self-sufficiency. One challenge in mentoring is identifying young people who project a sense that they don't need or want anybody, but who in reality do want such a connection. These young people may actually be masking trust or abandonment issues that prevent them from responding to needed intervention and support. Often, the role modeling of peers who are engaged in positive, successful mentoring relationships helps reluctant mentees to overcome their distrust of connecting with someone new.

Mentors also have ideas about what makes for a rewarding relationship. Mentors report wanting their mentees to trust them. The youth need motivation to follow through with commitments in the mentoring process. Mentors are understandably frustrated with mentees who fail to keep appointments or return phone calls.

While it is true that many children and adolescents could benefit from a caring relationship with a mentor, the harsh reality is that in most communities there are many more young people urgently needing mentors than there are mentors to match with them. According to the Harvard Mentoring Project, of the 17 million at-risk children in the United States, only 2.5 million served are currently engaged in a mentoring relationship. Reglin (1998, pp. 74–75) suggests giving priority to students who exhibit one or more of the following characteristics:

- One-parent family, with little or no support
- No parents, being raised by someone else with little or no support
- Intact family with history of drug or alcohol abuse
- Poor attendance at school
- High level of hostility
- Frequent trips to the principal's office
- Numerous detentions, suspensions, or expulsions
- Poor attitude
- Lack of self-esteem
- Inability to take risks

MENTORING RELATIONSHIPS TAKE DIFFERENT FORMS

Mentoring is not a unified concept and it takes a variety of forms. Just as an understanding of what constitutes successful youth development changes with societal trends, so do views of the nature of the mentoring relationship. Different types of mentoring programs are needed in different areas and for different populations. This calls for variations in the roles of mentors, the intensity of the mentoring relationship, and the desired outcomes.

The following are typical variations of mentoring that can be found throughout the mentor-mentee arena. These differences correspond to various dimensions such as the formality of the relationship, the focus of the program, the age and experiences of the mentor, and the particular structure of the mentoring program.

Natural Mentoring versus Formal Mentoring

Despite popular perceptions that young people are alienated from their parents and families, parents continue to rate as the most significant adults in the lives of adolescents, followed by other adult relatives (Galbo, 1986). Additionally, youth appear to forge positive relationships with other adults, including family friends, neighborhood residents, teachers, and religious leaders. This suggests that mentoring may occur as a natural process wherein members of the community offer guidance and support to youth. For example, urban African American communities may often include extended interpersonal support networks. In the past, elders in these communities who sought to foster the development and success of youth retained titles such as "Othermother," "Old Head," or "Fictive Kin" (Collins, 1987; Utsey, Howard, & Williams, 2003). Many of these traditions continue today. This is known as the concept of "child-keeping" and includes the informal fostering of children in the African American as well as in the Latino communities. Additionally, the Latino community often includes an extended kinship system wherein nonparent adults (such as godparents) accept responsibility for the growing child. Such natural mentors appear to offer a valuable protective influence on the lives of minority youth (Klaw, Rhodes, & Fitzgerald, 2003; Rhodes, Contreras, & Mangelsdorf, 1994; Rhodes, Ebert, & Fischer, 1992).

In one study, 45 percent of African American adolescent mothers reported having a natural mentor; that is, a nonparent/guardian older person to whom they turned for support and guidance (Rhodes et al., 1992). These relationships were marked by a sense that the young women could count on these individuals, believed that the individuals cared deeply about them, and inspired them to do their best. These natural mentors tended to be females who lived in the same neighborhood and were seen at least once a week. In a study of adolescent Latina mothers, 35 percent could identify a natural mentor, and again, these mentors were predominantly older women with whom the young women met at least once a week (Rhodes et al., 1994). An overwhelming majority of these young women expressed the intent to maintain this relationship for life.

Of course, natural mentoring is not necessarily always healthy and prosocial—for example, when an adult engages in criminal activity and then mentors and encourages young people to become partners in crime. Youth gangs, albeit extending camaraderie and protection, also may provide a negative form of "natural" mentoring when the mentoring includes criminal and illegal activity.

It remains unclear whether natural mentors make up for a lack of natural support or provide an important supplement to existing support (Rhodes et al., 1994; Rhodes et al., 1992), although there is convincing evidence that such individuals do not simply replace absent or uninvolved parental figures. Rather, natural mentors appear to provide opportunities for young people to process relationship problems and thus develop an enhanced ability to benefit from existing social connections (Rhodes et al., 1992).

Despite the many benefits of natural mentoring, and the frequency with which this form of mentoring relationship occurs, the popularity of formal mentoring programs has grown in recent decades. For reasons mentioned previously, many young people simply do not have access to positive adult mentors in the natural course of their lives. Formal mentoring programs operate under the assumption that the benefits of natural mentoring can be replicated in prearranged relationship "matches." These matches entail a third party, such as an agency, bringing together a young person and an adult who previously did not know each other. It is hoped that, with careful cultivation, meaningful relationships can grow. With formal mentoring programs, goals and objectives are often predetermined, even if only in a broad sense. When compared with natural mentoring, the contact between mentor and protégé may be less frequent and intense and the overall relationship may be of shorter duration. Formal mentoring programs are variously distinguished, based on both the focus of the relationship and the format of the mentoring program.

Variations in Program Goals

Broadly speaking, mentoring projects may be instrumental or psychosocial in focus.

Instrumental Mentoring: Instrumental mentoring is characterized by activities such as advising, teaching, coaching, guiding, and advocating (Powell, 1997). The instrumental philosophy includes both career and academic mentoring. Career mentoring focuses on exposure to the world of work, learning about a vocation and advancing in a profession, whereas academic mentoring is concerned with instruction and promoting development in the educational arena (Cannister, 1999).

Academic mentoring often includes a tutoring or skills-development component, such as learning to read, developing homework skills, or encouraging math achievement. This approach has been embraced nationally by the America's Promise initiative and has attracted the attention of many states seeking to use competitive grant opportunities to develop these programs in local school districts (Pringle, Anderson, Rubenstein, & Russo, 1993). Colleges and universities, likewise, are involved in various academic tutoring and mentoring programs (Calahan & Farris, 1990). In this model, the mentor becomes more than just an academic tutor; he or she becomes, in essence, an older friend.

In contrast, career mentoring targets skills related to the world of work. In keeping with the link between mentoring and career development, a vast number of mentoring programs link mentors from the business world with youth. This model uses local businesses that support the career development and job advancement of youth. Related experiences may range from time-limited job shadowing experiences to the provision of actual jobs for mentees. School-to-career and school-to-work initiatives have greatly expanded the concept of the business world mentoring young people.

Psychosocial Mentoring: From a philosophical standpoint, psychosocial mentoring encourages overall personal growth. The focus includes role modeling, counseling, or providing emotional support (Powell, 1997). The psychosocial mentor typically seeks to help change the mentee's general life situation by offering alternative perspectives on life and also by serving as a role model and support agent. This model emphasizes role modeling and the mentor-mentee *relationship*, rather than emphasizing specific skill development. The Big Brothers Big Sisters program is an example of a psychosocial mentoring approach.

TYPES AND VARIATIONS OF MENTORING PROGRAMS

This section contains a description of several forms of mentoring programs beyond the traditional adult-to-youth mentoring model. The formats outlined are not mutually exclusive, in that some programs combine formats.

Youth-to-Youth Mentoring

Thousands of formal mentoring programs exist linking a range of youth (pregnant teens, African American boys) and volunteers (elderly, peers, executives). Each approach to the mentor-mentee relationship brings with it unique benefits and challenges. Yet, whether the relationship is peer-to-peer, cross-age youth-to-youth, or youth-to-elder adult, benefits exist.

Some programs established to support children and youth, especially those in schools, use peer relationships in advising capacities. This advising connection often mirrors or becomes a distinct mentoring relationship. These programs typically go by the name of peer mentors, peer helpers, peer advisors, or peer counselors. Selected and supervised by (most often) the school counselor, peer advisors typically go through an intense training before being assigned to any advisees. Additionally, some middle or high schools will assign upperclassmen, whether formally or informally, to become mentors to incoming lowerclassmen. The "mentors" in these situations are typically students in leadership capacities in the school, including those students with high academic standing and/or those viewed as self-confident.

However, students other than those with the highest grades or self-esteem do, at times, also participate in mentoring. One example would be programs using at-risk students as tutors/mentors for other students in need. These at-risk students may receive mentoring themselves, often by adults. These young mentors may need close supervision in their role as mentor, but the older students' ability to provide services to younger students often helps them help themselves to grow and develop as healthy individuals. This is one of the hidden benefits for mentors involved in a mentoring relationship.

Perhaps even more than adults, peer mentors need extensive support. Therefore, the best peer mentoring programs include preservice training and ongoing debriefing and problem-solving sessions (Powell, 1997). Those peer mentors who may be at risk themselves may require ongoing reassurance of their own skills and capabilities as they engage in the mentoring relationship. There is some evidence that such peer mentoring programs are most effective when low-achieving students are matched with students much younger than themselves.

Cross-age tutoring traditionally involves linking students together across at least four grade levels to provide mentoring and academic support to the younger student. In the case of high school or middle school students, this normally involves tutoring at a school different than the one the mentor attends. Examples include high school students mentoring at the middle or elementary school levels and middle school students mentoring at the elementary school level. In the elementary grades, fifth graders, for example, are often linked with first or second graders to serve as reading tutors.

Intergenerational Mentoring

Intergenerational mentoring involves pairing a young person with a person from another generation, whether this be a college student, parental peer, or elder adult. Particularly popular in recent years is the youth-senior connection. Elders are the fastest-growing segment of the population in the United States. Census data indicate that in excess of 28 million Americans are over the age of 65, and projections suggest that this figure will double in the next 30 years (U.S. Bureau of the Census, 1992). Improved health care and increased longevity have created a vast pool of potential sources of social support for youth. In fact, there is evidence that volunteerism is greater among those over 60 years of age than among younger adults (Rogers & Taylor, 1997). Many of these elder volunteers are motivated by a desire to help others, and they appreciate the fact that volunteering gives them a sense of purpose, which in turn contributes to their own mental and physical health and vitality. The Center for Intergenerational Learning is an excellent resource for those interested in this form of mentoring.

Group Mentoring

Most of the curricula, literature, and research on mentoring focuses on a traditional one-on-one relationship between mentor and protégé. Yet, given the discrepancy between the number of young people desiring a mentor and the number of available mentors, it may be important to broaden the concept of mentoring to include other approaches. The concept of group mentoring is gaining in popularity, particularly in light of research indicating that caring adult-adolescent relationships do not necessarily need to be one-on-one to positively impact youth development (Roth et al., 1998). Indeed, it has been argued that the group format is more culturally congruent for African American youth (Utsey et al., 2003).

Group mentoring, by its very nature, requires fewer personnel resources as fewer mentors are needed to serve higher numbers of youth. Mentoring may take the form of an individual-team approach, wherein a group of young people connect with an individual or small number of individuals, much as in done in the classic style of mentoring (Philip & Hendry, 1996). The individual-team approach is common in specialized youth work or sports settings in which the mentors may not be much older than mentees.

Group mentoring is often found in youth religious or spiritual group settings. Cannister (1999) found that mentoring in a group seminar format enhanced religious and emotional well-being. Similarly, meetings of young people and role models in interactive group sessions appear to benefit ethnically marginalized youth in foster care (Utsey et al., 2003, Yancy, 1998). The research appears to support a blended mentoring approach—that is, something in between one-on-one and career-day programs in terms of cost and intensity of exposure.

Online and Telementoring

The advent of the World Wide Web and the proliferation of computers in society has opened the door to new avenues of mentoring. In particular, the idea of telementoring, also known as e-mentoring and online mentoring, is gaining popularity. This format possesses the potential to greatly expand the number of individuals involved in mentoring. Telementoring provides opportunities for a large population of previously untapped volunteers to become involved in mentoring, as many adults interested in mentoring often do not participate due to logistical concerns such as the feasibility of getting to the school campus during a busy workweek. Telementoring also creates new opportunities for elderly and disabled individuals to participate in mentoring relationships. Likewise, an online mentoring program may open doors to young people facing barriers to mentoring relationships, such as physical illness or rural living.

The flexibility of telementoring makes it appealing to both corporations and schools. Working within the parameters of general mentoring principles and e-mail/Web technology, specific schools and businesses can create unique programs suited to their particular needs. Telementoring initiatives may assist young people by focusing on any one of a variety of intervention areas such as skill building in academic subjects or career development and role modeling. The e-mail and Internet format naturally promotes computer literacy and keyboarding and Internet skills, while enhancing writing skills as students work to compose thoughtful, appropriate e-mail exchanges. While many online mentoring programs are school-based, telementoring components may also augment more traditional services provided by nonprofit organizations.

One popular telementoring format entails connecting school students with adult mentors from a local corporation, with the goal of bolstering the school-to-work connection. The corporation may solicit volunteer e-mentors who are then matched with a student or a classroom. At times, the corporation may supply funding and computers, along with technology expertise. Mentors and mentees communicate regularly via e-mail, often working on specific "assignments," such as collaborating on an interactive story. Periodic field trips to the work site may also occur, or mentors might come to lunch on the school campus once or twice a year.

To function successfully, online mentoring programs require, first and foremost, access to the necessary technology. Depending on its goals and the number of young people served, a telementoring program requires a sufficient number of computers with fully functional Internet access for mentees. Likewise, potential mentors must possess access to a computer with an Internet hookup. Securing and testing of the needed technology must occur prior to the launching of the mentoring program to ensure that the program can run smoothly without troublesome delays.

As with more traditional forms of mentoring, online mentoring requires that programs attend carefully to safety and ethical issues. Like direct contact mentoring, telementoring requires attention to screening, training, matching, and supervision. Often teachers perform the supervisory function, directing communication and monitoring e-mail communication. Protection of confidentiality also poses a significant concern, and program directors of telementoring programs must decide in advance who will have access to e-mail exchanges. Although assuring that the contents of e-mail messages will remain private between the mentor and mentee may foster open communication and sharing, such a policy makes it difficult to ensure that these interactions are appropriate and also complicates the monitoring of a student's progress toward skill-based goals.

While many anecdotal descriptions support the value of online mentoring for young people and businesses alike, there is, to date, little research evaluating the benefits of this emerging mentoring format. Published research suggests that such programs may play a role in improved student writing skills, social skills, and self-efficacy.

In 2001, MENTOR/National Mentoring Partnership's National E-Mentoring Clearinghouse assembled the E-mentoring Advisory Team, a representative group of nonprofit organizations and corporations with e-mentoring experience. These leaders established Elements of Effective Practice for E-mentoring programs, based on the 1991 Elements of Effective Practice that was developed by the National Mentoring Working Group. A downloadable version of these Elements of Effective Practice for E-mentoring is available at http://www.mentoring.org. For additional resources on e-mentoring, visit the National E-Mentoring Clearinghouse at www.mentoring.org or call MENTOR at (703) 224-2200.

There are several organizations with associated Web sites dedicated to the concept of telementoring:

- Service Leader maintains a valuable Web-based information resource for those interested in telementoring, including a comprehensive grid of key administrative tasks and numerous suggested activities for online mentoring programs.

- The National Mentoring Partnership hosts the National E-Mentoring Clearinghouse, which offers information, training, standards, and technical assistance related to online mentoring programs.

- The World Organization of Webmasters (WOW) Mentoring Program seeks to increase student exposure to the Internet by linking Web professionals with schools.

- The International Telementor Center provides resources and education related to online mentoring.

Interested readers are referred to chapter 6 in this text, "Selected Print and Nonprint Resources," for more information on these organizations.

GENDER DIFFERENCES AND MENTORING

It is important to recognize that gender differences may affect the course of the mentoring process and of the mentoring relationship. There is evidence that young males and females differ in the way they make use of and benefit from mentoring. These differences may reflect traditional gender socialization practices. More specifically, young boys in our society are often socialized to disconnect from relationships and sever emotional ties. Gurian (1999) refers to such youth as the "under-nurtured" boys. As part of this disconnecting and under-nurturing process, messages, subtle and not-so-subtle, socialize young men to be out-come—or results—oriented, whereas females are taught to pay more attention to what happens between people. Likewise, while females are typically socialized to value relationships, males are often encouraged to seek autonomy and independence.

Given these differences, boys and young men may be less inclined than girls and young women to view mentoring relationships as relevant (Philip & Hendry, 1996). Seeking support and guidance in the context of an affective relationship may, therefore, conflict with the male gender role. Thus, young men may feel most comfortable with "classical"-style mentoring programs. The classical style encompasses a specific goal or goals-directed relationship in which the mentor directly guides the pro-tégé toward a future objective. In contrast, research suggests that young women benefit from mentoring that emphasizes a *relationship* between the mentor and the protégé (Philip et al., 1996). These relationships pro-vide a young woman with a base from which she can explore the person she is becoming as she grows and matures.

Two research studies exploring the narratives of adolescent females revealed that young women have a desire to have someone listen to their thoughts and feelings (Schultz, 1999; Sullivan, 1996). The young women in the study also noted the rarity of such opportunities. The studies showed that, over time, these young women began to shut down—to silence their voices. This trend toward self-sufficiency and hesitance to trust appeared to reflect the girls' awareness of the potential for hurt and ridicule in close relationships. Schultz concludes that a grave need exists to create safe opportunities for girls and young women to develop nur-turing relationships within which to talk about aspirations. Mentoring can fill such a void.

Sullivan (1996) is concerned that adherence to a model of instrumen-tal mentoring may serve to unwittingly perpetuate the male-oriented status quo, much of which she feels is unhealthy for girls. She proposes that the character of a muse is a more appropriate metaphor than men-tor when it comes to the needs of young women. A muse denotes a mythological character that offers inspiration while recognizing the cre-ative potential of those whom they serve. In this relationship-oriented (muse) model, the focus moves to the girls' inner resources and poten-tials, rather than attempting to instruct girls in areas of a perceived deficit or to direct them toward a specific, concrete goal. This is particu-larly important given mounting evidence that as girls enter their teen years they may become more reluctant to show their true selves and more prone to censoring the expression of their thoughts and feelings. As an example of girls disconnecting from emotional connections if not properly nurtured, Sullivan cites Mary, a 10th-grade student: "I really don't tell anybody about anything."

CULTURAL DIFFERENCES AND MENTORING

Awareness and appreciation of cultural differences is essential to positive outcomes in youth mentoring. By 2010, one in three U.S. school-children will fit the census bureau definition of "minority" (U.S. Bureau of the Census, 1991); this underscores the importance of giving careful consideration to the best means of promoting optimal development for culturally diverse youth. Mentoring programs or interactions can provide significant help in realizing the potential of culturally diverse youth. Yet, those responsible for establishing and maintaining mentoring programs must recognize that the mentoring needs of young people in various ethnic groups may differ. For example, an African American youth may find mentoring in the form of an extended support network more in keeping with his or her cultural traditions (Powell, 1997; Utsey et al., 2003). In addition, unlike European American girls, African American girls tend to maintain strong self-esteem during adolescence. Nevertheless, African American girls tend to have lower academic self-confidence. Such differences will probably impact mentoring goals and definitions of mentoring success (Schultz, 1999). Awareness of such differences will be important for the mentors as well as for mentoring program implementers and managers.

One model that directly addresses cultural issues is the cultural empowerment model, identified by Mech and colleagues (1995). This approach links youth from a minority group with adult members of the same cultural group. This model seeks to overcome any negative messages that minority group members may receive from society about their culture or their ethnicity. The goal is to promote positive protégé identity, while encouraging ambitions and a sense of future possibilities. For example, Yancey (1998) describes a pilot program for a preventive mental health intervention called PRIDE (Personal and Racial/Ethnic Identity Development and Enhancement). Using successful, ethnically relevant role models, the program seeks to enhance the positive self-image of adolescents in foster care. Other cultural-empowerment programs include Rites of Passage (Detroit, Michigan) and Big Siblings (Gay and Lesbian Adolescent Social Services in West Hollywood, California).

A significant issue in mentoring youth from culturally diverse backgrounds is the question of racial or ethnic matching. The impact of the mentors' and youth's racial and ethnic background on the mentoring relationship remains unclear. Some argue that shared ethnic background is an essential prerequisite to the formation of an effective mentor-mentee bond. Indeed, the ability to empathize with a young person's experience plays a crucial role in the development of a positive mentor-mentee relationship. The argument for racial or ethnic matching highlights this point, emphasizing that, particularly for oppressed groups, individuals from divergent ethnic backgrounds would be hindered in their ability to form this empathic connection. Proponents of such matching also contend that individuals from a given ethnic group provide excellent role models for the young people in that group. In contrast, others express a belief that effective mentor-mentee relationships can be forged across ethnic boundaries, provided that mentors possess sufficient empathy, cultural sensitivity, and a sincere desire to understand their mentees' experiences. Such mentoring may also set the stage for mentees to become more comfortable with cultures and ethnicities different from their own.

While research on this debate is just beginning, there is emerging evidence that cross-ethnicity matches can provide some benefits (Ferguson, 1990; Morrow & Styles, 1995; Rhodes, Reddy, Grossman, & Lee, 2002). Other research suggests that the impact of ethnic matching is not consistent, and may be influenced by other factors such as the gender or age of the mentee, parental attitudes about cross-race matching, or the particular method used to establish match success.

MENTORING SEXUAL MINORITY YOUTH

Given that an estimated 10 percent of the U.S. population is lesbian or gay, it is highly likely that programs targeting adolescents are likely to serve sexual minority youth. In fact, the isolation, discrimination, and prejudice these young people encounter may heighten the potential value of a supportive, nonjudgmental, and caring adult in their lives. At present, research on mentoring relationships with sexual minority adolescents is virtually nonexistent. Yet, mentoring programs would benefit from addressing the needs of this population. Linda Jucovy (2000) offers valuable tips for training mentors to work with lesbian or gay young people. She suggests that agencies discuss their diversity policy and confidentiality requirements, including the needs of sexual minority youth, while providing a forum to explore issues such as inclusive language, the volunteer's attitudes toward varying sexual orientations, or how to respond appropriately when a mentee shares information about sexual orientation or gender identity.

CONCLUSION

Mentoring is a time-tested strategy for promoting youth development. It is an intervention especially suited to the current needs of young people in this country, and it provides benefits for both the mentor and the mentee. Mentoring may occur naturally or be the result of a formal "match." The relationship may focus on diverse outcomes and take many different forms. While a wide variety of mentoring programs appear to benefit young people, mentoring is not without risks, and careful guidelines must be followed when implementing a mentoring program. The particulars of implementing a mentoring program are outlined in chapter 2.

REFERENCES

Calahan, M., & Farris, E. (1990). *Higher education surveys report: College sponsored tutoring and mentoring programs for disadvantaged elementary and secondary students.* Rockville, MD: Westat.

Cannister, M. W. (1999). Mentoring and the spiritual well-being of late adolescents. *Adolescence, 34,* 770–779.

Collins, P. H. (1987). The meaning of motherhood in black culture and black mother/daughter relationships. *Sage, 4,* 3–10.

Dondero, G. (1997). Mentors: Beacons of hope. *Adolescence, 32* (128), 881–886.

Ferguson, R. F. (1990). *The case for community based programs that inform and motivate black male youth.* Washington, DC: Urban Institute.

Freedman, M. (1993). *The kindness of strangers: Adult mentors, urban youth, and the new voluntarism.* New York: Cambridge University Press.

Galbo, J. J. (1986). Adolescents' perceptions of significant adults: Implications for the family, the school, and youth serving agencies. *Children and Youth Services Review, 8,* 37–51.

Garbarino, J. (1999). *Lost boys: Why our sons turn violent and how we can save them.* New York: Free Press.

Gurian, M. (1999). *A fine young man: What parents, mentors and educators can do to shape adolescent boys into exceptional men.* New York: Putnam.

Jucovy, L. (2000). *Mentoring sexual minority youth.* Portland, OR: Northwest Regional Educational Laboratory.

Klaw, E. L., Rhodes, J. E., & Fitzgerald, L. F., (2003). Natural mentors in the lives of African American adolescent mothers: Tracking relationships over time. *Journal of Youth & Adolescence, 32*, 223–232.

Larson, R. W. (2000). Toward a psychology of positive youth development. *American Psychologist, 55*, 170–183.

Lee, J., & Cramond, B. (1999). The positive effects of mentoring economically disadvantaged students. *Professional School Counseling, 2*(3), 172–178.

McLearn, K. T., Colasanto, D., & Schoen, C. (1998). *Mentoring makes a difference.* New York: Commonwealth Fund.

Mech, E., Pryde, J. A., & Rycraft, J. R. (1995). Mentors for adolescents in foster care. *Child and Adolescent Social Work Journal, 12*(4), 317–328.

Morrow, K. V., & Styles, M. B. (1995). *Building relationships with youth in program settings: A study of Big Brothers Big Sisters.* Philadelphia: Public/Private Ventures.

Mrazek, P. J., & Mrazek, D. A. (1987). Resilience in child maltreatment victims: A conceptual exploration. *Child Abuse and Neglect, 11*, 357–366.

Philip, K., & Hendry, L. B. (1996). Young people and mentoring: Towards a typology? *Journal of Adolescence, 19*, 189–201.

Powell, M. A. (1997). *Academic tutoring and mentoring: A literature review.* Sacramento, CA: California Research Bureau.

Pringle, B., Anderson, L. M., Rubenstein, M. C., & Russo, A. W. (1993). *Peer tutoring and mentoring services for disadvantaged secondary students: An evaluation of the secondary schools basic skills demonstration assistance program.* Washington, DC: Policy Studies Associates. Sponsored by the U.S. Department of Education Office of Policy and Planning.

Reglin, G. (1998). *Mentoring students at-risk: An underutilized alternative education strategy for K–12 teachers.* Springfield, IL: Charles C. Thomas.

Rhodes, J. (2002). *Stand by me: The risks and rewards of mentoring today's youth.* Cambridge, MA: Harvard University Press.

Rhodes, J., Contreras, J. M., Mangelsdorf, C. (1994). Natural mentor relationships among Latina adolescent mothers: Psychological adjustment, moderating processes, and the role of early parental acceptance. *American Journal of Community Psychology, 22*, 211–228.

Rhodes, J. E., & Davis, A. B. (1996). Supportive ties between nonparent adults and urban adolescent girls. In B. J. R. Leadbeater & N. Way (Eds.), *Urban girls: Resisting stereotypes, creating identities* (pp. 213–225). New York: New York University Press.

Rhodes, J. E., Ebert, L., & Fischer, K. (1992). Natural mentors: An overlooked resource in the social networks of adolescent mothers. *American Journal of Community Psychology, 20*, 445–461.

Rhodes, J. E., Haight, W. L., Briggs, E. C. (1999). The influence of mentoring on the peer relationships of foster youth in relative and nonrelative care. *Journal of Research on Adolescence, 9*(2) 185–201.

Rhodes, J. E., Reddy, R., Grossman, J. B., & Lee, J. M. (2002). Volunteer mentoring relationships with minority youth: An analysis of same- versus cross-race matches. *Journal of Applied Social Psychology, 32,* 2114–2133.

Rogers, A. M., & Taylor, A. S. (1997). Intergenerational mentoring: A viable strategy for meeting the needs of vulnerable youth. *Journal of Gerontological Social Work, 28*(1–2), 125–1240.

Roth, J., Brooks-Gunn, J., Murray, L., & Foster, W. (1998). Promoting healthy adolescents: Synthesis of youth development program evaluations. *Journal of Research on Adolescence, 8*(4), 423–459.

Rutter, M. (1987). Psychosocial resilience and protective mechanisms. *American Journal of Orthopsychiatry, 57,* 316–331.

Schultz, K. (1999). Identity narratives: Stories from the lives of urban adolescent females. *The Urban Review, 31*(1), 79–106.

Smink, J. (1990). *Mentoring programs for at-risk youth: A drop-out prevention research report.* Clemson, SC: National Dropout Prevention Center. (ERIC Document Reproduction Service No. ED 318 931).

Soucy, N., & Larose, S. (2000). Attachment and control in family and mentoring contexts as determinants of adolescent adjustment to college. *Journal of Family Psychology, 14*(1), 125–143.

Sullivan, A. M. (1996). From mentor to muse: Recasting the role of women in relationship with urban adolescent girls. In B. J. R. Leadbeater & N. Way (Eds.), *Urban girls: Resisting stereotypes, creating identities* (pp. 226–249). New York: New York University Press.

U.S. Bureau of the Census. (1992). *Projections of the population of the United States by age, race, and sex, 1983–2080* (Current Population Report Series P-25). Washington, DC: G. Spencer.

U.S. Bureau of the Census, Economics and Statistics Administration. (1991). *1990 census profile: Race and Hispanic origin* (Number 2). Washington, DC: U.S. Government Printing Office.

Utsey, S. O., Howard, A., & Williams, O. (2003). Therapeutic group mentoring with African American male adolescents. *Journal of Mental Health Counseling, 25,* 126–140.

Werner, E. E. (1990). Protective factors and individual resilience. In S. J. Meisels & J. P. Shonkoff (Eds.), *Handbook of early childhood intervention* (pp. 97–117). New York: Cambridge University Press.

Werner, E. E. & Smith, R. S. (1992). *Overcoming the odds: High risk children from birth to adulthood.* Ithaca, NY: Cornell University Press.

Yancey, A. K. (1998). Building positive self-image in adolescents in foster care: The use of role models in an interactive group approach. *Adolescence, 33*(130), 253–267.

2

Formal Mentoring Program Guidelines

> I used to mess up a lot. Now I only mess up a little. My mentor has helped me to learn from my mistakes.
>
> Jeremy, 14 years old

While informal mentoring of children and youth (mentoring that happens on its own, or naturally) occurs frequently in all cultures, many states and localities are not leaving mentoring matches to chance. Instead, formal mentoring programs are being established in increasing numbers at schools, community youth centers, and even in business settings. This chapter takes a comprehensive look at formal mentoring programs, from the envisioning and creating of the program to the more practical elements of maintaining a mentoring program or raising funds to sustain the endeavor. In this chapter, the reader will find current information on the elements of effective practice in formal mentoring. In addition, the chapter covers procedures and processes essential to formal mentoring programs, including:

- Features of quality mentoring programs
- Initial development of formal youth mentoring programs
  - Determining the need for a formal mentor program
  - Recruiting the program development team
  - Developing a mission statement

- Formulating program goals and objectives
- Defining the target population
- Determining the location (site based or community based)
- Establishing the program structure
- Developing a budget and pursuing funding
- Mentors: A core component
  - What it takes to be a good mentor
  - Mentor recruitment
  - Mentor screening
  - Mentor training and orientation
- Mentees and protégés
  - Recruitment of children and adolescents
  - Preparation of participating children and adolescents
- The mentor-mentee connection
  - Making a mentoring match
  - Helping to establish and maintain a relationship
  - Monitoring and supervising mentoring matches
  - Terminating a mentoring match
- Risk management
- Common problems in mentoring and mentor programs
  - Scarcity of mentors
  - Inadequate screening
  - Mentors' relationship with mentees' families
  - Commitment to the relationship
  - Relationship development
- Evaluation

FEATURES OF QUALITY MENTORING PROGRAMS

Developing a formal mentoring program to support children and adolescents is a time-consuming task. The components of program development are many. Fortunately, directors of mentoring programs do not need to start from scratch when developing program standards. Most mentoring organizations and initiatives use existing knowledge about mentoring to outline crucial aspects of quality mentoring programs. The National Mentoring Partnership's Elements of Effective Practice requirements are reproduced in Appendix A. The Academic Volunteer Mentoring Support Program (AVMSP) Quality Standards are reproduced in Appendix B. The information provided in both documents may serve as a template for emerging mentoring programs. In addition, these features of quality programs are integrated into the following section.

Initial Development of Formal Youth Mentoring Programs

This section focuses on the development of formal mentoring programs and the steps individuals or organizations must take to ensure the creation of effective programs that positively impact the lives of children and youth.

Mentoring-program development requires a vision, a strategic plan of action, and the development of partnerships with other like-minded groups. The process typically begins with an assessment of the need for mentoring in the community. Following from the needs assessment, the program vision or mission broadly details the overriding purpose of the mentoring effort. More specifically, development of a mentoring program requires assessment of community needs, formulation of a mission and goals, delineation of a target population, recruitment of the program development team, establishment of the program structure, determination of the management structure, formulation of standards for effective practice, and establishment of a setting for the program.

Determining the Need for a Formal Mentor Program

Any credible program begins with an assessment of community and youth needs. Mentoring programs can address a wide variety of youth issues. They may focus on career development, academic achievement, psychosocial issues, or any combination of these areas. It is, therefore, important to determine what the specific needs are for particular young people in a given community. A prospective program also needs to determine the demographic characteristics of the youth served, such as age and gender.

For example, community members may have concerns about whether local youth are, in a broad sense, developing optimally. Or, concern may emerge about young people engaging in a particular high-risk behavior, such as substance abuse. In either case, the interventions could vary, and, while mentoring may be appropriate, it is not the only option for addressing such issues. Before pursuing any intervention, it is essential that the involved parties carefully examine the specific nature of the concerns. A needs assessment allows community members to clarify presenting issues and more specifically define the target of the intervention, as well as the intervention strategy (mentoring, for example) that is most appropriate.

Potential elements of a needs assessment include interviews with key community members, surveys of relevant individuals or institutions, focus groups, and the examination of community statistics (such as graduation rate, juvenile citations, school performance measures, etc.). In gathering such information, the goals are to clearly define the specific nature of the presenting concern.

Recruiting the Program Development Team

Successful mentoring programs grow from effective program development teams. The program development team is responsible for the development of a realistic, reachable operational plan for the program. As it develops the vision and the mission of the program, the team should also develop goals, objectives, and timelines for the implementation of all aspects of the operational plan. The program development team should also develop a list of possible funding opportunities and other resources. Services groups such as Kiwanis, Rotary, Soroptomist, and the like are valuable sources of team members for the mentoring program development task. When forming a program development team, recruitment of members from the target group and greater community is also essential.

Developing a Mission Statement

Upon completion of a needs assessment, targets of the program, in terms of goals and population, emerge. A mission statement helps integrate these findings into a cohesive sense of purpose. A mission guides the formal mentoring program and keeps it on track so that the program effectively and consistently pursues its intended goals. Creating a mission statement requires forecasting the future or, in the case of a vision for a mentor program, "seeing" youth making positive changes and having more viable options in the future as a result of the mentoring interventions.

Many formal programs ultimately fail because they do not narrow their focus enough to be successful. When an assessment indicates that a myriad of needs exist for children and youth in a school or community, it is understandable that well-intentioned program directors would want to try to meet as many of those needs as possible. However, by trying to take on too many problems or need areas, programs may ultimately end up meeting few of the needs.

Each mentoring program should possess a clearly defined mission, that is, a statement about what the organization seeks to accomplish. The mission encompasses the rationale behind the program and the nature of the services offered, as well as its goals, objectives, and target population. Failure to attend to this crucial first step potentially impacts the success of the entire mentoring program.

Formulating Program Goals and Objectives

A key element of the mentoring process is the setting of goals for the program and for the young people it serves. As is usually the case in intervention programs of all types, creators of mentoring programs must carefully delineate desired outcomes for the participating youth and mentors. Attention to outcomes and goals allows for appropriate assessment and monitoring and helps ensure that the program is working toward its desired end. Mentoring programs have the potential to serve a variety of goals and objectives, including:

- Academic improvement (basic skills, attendance, school-related behavior, etc.)
- Drop-out prevention
- Career success and employment assistance
- Socialization
- Skill development
- Enhanced self-esteem
- Exposure to positive role models
- Social and cultural enrichment

While the mentoring program structure will typically prescribe some goals, it is often useful for individual mentor-mentee pairs to negotiate more individually tailored goals themselves. Taylor and colleagues (Taylor, LoSciuto, Fox, Hilbert, & Sonkowsky, 1999) found that a predictor of satisfaction in mentoring relationships was helping the mentored youth set reasonable, attainable goals.

Defining the Target Population

In the establishment of a formal mentoring program, a crucial decision is the determination of which particular young people will be mentored and who will serve as mentors. The needs assessment conducted in the target community or service area should direct attention to the area of greatest need, be it preventing gang membership, raising academic scores, increasing retention and graduation rates, preventing pregnancy, or any of an array of possibilities. Clearly identifying the target group allows the program to focus on a narrower range of objectives, more easily recruit mentors who can help children and youth in the specific areas, and attract the attention of funders or fundraising organizations that have the capacity to sustain the program financially.

Determining the Location (Site Based or Community Based)

An issue that needs much consideration in the establishment of a mentoring program is the site of mentor-protégé meetings. Broadly speaking, mentoring programs may be community based or site based. In community based mentoring programs, the program does not determine the location of the mentoring activities and interactions. Rather, the mentor and mentee determine where in the community they will meet. The precise meeting place may vary from week to week, based on the needs or interests of the match.

In site based mentoring programs, the mentoring activities consistently occur at a predetermined location. Common site options include schools, houses of worship, businesses, residential locations (e.g., group home, juvenile hall, or youth shelter), or youth service agencies (e.g., Boys and Girls Club or the YWCA). For some site based programs, any deviation from on-site activities occurs only as a supervised group activity. In other site based programs, there is a combination of the two modes, with regular mentoring occurring on site and extra mentoring activities occurring in the community. For example, an academically focused program may require the mentor to meet weekly at the mentee's school, while also permitting the option of engaging in less formal mentoring activities, such as attending a baseball game, away from school.

When determining a meeting location, it is important to consider such factors as funding, site availability, and program goals. For example, if the focus of the program is on academic issues, the school may be the most logical site for mentoring to take place. In contrast, a mentoring

program that emphasizes cultural enrichment may encourage participants to explore interests in the community and beyond.

Establishing the Program Structure

In order to be effective, mentoring programs require a program structure that supports participants in pursuing the mission and goals of the
program. The management and coordination of the mentoring program
play a vital role in the success of the program. Many programs benefit
from appointing a project or program coordinator.

Typically the program coordinator for a child and youth mentoring
program has overall responsibility for the essential elements of the program, including envisioning, developing, implementing, and evaluating
the entire program. Specific elements of the program coordinator position might include:

- Responsibility for meeting program goals and objectives
- Recruitment, screening, and training of volunteer mentors
- Recruitment, preparation, and encouragement of the children
  being mentored (mentees)
- Matching and providing ongoing support of the mentoring rela-
  tionship, including primary contact with all participants and the
  overall case management of the mentoring match
- Budget preparation and oversight
- Program evaluation coordination
- Fundraising and coordination of grant-writing activities
- Risk management and crisis intervention for situations both pro-
  grammatic and related to a specific match relationship
- Publicity for the program
- Development and execution of recognition and celebration activ-
  ities designed to encourage all stakeholders

It is evident that the role and function of the program coordinator is
broad based. Care must be given to the recruitment and retention of
individuals with the capacity to carry out this assignment. In many organizations the tasks are divided among two program coordinators or are
shared by an executive director and a program coordinator.

The community in which the mentoring project is embedded forms an
important element of the program structure. When establishing a men-

toring program, it is important to clarify all potential community stake-holders, or people and agencies with a vested interest in the program. Stakeholders may include parents, school personnel, the police department, businesses, community-service organizations, religious organizations, civic groups, and local government.

Key organizational structures include careful screening, orientation, and training, as well as support and supervision of volunteers by program staff (Roth, Brooks-Gunn, Murray, & Foster, 1998). An evaluation of the Big Brothers Big Sisters program indicated that program infrastructure was crucial to attaining program goals (Tierney, Grossman, & Resch, 1995). Mentors who feel supported by project staff are more likely to remain connected to the program and to effectively pursue the program's mission. Because mentoring efficacy is related to relationship longevity and consistency, mentoring programs must focus on strengthening infrastructure and improving program practices in support of this process. Embedding mentoring projects with existing programs and institutions is one way to create this supportive context.

The most effective mentoring programs exist as part of a comprehensive approach integrated with other program components. Such agency linkages provide stability. For example, tutoring-focused mentoring programs depend on the positive involvement and participation of teachers, as mentoring should not and cannot be a substitute for quality instruction (Pringle, Anderson, Rubenstein, & Russo, 1993). With in-school peer tutoring/mentoring programs, teachers should be informed of project goals, as well as of the teacher's role of supporting and role modeling for the tutor.

Collaboration of mentoring programs with colleges, universities, and other professional organizations is becoming increasingly popular. Inter-agency partnerships contribute greatly to effective intergenerational mentoring programs (Rogers & Taylor, 1997).

Developing a Budget and Pursuing Funding

Money is an important consideration in the establishment and maintenance of a formal mentoring program. Few programs are able to start up, much less endure past the first year, without a source of funding. Funds are needed to hire a coordinator, establish an office and a place to mentor children, provide mentoring and office supplies, attend workshops for program development, and provide activities to celebrate and appreciate the mentors and their mentees. Although exact figures are unclear and will vary from location to location, the Big Brothers Big Sisters of America organization estimates that the cost of establishing and monitoring a relationship is $1,000 per match. The California Governor's Office of the Secretary of Education has established a value of $500 per year per match for the state's Academic Volunteer Mentoring and Tutoring Program. These amounts are for mentoring enterprises that utilize unpaid mentor volunteers. For programs that pay the mentor a stipend, or at least provide transportation and activities reimbursement, the cost of sustaining the program will be higher.

Sustaining program viability therefore becomes essential in mentoring programs. In order to fulfill the mission of the mentoring program, sufficient funds must be available to continue the operation. Many mentoring programs were initiated on the basis of local, state, federal, or private grant proposal funds. In a grant proposal, the agency—public or private—typically identifies a need area and invites the public or private agencies to submit proposals. The invitation is typically called an RFP (request for proposals) or an RFA (request for applications). Proposals submitted may be replications of existing mentoring models with proven track records of success; or the proposal may be a unique, innovative approach to mentoring that is compatible with the specific needs of the children and youth in a particular school or organization. The submitted proposals (varying in size and complexity depending on the request of the potential funder) will typically go through a review process before funding decisions are made. Technical assistance is often available to help organizations complete the proposal requests. A sample of a funded mentoring grant proposal is provided in Appendix C.

Developing a mentoring program or sustaining an existing mentoring program on grant funds has advantages and disadvantages. The advantages are readily evident. Grants provide an immediate financial start for new programs and the alliance with the funding agency (if the organization is well known) may lend an instant level of credibility. Additionally, the requirements for successful grant proposals typically include developing goals, objectives, activities, timelines, and a plan for evaluation, and having these elements in place is an advantage. Furthermore, the requirement of regular reports (usually quarterly) to an external reviewer will force mentoring programs to develop careful, organized records.

Surprisingly, there are also disadvantages to relying on grant funds for program sustenance. Grant funding can be quite lucrative and is usually provided in the form of outright gifts with no concern about repayment. However, grant proposals are typically complicated and time consuming to write, and developing these proposals often falls to overburdened staff who may have little or no training in grant writing. Additionally, most grant periods are short (one to three years) and are frequently non-renewable. Furthermore, expenditures are restricted to the line items on the grant budget and to the time frames specified in the grant budget, allowing no room for flexibility.

MENTORS: A CORE COMPONENT

A mentoring program is only as good as the mentors it recruits and retains. This section focuses on aspects of the mentor in the mentoring of children and youth.

What It Takes to Be a Good Mentor

Successful mentors have successful mentoring relationships. The selection of appropriate mentors will depend in large part on the specific mission of a given mentoring program. For example, a mentoring program aimed at promoting career development will most likely seek relevant career role models for young people. Nevertheless, research indicates that certain mentor qualities promote successful mentoring relationships across various types of mentoring programs. Successful mentors have the following characteristics in common:

• *Youth driven and youth centered:* Successful mentoring relationships are "youth driven" (Rogers & Taylor, 1997). That is, they consider the interests and needs of the youth. Adults who approach the mentoring relationship from the perspective that they, the adults, know what the young person needs and then attempt to dictate activities and goals are likely to have dissatisfied mentees. Understandably, young people do not need another adult telling them what they should be doing, whether that "should" is about a particular activity or broader life goals. It is unfair to assume that young people will be motivated to pursue activities in which they have no interest. Because adults, children, and adolescents may have very different ideas about what constitutes a "fun" activity, successful mentoring relationships require open communication and negotiation. Thus, effective mentoring relationships allow the young person to determine much of the pace of the relationship and the types of activities that are undertaken.

Ineffective mentors try to change the youth, whereas effective mentors focus on developing a trusting relationship. From the trusting relationship, the desire on the part of the youth to make positive life changes is often a natural sequence. A young person facing a roadblock in life is better served by someone who actively listens and helps him or her generate solutions to the problem. Mentors help young people understand the consequences of their actions and explore alternative options, and they manage to do this without coming across as critical or disapproving. In sum, effective mentors genuinely like children and are open to experiencing new and different things, including engaging in activities that young people find appealing.

• *Active listeners:* Over and over again, youth report that they primarily want adults to listen to them. Active listening does not always come naturally, and many mentors find that they benefit from formal training in listening skills. The mentor must be able to communicate with young people and understand their concerns. Particularly for young girls, whose voices are often silenced as they enter adolescence, the ability to speak freely and to be heard and validated is key to a successful mentor-mentee connection.

• *Go slow:* Pacing is also an important part of the mentoring relationship. Successful mentors do not rush the formation of a relationship with their mentee. They understand that building a relationship may take time, and they tolerate potential disappointment without taking it out on the child. The mentoring relationship is not undertaken to meet the needs of the adult, and appropriate mentors have appropriate adult relationships through which to meet their own social needs.

• *Make connections:* Mentors who successfully engage with a particular youth generally understand that person's background and experience. These mentors possess the ability to empathize with the young person's experience. This may occur naturally, as is the case when the mentor's life experiences mirror those of his or her mentee. In other cases, mentors need to educate themselves about their mentee's life experiences. While mentors by definition possess attributes and skills that are beyond those of the protégé, the gap in terms of social distance must not be too great (Flaxman, Ascher, & Harrington, 1988). Young people report that they appreciate the opportunity to interact with people who "made it" despite negative experiences similar to their own (Yancey, 1998). When significant differences exist, it is essential that the mentor accept the youth as he or she is and possess a level of comfort with these differences. When a mentor accepts his or her mentee as a person, he or she inspires self-confidence. When mentors set the clear, high expectations associated with mentoring, mentees then feel confident, both in their own ability to achieve these goals and in the mentor's support.

• *Adequate time:* Other qualities important in a mentor are motivation, dependability, and availability. That is, mentors need a genuine interest in spending time with youth. They must recognize the importance of consistency and have the time available to allow such regular contact to occur. A prospective mentor with the best of intentions and a great deal of interest, but a hectic life schedule, may need to consider whether the time is there to devote to a mentoring relationship. Although the time involved is usually not excessive, the importance of consistency requires that mentoring be integrated into existing commitments.

• *Dependability and mutual respect:* A number of studies have examined what young people themselves value in relationships with nonrelated adults. It appears that young people value adults who are trustworthy, faithful, open-minded, and intelligent. Adults who possess a wide array of life experiences, as well as an interest in and willingness to spend time with youth, most often attract the interest of young people. Adolescents, in particular, desire respect and treatment as equals, and report status differences as a key barrier to engaging in relationships with adults (Gottlieb & Sylvestre, 1996). In other words, young people feel that they have few opportunities to engage with adults or get to know them outside of their role as authority figures. This, in turn, leaves the young person feeling inferior, and also results in a one-dimensional view of the adult. Yet, adolescents desire a more mutual relationship with adults and place particular value on the adult's willingness to self-disclose (Gottlieb & Sylvestre; Sullivan, 1996; Yancey, 1998). When young people hear about an adult's personal interest, or struggle with a difficult experience, they come to see adults as people whom they themselves might become. They learn about the challenges and rewards life presents in adulthood, as well as ways to overcome struggles. In describing breakthroughs in their relationships with meaningful adults, many young people noted particular instances in which the adult let his or her guard down and shared personal information or otherwise stepped outside of the typical adult role (Gottlieb et al.; Philip & Hendry, 1996). To the youth, this conveyed that the adult trusted him or her.

• *Other factors:* Beyond these global qualities, the type of person suited to mentor will depend on the particular focus and goals of the specific mentoring program. In addition, mentors often need to be willing and able to conform to a variety of requirements. These requirements include practical details. For example, when transportation of mentees is an anticipated aspect of the mentoring process, the volunteer must have access to a valid driver's license, a car, and appropriate auto insurance. Typically, the absence of a criminal history is mandated, and most programs now screen volunteers via a police background check.

The Mentoring Center of Oakland, California, maintains that one's own life experiences in working and living qualify one to be a mentor. The best mentors, according to the Center, are people who like kids and are contagiously enthusiastic about life. The Center cites the following five categories as the characteristics of what makes a mentor:

1. A role model providing a model for appropriate behavior and attitudes
   - Inspiring admiration and desire for emulation
   - Possessing qualities that the youth desires for himself or herself
   - Expanding the youth's perspective and definition of adulthood
2. A teacher helping youth to acquire knowledge, information, or skills
   - Showing youth how to do things
   - Participating with youth in learning new things
3. A companion enjoying doing things with youth
   - Sharing interest and experience with youth
   - Spending time talking with youth
4. A support boosting self-esteem, conveying warm caring about the youth as a person
   - Giving support to the young person's efforts
   - Listening to youthful ideas and concerns
   - Expressing belief in the youth's abilities
5. A resource providing opportunities for the youth to try new things
   - Introducing youth to new ideas, places, interests
   - Suggesting new sources of information, including people sources

Mentor Recruitment

Recruiting and maintaining mentors is a major challenge for a mentoring project. Mentor programs may recruit mentors formally or informally.

There are a variety of strategies available to assist in the recruitment of mentors. These strategies include:

- Advertisements and/or human interest stories in newspapers and other media
- Public awareness campaigns
- Public service announcements
- Announcements and/or guest speakers targeted to community-oriented organizations such as churches, social service agencies, and fraternal organizations
- Outreach to local businesses
- Personal contacts/outreach to potential mentors
- Referrals from other mentors
- Integration of mentoring programs with existing organizations such as corporations or colleges and universities

When a program is targeting a certain type of mentor, advertisements and announcements in venues employed by that population is most appropriate. For example, a program seeking to recruit gay and lesbian mentors would do well to focus recruitment efforts on this population. Similarly, there is evidence that the recruitment of elder volunteers calls for unique strategies such as creating personal relationships with elder organizations and churches (Mecartney, Styles, & Morrow, 1994).

Ongoing recruitment campaigns require some sort of publicity materials. It may help an organization to have program logos, as well as a motto that captures attention. Print materials such as business cards and brochures ensure that interested parties may receive contact and program information easily. A video about the program also provides a useful means of conveying program information to potential mentors. The logo and slogan may be presented on a variety of publicity materials, such as balloons, pins, and T-shirts.

It is essential that, during the recruitment of mentors, expectations and goals be clearly conveyed to prospective mentors. In an effort to attract much-needed mentors, it may be tempting to minimize the expenditure of time and energy required by the mentor, or to oversell the potential gains to the mentor or mentee. Mentoring requires a notable investment by the mentor. It is also not a miracle cure-all for the troubles facing today's young people. A mentor recruited under false expectations may become disillusioned and prematurely terminate a mentoring relationship. For these reasons, it is important to clearly and honestly address issues of expectations and potential impact early on. For example, potential mentors should know the time commitment for each mentoring session and the expected frequency of such meetings. The period of time that volunteers are committing to in terms of their involvement should be specified. Most commit to at least one year, although some organizations require a three- to five-year commitment.

At times, incentives such as stipends or university credits are used to attract potential mentors. For elders, stipends may be particularly effective, as they help cover expenses and provide added revenue for individuals living on a fixed income. An example of such a program is the Foster Grandparent Program, a national initiative that places low-income seniors with needy children. Originally developed for the mentoring of the developmentally disabled residing in state facilities, in recent years some of the programs have reached out to children with special needs who attend public schools. Some evidence suggests that making personal contact is essential to the recruitment of older adults (Rogers & Taylor, 1997). Incentives for recruiting elder mentors include the creation of social opportunities and locating the program in an accessible facility (Rogers et al.). See Appendix D for a sample recruitment letter.

Mentor Screening

Mentoring programs are obligated to screen personnel and potential mentors prior to matching these individuals with youth. With mentoring that takes place in a group or public setting such as a school, a basic screening involving a written application, a personal interview, and reference checks may suffice. Health screening, such as a tuberculosis test, is typically needed. The extent of the screening process may depend on the level of intimacy expected for the mentoring relationship and/or the amount of time the mentor and mentee spend alone. This process may include a motor vehicle check or fingerprinting and a criminal history review.

In addition to discerning whether or not the mentor is a safe, responsible adult, the screening process explores the mentor's potential ability to help the mentee reach program goals and the likelihood that the mentor can follow through with program requirements in a consistent fashion. Exploring a potential mentor's motivation for participation may help assess suitability for a particular program. For example, potential volunteers with self-centered motives or ones who profess a desire to "save" a child may ultimately prove inappropriate. Some mentor programs require a home visit to evaluate potential safety hazards. This is especially important if the program permits the mentee to visit the volunteer's home. In many cases it is useful to explore a potential volunteer's history of personal relationships, as this may provide clues as to the suitability of the person as a mentor. Adults who report limited peer friendships, lack of a social support system, or few long-term relationships may prove inappropriate. Likewise, volunteers who show evidence of inappropriate boundaries, limited social skills, or deficits in understanding developmental issues may experience difficulty as mentors. Because of the time commitment involved in a thorough application and screening process, many unsuitable mentors may self-select out of participation during the process.

See Appendix E for a sample mentor application and Appendix F for a sample mentor profile sheet.

Mentor Training and Orientation

Mentoring programs vary greatly in the degree of training, supervision, and orientation provided. Yet, it is clear that attention to these issues is essential to the maintenance of an effective mentoring program.

Orientation is relevant to both mentors and mentees. A careful introduction to the mentoring process in general, as well as to specific program goals and policies, plays a significant role in ensuring that the match is successful. Participants may benefit from a review of the history of the program, as well as its goals and structure. All involved parties, such as mentors, mentees and families, should be familiar with program policies, including the roles, responsibilities, and expectations of participants. Participants should clearly understand program guidelines for issues such as confidentiality, liability, and crisis management. It is advisable that programs have their policies available in writing.

Orientation should also include education regarding the challenges of mentoring, so that participants do not become disillusioned. Training in relationship skills, such as rapport building, effective communication, and active listening may help. In particular, training regarding the characteristics of effective mentors is essential. Training should emphasize the importance of relationship development and provide opportunities to explore factors that impact this process. For example, mentors might benefit from exploring their expectations of the mentoring relationship and examining how expectations influence mentor-mentee interactions.

Diversity awareness and cross-cultural sensitivity training are also important, particularly if mentor-mentee matches will entail diversity of such characteristics as ethnicity, age, or socioeconomic background.

Many participants may benefit from training related to the program's target population, in terms of both general developmental issues and specific youth challenges (self-esteem, violence, sexuality, substance use, career development, etc.). Any program working with children requires that staff and mentors be familiar with child abuse reporting procedures, particularly if the program focuses on children at risk for abuse.

Specifically targeted programs will also have unique orientation needs. For example, with intergenerational mentoring, it is essential that the elders receive training regarding the developmental needs of youth, as well as on issues such as contemporary youth culture. Training may be part of the orientation and it may be provided throughout the course of participation in the mentoring program. Training may include assistance with specific skill development, such as listening skills, or education regarding relevant resources.

Research suggests that "failed" matches tend to occur in programs in which program staff do not make regular contact with volunteers (Sipe, 1996). Consistent contact provides information on whether or not the participants are actually meeting regularly and adhering to program guidelines. Ongoing monitoring and support may include scheduled phone calls, progress notes/activity logs maintained by the mentor, group supervision, and face-to-face meetings of supervisors with mentors, protégés, and possibly parents. They also provide opportunities to check for possible problems, such as overinvolvement with the child. Many mentor programs also include regular mentor recognition events, as well as newsletters or other mailings to involved parties and program supporters.

MENTEES AND PROTÉGÉS

This section focuses on the heart of the formal mentoring program: the youth and children being mentored (the mentees or protégés) and the adults or older youth providing the mentoring component.

Recruitment of Children and Adolescents

Once a program has determined its "target population"—which is to say, the type of problem or need it hopes to address (low achievement, teenage pregnancy, fatherless boys, etc.)—and the location of the mentoring program, active recruitment of potential mentees can take place. In locations where mentoring programs have already been successfully developed, recruitment of potential mentees is typically easily accomplished. When children or their families see others being helped through mentoring, they typically self-refer or respond favorably to a mentoring proposal.

With new programs or in new locations, the recruitment may take some time. In a year 2000 survey at Flowery Elementary School in Boyes Hot Springs, California, 97 percent of the children at the school listed mentoring as a top choice in terms of "what I need to help me succeed in school." At the time of the survey, Flowery's school-based mentoring program had completed its fourth year. At a nearby neighborhood school, El Verano Elementary School, where no program existed, only 2 percent of the students identified mentoring as a needed school support. The following year, upon implementation of a school-based mentoring program at El Verano, the number of students listing mentoring as important to them rose to 70 percent.

See Appendix G for a sample mentee application.

Preparation of Participating Children and Adolescents

As with any new endeavor, children and youth who are prepared to be "good mentees" will be more likely to see good results from the beginning. Some programs have developed a "mentoring success" pre-entry program to accomplish this preparation. Included in such preparation is a discussion of what to expect from mentoring and the responsibility of both the mentor and the mentee in the relationship. As to the latter's responsibility, typically the mentee's role is to cooperate with the mentor; attempt to establish a good relationship with the mentor; agree to work on goals for self-improvement, scholastic achievement, or increased positive behavior; and to have fun in the process.

Specific mentoring programs call for targeted orientation needs. For example, with intergenerational mentoring programs, youth benefit from training with regard to aging, especially information combating the myths about aging.

THE MENTOR-MENTEE CONNECTION

The essence of any mentoring program is the connection forged between a young person and his or her mentor. In a formal mentoring program, relationships are artificially created. Thus, great care is required to nurture and develop a caring connection between two strangers.

Making a Mentoring Match

The most effective mentoring programs attend carefully to the process of matching mentors with mentees. Many factors go into making an appropriate mentor-protégé match. In addition to the personal characteristics of each party, as noted previously, attention must be paid to how these two unique personalities will come together. Consideration of program goals is also important, and it is often useful to articulate a rationale for forming matches. In terms of developing a relationship, commonly noted influences include similarity in cultural background, gender, language, life experience, and economic background. Yet, research suggests that factors such as age, gender, or ethnicity do not link strongly with outcome factors such as frequency of meetings, match length, or match effectiveness (Sipe, 1996). In fact, none of these factors appears more important than the ability to listen and understand the experience of the young person.

Often, pairing youth and adults with similar interests and hobbies may be useful. Practical issues such as geographic proximity and schedule coordination are essential to consider. For more formal programs espousing specific goals, it is important that the potential mentor possess skills or qualities that relate to program goals. It may also be useful to allow the protégé input into the mentor selection process. The Big Brothers Big Sisters program attends carefully to the matching process and includes consideration of parental approval of the match. At the outset of the match process, establishing a mutual agreement between parties may be beneficial.

Helping to Establish and Maintain a Relationship

Effective mentoring programs need to focus on creating sufficiently intense and enduring relationships, especially since the length of the mentoring relationship appears crucial to the degree of positive impact. One study found that the most positive outcomes for youth occurred when the relationship averaged 24 to 30 months (Royse, 1998). More recently, an impact study of Big Brothers Big Sisters programs found that mentoring relationships continuing a year or longer were associated with the greatest number of gains for adolescent mentees (Grossman & Rhodes, 2002). In contrast, fewer positive gains were found for young people engaged in shorter mentoring relationships. Early termination corresponded to a decrease in performance on some indicators of functioning.

One major challenge for mentoring programs is the potentially difficult process of developing a relationship between mentor and protégé. It is important to remember that formal mentoring programs depend on contrived relationships. In other words, two unfamiliar people come together with the expectation that they will bond in some meaningful way. This alone is no small task. Add to this the idea that this relationship will somehow be transformative for both parties, and the pressure on this artificially created match mounts. Often, in an effort to recruit much-needed volunteers, mentor programs understandably highlight the positives of mentoring programs for both parties. While those positives are present, it is important for mentor and protégé to enter the relationship aware of the challenges that lie ahead.

It can be awkward to develop a relationship with any new person, mentor or other. Not uncommonly, mentoring relationships take time to develop and this pattern often relates to issues of intimacy and trust. This difficulty compounds when significant differences between participants, such as age, create artificial barriers. Many mentors approach the mentoring process with the idea that they will contact an eager young person who, in turn, will instantly engage. Yet, for every child who immediately embraces the relationship, there is another who holds back. This may be especially true for mentor programs targeted to specific at-risk populations. For example, emerging risk factors for early termination include exposure to ongoing emotional, sexual, or physical abuse, as well as being part of the older adolescent age bracket (Grossman et al., 2002). For young people who find it difficult to engage, resistance to forming a relationship may manifest itself in unreturned phone calls, missed appointments, or awkward silences during meetings. However, resistance can be a normal part of the mentoring process.

Unfortunately, when volunteers are not informed in advance about this process and the difficulties of establishing a comfortable relationship, they may feel discouraged and perhaps abandon the relationship altogether. This is one reason why training, supportive infrastructure, and ongoing support are so essential to an effective mentoring experience. In fact, Public/Private Ventures, a major force in mentoring research, concluded that mentor support is one of the most important factors contributing to mentor-mentee relationship building (Sipe, 1996). According to one estimate, 50 percent of mentoring relationships fail (Freedman, 1993). Findings for a mentoring program at an alternative school for pregnant and parenting adolescents indicate that 20 percent of the relationships terminated after only a few months (Rhodes & Davis, 1996). The authors express the belief that such high termination rates relate, in part, to the expectations of the volunteers, as well as to youth perceptions that factors related to social distance rendered the mentors "out of touch" with their experiences and problems.

Other very basic factors influence the quality and duration of the mentoring process. Basic elements such as transportation, physical space, and coordination with parents influence the ease and therefore the regularity of mentor-mentee meetings.

Monitoring and Supervising Mentoring Matches

Formal child and youth mentoring matches require formal monitoring processes. In many programs, a program coordinator supervises all mentoring activity (any interaction between the mentor and the mentee). In other programs, supervision is from a distance, with the actual activities between the mentor and mentee taking place unobserved. But even in these cases the mentor should have regularly scheduled consultations or check-ins with the staff of the mentoring program. For example, first-year matches in the Big Brothers Big Sisters program require monthly phone check-ins with both mentor and mentee by program staff. In many formal programs, mentee contact records are kept, along with a tracking system for ongoing assessment of the relationship, its frequency, and content.

Because maintaining mentor motivation is central to the mentoring process, many mentoring programs advocate the inclusion of regular mentor appreciation activities such as appreciation dinners, certificates, or thank-you announcements in local newspapers.

Terminating a Mentoring Match

A mentoring match may end naturally, as when the mentee achieves his or her preset goals or when the mentor fulfills his or her predetermined program commitment. At other times, the match may end prematurely—for example, if the mentor or mentee withdraws commitment to the program.

Premature termination is often a result of inadequate preparation (by the mentoring program staff) of the mentor or mentee—or both—as to the roles and responsibilities of each person in the relationship. There may be unrealistic goals expected from the match. When these expectations are not realized, either party may withdraw in disappointment or frustration.

Regardless of the reason, if the relationship "doesn't work" even when attempts have been made to encourage or to mediate between the mentor and mentee, it is usually best to end the relationship. In that situation, the program coordinator or designee should meet with the mentor and the mentee separately and discuss the end of the relationship. Individuals should be encouraged to try again with another match, either immediately or after a short time.

If a mentoring relationship must be terminated prematurely, extra care should be taken with the termination process, especially as it relates to the young person involved. Any termination discussions must be private and confidential. Counseling or support must be offered to the mentee if needed to work through the process of termination. The mentee will often feel that he or she has done something wrong and must be reassured by the mentoring staff. The program should offer the mentee assistance in completing the goals he or she had expected from the terminated relationship.

One or both of the parties involved in mentoring may feel disappointed if the mentoring match ends prematurely. In a youth mentoring program, the emphasis of support will focus on the mentee under such circumstances. The self-worth of the child or youth must be considered in the transition, with care taken to help the mentee adjust to the disappointment and ensure that the child's sense of empowerment remains intact.

Even when the relationship ends without problem—when caused by an unexpected event such as relocation on the part of the mentor, for example—care must be taken to support the mentee. Plans for follow-up communication between the (now former) mentor and mentee should be instituted. E-mails can be exchanged, along with letters or postcards. Telephone contact may also be a part of the transitioning-out phase. The same should be true in the case of the mentee moving from the area, although confidentiality may prevent the mentor from obtaining the mentee's new address. In most cases the original school or organization will be able to forward mail for the mentee to the new location.

Regardless, an exit interview is an expected procedure at the end of any mentoring relationship, but especially so in case of premature termination. These private and confidential interviews should be completed with the mentee, mentor, and staff. Depending on the nature of the termination, individual or group exit interviews may be conducted. A group interview is most appropriate in the case of a logical termination of a mutually satisfying mentoring relationship.

RISK MANAGEMENT

Despite the many benefits of mentoring, the process of joining a young person and adult in a caring relationship also comes with certain potential risks. Mentor programs have an obligation to attend to potential harm that may befall mentors and mentees, and to take steps to minimize the chance of such harm occurring. The term "risk management" refers to steps taken to address the possibility that a future event may lead to harm (White, Patterson, & Herman, 1998).

A key element of risk comes in the potential violation of the core trust that is so crucial to the mentoring relationship. For example, a mentor who repeatedly fails to keep commitments to the mentee may do more harm than good. All mentoring programs must take steps to guard against violations of the trust bond.

The section below addresses 10 concepts for mentoring-related risk management, as outlined by White and colleagues (1998). Readers interested in exploring this issue further can consult their book, *More Than a Matter of Trust: Managing the Risks of Mentoring*.

1. *Choose your mission, choose your risks:* Each particular programmatic mission carries with it unique risks. For example, the risks of an academic mentoring program may differ markedly from those of a program addressing adolescent substance abuse. When an organization remains focused on its mission it is better able to appropriately use resources and meet its goals. In addition, a focused organization can possess more awareness of its limitations and risks, and take a careful approach to minimizing potential harm.

2. *Collaborate with care:* Many excellent mentoring programs entail collaboration among agencies. While such collaboration often strengthens a mentoring program, it also brings with it potential areas of difficulty. In collaborative relationships, differ-

ent parties may espouse different goals and agendas, leading to a clouding of the program focus. Tension may lead to disagreement. Confusion about roles and responsibilities is more likely. Careful selection of potential partners, along with an open communication channel among those who collaborate, is essential. A written agreement can help clarify duties and responsibilities for collaborating parties, and a frank discussion of liabilities and commitments to handling such issues should occur at the outset of the collaborative relationship.

3. *Understand your clientele:* A mentoring program with a clearly defined mission statement will most likely target a specific group of individuals. These individuals will, in turn, possess particular assets and needs. Mentoring programs must consider these unique needs and make sure that the program is equipped to deal with them.

4. *Select your personnel:* As noted previously in the section on screening, careful selection of personnel and mentors is essential. Mentoring programs have an obligation to screen involved parties on relevant information to protect the clientele and the organization. A written application, face-to-face interviews, and reference checks should always be included. Criminal background checks will only show if the person has been arrested for criminal behavior.

5. *Establish boundaries of appropriate behavior and activities:* Both mentors and mentees should know what is expected of them. This includes goals and objectives, which, in turn, suggest appropriate activities. Participants should be clearly informed regarding acceptable and unacceptable activities. Potential areas for consideration are the appropriateness of gift giving or overnight stays. The role, if any, of the mentee's family should also be delineated. Clarification of appropriate meeting places and activities is also essential. Mentors transporting youth or engaging in potentially risky behaviors, such as water sports, should understand expectations regarding appropriate safety precautions.

6. *Supervise and train:* Mentoring organizations need to continuously monitor their programs to ensure that participants are doing what they should be doing. This includes general oversight of the overall program, as well as specific supervision of

individual activities and/or relationships. Training, orientation, and ongoing supervision are crucial for staff, mentors, and mentees, as are monitoring of facilities and other programmatic components.

7. *Manage your administrative function:* This element refers to the overall program structure and function. Key issues include information management, record keeping, documentation, and transportation policies and procedures.

8. *Plan for your crisis:* A crisis, by definition, is a sudden situation that poses potential threat or risk to your program's future. The best way to manage this risk is to plan in advance. Mentoring organizations should brainstorm the types of crises that may potentially occur and develop a specific plan for dealing with such crises.

9. *Evaluate your program:* As noted previously, evaluation is an important component of ensuring that a mentoring program is effectively meeting its goals. Evaluation can also help explore the possibility that the program is causing any harm to involved parties. Carefully gathered evaluation information can be integrated back into the program to improve functioning.

10. *Finance your risk:* Once the program directors understand managing risk, they must consider how they will finance both steps to reduce these risks and means for compensating for actual losses. This includes careful consideration of the insurance needs of the organization and its participants. Liability insurance adequate to cover mentor/mentee activities is advisable, but may be difficult or very expensive to attain. Programs that adopt sound hiring, training, and supervision policies and procedures will be in a stronger position to manage risk.

COMMON PROBLEMS IN MENTORING AND MENTOR PROGRAMS

Despite the significant promise of mentoring, the seeming simplicity of the concept (that is, matching an eager volunteer with a needy young person) belies the complexity of creating and maintaining effective mentoring programs. A few of the most common potential problems will be discussed in this section.

Scarcity of Mentors

A major challenge for mentoring programs is the scarcity of volunteer mentors. While about one-third of all two- and four-year colleges in the United States sponsor mentor/tutor programs for elementary and secondary school students, of these, one-third reported that they had insufficient tutors/mentors to meet the need (Calahan & Farris, 1990). Similarly, in an evaluation of a one-year mentoring/tutoring demonstration, there was a trend of schools reporting difficulty in recruiting enough mentors (Pringle et al., 1993). Like many mentoring programs, the Big Brothers Big Sisters program often encounters a shortage of volunteers in general, but male volunteers in particular. In one evaluation, 90 percent of the girls in the Big Brothers Big Sisters program were matched, as compared to 75 percent of the boys (Tierney et al., 1995).

Furthermore, mentoring programs are concerned not only with recruiting a large number of mentors, but also with attracting individuals who are appropriate for the program, both in terms of general suitability for work with youth and the ability to contribute to specific program goals. Programs may be attempting to recruit mentors of specific ethnicities or language groups due to the individual children's needs or preferences. Students may need tutoring in specific areas (math or science, for example) or desire a mentor with specific skills (technology or computer skills, for example) or a mentor who can serve as a role model for a specific career path (a farmer or an attorney, for example). In those situations, it is not just a matter of matching an adult with a child; rather, a very specific volunteer is needed.

Inadequate Screening of Mentors

Not taking the time to thoroughly screen mentors can create many problems, time-consuming and potentially serious, for a mentoring program. Three areas must be evaluated when screening volunteers for a mentoring program: (1) Safety is the first and foremost concern. The potential mentor must be appropriately screened (including a criminal background check and checking references) to ensure that the volunteer has good intentions, a healthy lifestyle, and good judgment; (2) The motivation of the volunteer is also important. In screening mentors, staff should ascertain why the person has been drawn to the mentoring program. For example, an individual with unresolved and/or unmet personal or relationship needs who is seeking to meet these needs through mentoring is an inappropriate mentor for a young person, as the individ-ual's neediness will negatively impact his or her role as a mentor; and (3) Checking out the track record of reliability and consistency of the poten-tial mentor is another screening task. Consistency in seeing a mentee is necessary if a mentor is going to establish trust and credibility with the child. A mentor who is unreliable and does not follow through with his or her mentee can do much harm to the child and will impact the men-toring relationship. A secure and trusting relationship is built only when the young person is assured that he or she can trust his or her mentor to do what the mentor promised to do.

The Mentor's Relationship with the Mentee's Family

Another area of potential concern is the mentor's relationship with the mentee's family members. An important but often unachieved task of the mentoring relationship is finding a level of engagement with the mentee's family that is comfortable for both mentor and mentee. While a young person may want his or her mentor to get along with family members, it is also common for the youth to want to keep this relationship separate or "special." Particularly for adoles-cents, who are in the process of disengaging from family life, there may be a need to isolate the mentor from family life. In some cir-cumstances, it may be the mentor who seeks to maintain distance from the family, particularly if he or she perceives that the family has a less than desirable influence on the young person. Mentors should be cautioned to guard against such positions, as the attitude and feel-ings may be transparent enough to the young person to cause poten-tial harm to the mentor-mentee relationship. Mentors may also strive to create firm boundaries when they perceive the family as pulling them into activities that are outside of the mentoring role, such as child care or "chauffeur service." Conversely, it may be that the fam-ily members put up a wall to the mentor who desires to engage with them. This can occur for a variety of reasons, including insecurity, embarrassment, jealousy, and/or mistrust. In many cases, adopting a nonjudgmental attitude toward the family can break down these bar-riers. By accepting the family's boundaries and pacing regarding allowing someone new into the family system, the mentor may find that the family is eventually open to the role that the mentor has in the life of the child.

Failure to Meet Participant Expectations

Often mentoring relationships fail because one or both of the parties involved, the mentee or the mentor, expected something different from the relationship. In the case of the mentee, the child or adolescent may have thought that the mentor would provide things for him or her (either relationship-wise or material items) that just did not happen. Often children think magically and imagine, "If I only had a mentor, all my problems would go away." The mentee may have projected the attributes or personality of another relationship (real or imagined) upon his or her mentor and the mentor never matched up. In any case, adequate preparation of the mentee, including a discussion about what he or she might receive from the relationship, along with follow-up and support for the duration of any match to circumvent potential problems, will go a long way in sustaining the relationship.

As for the volunteer adult mentors, they, too, often have unrealistic expectations about the relationship. Mentors may feel unappreciated and even "used" at times by their mentees, especially in the beginning phases of the relationship. Young people are often brought into a mentor program because they have had unsatisfactory relationships in the past, and they may not know how to engage in a mutually satisfying friendship. Some mentors have lamented that their mentees do not express their positive feelings in words, actions, or even facial expressions, making it difficult for mentors to know if the young people even want them to continue in the match. In academic tutoring and mentoring programs, mentors are often asked to tutor in subjects that they do not feel adequate to tutor. Whatever the source of the dissatisfaction or the unmet expectation, communication is always the lifeline. Most programs have set up monthly meetings in which issues of this nature are discussed. Since the problems are commonplace, many programs set up age-appropriate (depending on whether the discussion is for the mentors, the mentees, or both) in-service training sessions to discuss topics such as how to get more satisfaction from the mentoring relationship.

The Commitment to the Relationship Is Not Strong

A relationship takes time to develop. Many matches of mentors and mentees take months, even years, for the comfort level and the trust to fully develop. For this reason, some organizations are reconsidering their policy of having shorter-term commitments from mentors (typical commitments are six months to one year, with longer commitments encouraged) and are asking for at least three-year commitments. One mentor tells a familiar story of it taking one solid year of weekly meetings before the mentee would initiate conversation. Four years into the relationship, the bond is strong, the mentee secure that this person is not going to leave him, and the mentee self-initiates contact several times a week.

Mentors should always self-examine to see if there is something amiss in the relationship if it is not developing in a strong or satisfactory manner over time. Consulting with the program coordinator and meeting with other mentors to discuss mutual concerns at program in-services is an excellent, proactive approach to developing stronger bonds with a mentee. Of course, it goes without saying that keeping commitments to the mentee, treating him or her in a cordial and respectful manner at all times, and modeling enthusiasm and warmth to the mentee are also essential.

The Mentoring Relationship Does Not Develop

Occasionally, even given warmth, time, dependability, and caring on the part of the mentor, the relationship never develops. If a mentee or a mentor has concerns in this area, he or she should schedule a meeting (individually or, less often, together) with the program coordinator to see if something can be resolved or an element infused into the relationship to make it work. If both parties are committed to working on the relationship, it will probably ultimately be successful. If, however, it is determined that the match should be rescinded, care must be taken to ensure that the child or mentee primarily, and the mentor secondarily, is supported through any termination process (see section on termination).

EVALUATION

In order to determine whether or not a program is achieving its mission, an evaluation is needed. Ideally, an evaluation system is in place prior to the start of a mentoring program. This will allow a natural process of gathering evaluative information to occur in a smooth and consistent fashion. Evaluation questions should flow logically from the program's mission statement and link directly to goals and objectives. Organizations need to consider what evidence might indicate that goals and objectives are being met, and how to access that evidence. Evaluation should include short- and long-term outcomes.

Program efficacy, or the degree to which the program achieves its mission, includes both attainment of desired outcomes (outcome evaluation) and relative efficacy of the program process (process evaluation). The exact nature of outcome evaluations for mentoring projects depends on the specific goals of the program. Typically, mentoring outcome studies have examined variables such as:

- Attitudes about school or work
- High school drop-out rate
- Attendance
- Test scores and grades
- Completion of schoolwork
- Study and organizational skills
- Disciplinary referrals
- Drug and alcohol attitudes and usage
- Behavior problems
- Life aspirations
- Relationships with family and peers
- Self-confidence and self-esteem
- Communication skills

One way to effectively evaluate outcomes is to compare youth who were mentored to those who were not mentored. Another method involves looking at the progress of mentored youth over the course of the relationship. For example, adolescent attitudes about careers may be assessed prior to initiating the mentoring relationship and compared to attitudes toward careers after one year of mentoring.

In contrast, process evaluation attends to the program's overall operation. Questions might include:

- How effective is the program in recruiting mentors?
- Does the match process proceed smoothly and efficiently?
- Are the screening procedures for mentors adequate?
- How satisfied are participants or stakeholders with the program?
- What are the program drop-out rates for mentors? Mentees?

- What is the frequency and duration of mentor-mentee meetings?
- What activities do matches engage in during their time together?

OVERALL CHECKLIST: THE NUTS AND BOLTS FOR MENTORING PROGRAMS

The National Mentoring Working Group, convened by United Way of America and MENTOR/National Mentoring Partnership, developed the following checklist in 1990 for developing an effective mentoring program. The 2003 Elements of Effective Practice, 2nd Edition, is available from the National Mentoring Partnership at http://www.mentoring. org/common/effective_mentoring_practices/pdf/effectiveprac.pdf).

Does your program have the following?

1. A statement of purpose and long-range plan that includes:
   - Who, what, where, when, why and how activities will be performed.
   - Input from originators, staff, funders, potential volunteers, and participants.
   - Assessment of community need.
   - Realistic, attainable, and easy-to-understand operational plan.
   - Goals, objectives, and timelines, for all aspects of the plan.
   - Funding and resource development plan.

2. A recruitment plan for both mentors and participants that includes:
   - Strategies that portray accurate expectations and benefits.
   - Year-round marketing and public relations.
   - Targeted outreach based on participants' needs.
   - Volunteer opportunities beyond mentoring.
   - A basis in your program's statement of purpose and long-range plan.

3. An orientation for mentors and participants that includes:
   - Program overview.
   - Description of eligibility, screening process, and suitability requirements.

- Level of commitment expected (time, energy, flexibility).
- Expectations and restrictions (accountability).
- Benefits and rewards they can expect.
- A separate focus for potential mentors and participants.
- A summary of program policies, including written reports, interviews, evaluation, and reimbursement.

4. Eligibility screening for mentors and participants that includes:
   - An application process and review.
   - A face-to-face interview and home visit.
   - Reference checks for mentors, which may include character references, child abuse registry check, driving record checks, and criminal record checks where legally permissible.
   - Suitability criteria that relate to the program statement of purpose and needs of the target population. Could include some or all of the following: personality profile; skills identification; gender; age; language and racial requirements; level of education; career interests; motivation for volunteering; and academic standing.
   - Successful completion of pre-match training and orientation.

5. A readiness and training curriculum for all mentors and participants that includes:
   - Trained staff trainers.
   - Orientation to the program and resource network, including information and referral, other supportive services, and schools.
   - Skills development as appropriate.
   - Cultural/heritage sensitivity and appreciation training.
   - Guidelines for participants on how to get the most out of the mentoring relationship.
   - Do's and Don'ts of relationship management.
   - Job and role descriptions.
   - Confidentiality and liability information.

- Crisis management/problem solving resources.
- Communications skills development.
- Ongoing sessions as necessary.

6. A matching strategy that includes:
   - A link with the program's statement of purpose.
   - A commitment to consistency.
   - A grounding in the program's eligibility criteria.
   - A rationale for the selection of this particular matching strategy from the wide range of available models.
   - Appropriate criteria for matches, including some or all of the following: gender; age; language requirements; availability; needs; interests; preferences of volunteer and participant; life experience; temperament.
   - A signed statement of understanding that both parties agree to the conditions of the match and the mentoring relationship.
   - Pre-match social activities between mentor and participant pools.
   - Team building activities to reduce the anxiety of the first meeting.

7. A monitoring process that includes:
   - Consistent, scheduled meetings with staff, mentors, and participants.
   - A tracking system for ongoing assessment.
   - Written records.
   - Input from community partners, family, and significant others.
   - A process for managing grievances, praise, re-matching, interpersonal problem solving, and premature relationship closure.

8. A support, recognition, and retention component that includes:
   - A formal kick-off event.
   - Ongoing peer support groups for volunteers, participants, and others.

- Ongoing training and development.
- Relevant issue discussion and information dissemination.
- Networking with appropriate organizations.
- Social gatherings of different groups as needed.
- Annual recognition and appreciation event.
- Newsletters or other mailings to participants, mentors, supporters, and funders.

9. Closure steps that include:
- Private and confidential exit interviews to de-brief the mentoring relationship between:
  - participant and staff.
  - mentor and staff.
  - mentor and participant without staff.
- Clearly stated policy for future contacts.
- Assistance for participants in defining next steps for achieving personal goals.

10. An evaluation process based on:
- Outcome analysis of program and relationship.
- Program criteria and statement of purpose.
- Information needs of board, funders, community partners, and other supporters of the program.

REFERENCES

Calahan, M., & Farris, E. (1990). *Higher education surveys report: College sponsored tutoring and mentoring programs for disadvantaged elementary and secondary students.* Rockville, MD: Westat.

Flaxman, E., Ascher, C., & Harrington, C. (1988). *Youth mentoring: Programs and practices.* New York: ERIC Clearinghouse on Urban Education at Columbia University.

Freedman, M. (1993). *The kindness of strangers: Adult mentors, urban youth, and the new voluntarism.* New York: Cambridge University Press.

Gottlieb, B. H., & Sylvestre, J. C. (1996). Social support in the relationships between older adolescents and adults. In K. Hurrelmann & S. F. Hamilton (Eds.), *Social problems in social contexts in adolescence* (pp. 153–173). New York: Aldine de Gruyter.

Grossman, J. B., & Rhodes, J. E. (2002). The test of time: Predictors and effects of duration in youth mentoring relationships. *American Journal of Community Psychology, 30,* 199–219.

Mecartney, C. A., Styles, M. B., & Morrow, K. V. (1994). *Mentoring in the juvenile justice system: Findings from two pilot programs.* Philadelphia: Public/Private Ventures.

Philip, K., & Hendry, L. B. (1996). Young people and mentoring: Towards a typology? *Journal of Adolescence, 19,* 189–201.

Pringle, B., Anderson, L. M., Rubenstein, M. C., & Russo, A. W. (1993). *Peer tutoring and mentoring services for disadvantaged secondary students: An evaluation of the secondary schools basic skills demonstration assistance program.* Washington, DC: Policy Studies Associates. Sponsored by the U.S. Department of Education, Office of Policy and Planning.

Rhodes, J. E., & Davis, A. B. (1996). Supportive ties between nonparent adults and urban adolescent girls. In B. J. R. Leadbeater & N. Way (Eds.), *Urban girls: Resisting stereotypes, creating identities* (pp. 213–225). New York: New York University Press.

Rogers, A. M., & Taylor, A. S. (1997). Intergenerational mentoring: A viable strategy for meeting the needs of vulnerable youth. *Journal of Gerontological Social Work, 28*(1–2), 125–1240.

Roth, J., Brooks-Gunn, J., Murray, L., & Foster, W. (1998). Promoting healthy adolescents: Synthesis of youth development program evaluations. *Journal of Research on Adolescence, 8*(4), 423–459.

Royse, D., (1998). Mentoring high-risk minority youth: Evaluation of the Brothers project. *Adolescence, 33,* 145–158.

Sipe, C. (1996). *Mentoring: A synthesis of P/PV's research: 1988–1995.* Philadelphia: Public/Private Ventures.

Sullivan, A. M. (1996). From mentor to muse: Recasting the role of women in relationship with urban adolescent girls. In B. J. R. Leadbeater & N. Way (Eds.), *Urban girls: Resisting stereotypes, creating identities* (pp. 226–249). New York: New York University Press.

Taylor, A. S., LoSciuto, L., Fox, M., Hilbert, S. M., & Sonkowsky, M. (1999). The mentoring factor: Evaluation of the Across Ages intergenerational approach to drug abuse prevention. *Child and Youth Services, 20,* 77–99.

Tierney, J. P., Grossman, J. B., & Resch, N. L. (1995). *Making a difference: An impact study of Big Brothers Big Sisters.* Philadelphia: Public/Private Ventures.

White, L. T., Patterson, J., & Herman, M. L. (1998). *More than a matter of trust: Managing the risks of mentoring.* Washington, DC: Nonprofit Risk Management Center.

Yancey, A. K. (1998). Building positive self-image in adolescents in foster care: The use of role models in an interactive group approach. *Adolescence, 33*(130), 253–267.

3

Individuals and Professional Organizations Making a Positive Impact on Youth and Children through Mentoring

I've been really thankful for the mentoring program. My child has truly bonded with her mentor, and she has been exposed to new experiences. She is learning to play the guitar. With the support of her mentor, she has improved academically and stayed on task in class. She has gone from failing grades to making the honor roll, and recently told her mentor, "I really like the feeling of succeeding." Her mentor has taken a genuine interest in her; she is part of our family.

Parent

This chapter presents biographical and organizational summaries of major contributors to youth mentoring. Featured are key individuals, programs, and organizations that have made positive impacts on the lives of children and youth through both formal and informal mentoring efforts.

The organizations and programs ("Programmatic and Organizational Leaders in the Field") featured in this chapter were selected for their mentoring innovations, demonstrated successful outcomes, ability to be replicated, and leadership modeling in the field of youth mentoring. The list is representative, but not exhaustive. There are many exemplary individuals and programs currently active in the field of mentoring. Space limits allow only a few of the many exemplars to be highlighted. The individuals identified in this chapter ("Leaders in the Field") are known nationally for their innovation and effective contributions to the field of formal mentoring programs, for the role modeling of their mentoring efforts, and for their commitment to children and youth mentoring in general. The collective contributions of all featured in this chapter have enabled other localities to replicate youth mentoring innovations and have laid the groundwork for supporting children and youth for years to come.

In addition, following the "Leaders in the Field" section, two vignettes are presented to offer a more personal glimpse into the nature of the mentoring relationship, permitting the reader to view the concept through the eyes of the mentee and the mentor. These contributions, entitled "The Faces of Mentoring," are not a composite; rather, they are life stories about real people, mentees and mentors, involved in a formal school- or community-based mentoring program relationship. To protect the privacy of the individuals highlighted in "The Faces of Mentoring," identifying information has been changed.

LEADERS IN THE FIELD OF CHILDREN AND YOUTH MENTORING

Linda Alioto-Robinson

One to One/Massachusetts Mentoring Partnership

Linda Alioto-Robinson has gained national recognition for her expertise in the areas of mentor program design and development, collaborative partnerships, fundraising, and mentor/volunteer training. Since 1991, she has been the executive director of Greater Boston One to One, a model mentoring program, and part of the Massachusetts Mentoring Partnership. Alioto-Robinson has guided Greater Boston One to One in providing mentoring assistance to thousands of young people and serving as a model to the nation. Originally a social worker in a Boston settlement house, and later a school administrator and the director of a public school drop-out prevention initiative, Alioto-Robinson has worked with youth and families since 1975. She has experience in facilitating effective outcomes both with inner-city youth and their families, and with the institutions that provide services to these individuals. Alioto-Robinson has a professional record of success with programs that address the needs of at-risk youth. She consults with mentoring programs and is affiliated with the National Mentoring Partnership.

DeVone L. Boggan

The Mentoring Center

DeVone Boggan is the executive director of The Mentoring Center, an advocacy, research, and resource center providing national technical assistance and training for mentoring program staff, boards, and mentors. His leadership and commitment to mentoring has set a standard for mentoring in general and for the mentoring of incarcerated youth, in particular. A founding member of the National Mentoring Technical Assistance Corps and a member of the National Forum for Black Public Administrators, Boggan has also served as a consultant to the White House on the National Advisory Council on Violence against Women and Children. Boggan has been instrumental in the formation of local and regional mentoring coalitions. His efforts to recruit thousands of mentors in the Bay Area of Northern California have inspired mentoring organizations throughout the nation to do likewise in their own communities. Boggan's experience, leadership, and advocacy efforts in the mentoring arena have placed him in high demand as a youth development policy advocate, organizational development consultant, and trainer. Boggan has coauthored three mentoring publications: *Classification of Mentoring Relationship Types, Final Report—Mentoring Service Delivery Systems,* and *Framework for Mentorology.* He is a graduate of the University of California at Berkeley.

Travis Ann Cain

Office of Juvenile Justice and Delinquency Prevention

Travis Ann Cain has long been acknowledged as a leader in the field of child and youth mentoring for her role in creating the National Youth Network, a youth-adult partnership program sponsored by the Department of Justice. Cain currently directs one of the most far-reaching government sponsored mentoring programs, the Juvenile Mentoring Program (JUMP), which operates out of the Office of Juvenile Justice and Delinquency Prevention (OJJDP) in the U.S. Department of Justice. JUMP serves troubled youth in school or community settings, providing mentors and mentoring interventions. In addition to being responsible for the overall planning, development, and management of JUMP funding and implementation, Cain also had oversight of the National Crime Prevention Council and the Teens, Crime and Community program. Her professional background in the area of juvenile delinquency and delinquency prevention is considered an asset to the field of youth mentoring. JUMP outcomes have demonstrated that positive relationships with caring adults can make an important difference in the lives of at-risk children. Cain is a graduate of St. Mary's University, San Antonio, Texas.

Kay Coffin

Big Brothers Big Sisters

Kay Coffin is acknowledged as a leader in the area of mentoring for her successful efforts in youth mentoring in general and her ability to develop innovative and sustainable youth support programs. Coffin has been the executive director of Big Brothers and Big Sisters of Fresno, King, and Madera Counties (California) since 1998 and has developed numerous innovative mentoring programs including Kids with Character, Independent Living Skills Mentoring Program, and Student Tutoring and Resources Training. Coffin is a member of the California Mentor Council, where she chairs the Quality Assurance and Training committees.

Joyce Corlett

Big Brothers Big Sisters of America Federation

Joyce Corlett is noted for her visionary work in the field of children and youth mentoring. Corlett is the director of Program Development for the Big Brothers Big Sisters Federation and is a widely recognized leader in community-based youth mentoring programs. Both Corlett's leadership role in Big Brothers Big Sisters of America and her vision and expertise are considered models for community-based child and youth mentoring organizations. Corlett's experiences are in the area of one-to-one youth mentoring, mentees' needs assessment, volunteer mentor components (recruitment, screening, training, and supervision), and mentoring program infrastructure and board oversight. The groundbreaking work by Corlett and her colleagues on the foundations of mentoring projects has facilitated the establishment of replicable youth mentoring programs.

Ernest K. Coulter (1871–1952)

Big Brothers Innovator

Many have called Ernest Coulter the "father" of the Big Brothers of America concept. As a clerk in the New York City Children's Court,

Coulter daily witnessed the effects on children who were left unsupported and unsupervised. Rather than merely lamenting, Coulter took action on the boys' behalf: He is credited with founding the New York chapter of Big Brothers in 1904, an organization that later became the Big Brothers Big Sisters of America. Coulter is said to have inspired the Big Brothers movement during a speaking engagement with city civic and business leaders. At this meeting, he challenged influential New York residents to mentor the delinquent boys who were brought through the New York City Children's Court system. Coulter's moving challenge is evident in a quote typically attributed to this meeting: "There is only one way to save [that] youngster, and that is to have some earnest, true man volunteer to be his Big Brother, to look after him, help him do right, make the little chap feel that there is at least one human being in this great city who takes a personal interest in him." It has been traditionally reported that most, if not all, of the men present in the meeting that day answered Coulter's challenge. Coulter went on to establish a formal organization to support young boys, which eventually became known as Big Brothers of New York. (For more information, see the section on Big Brothers Big Sisters of America.)

H. Stephen Glenn

Author, Educator, Psychologist

Family psychologist and educator H. Stephen Glenn is internationally recognized for his contributions to the development and identification of prevention/intervention strategies for use in youth mentoring. He is the author and/or coauthor of a range of resource materials widely used by mentoring organizations and mentors, including *Raising Self-Reliant Children in a Self-Indulgent World* (1998), *Positive Discipline in the Classroom* (revised, 2000), *Positive Discipline A–Z* (1993), *Positive Discipline for Blended Families* (1997), and *7 Strategies for Developing Capable Students* (1998); he is also the author of several training series, including *Developing Capable People*. His books and professional development training have contributed to the foundation of state and community volunteer mentor training programs. A frequent speaker, his presentation venues have included the White House, where he was honored as one of the nation's most outstanding family life and prevention professionals. Glenn has served on many national boards related to the field of mentoring. Included in his board service are the National Association for Self-Esteem, and the

National Association for Children of Alcoholics. Glenn has also been the director of the National Drug Abuse Center for Training and Resource Development in Washington, D.C.

Darryl C. Green

Casey Family Services

Currently with Casey Family Services, Baltimore Division, Darryl Green is the cofounder of TEAM, The Empowerment of African-American Males. Among his many areas of expertise and leadership is in the development of programs supporting at-risk youth, especially youth of color. Green's emphasis on youth has been reflected in his career path, including his past work as program coordinator for Project RAISE (Maryland Mentoring Partnership), an acclaimed child and youth mentoring program designed to improve the future options and quality of life for inner-city disadvantaged students. Green's areas of expertise and experience include conflict management, assertiveness training, and the development of self-esteem in youth. A frequent lecturer, Green continues to contribute to the area of youth mentoring through workshops on designing and developing formal mentoring programs, including how to recruit, train, and retain volunteer mentors.

Michael Gurian

Author

Michael Gurian has made far-reaching contributions to the field of youth mentoring by his professional writings, many of which are considered essential to understanding the social, emotional, and developmental phases experienced by young boys and girls. A social philosopher, family therapist, educator, and the best-selling author of 15 books, Gurian founded the Gurian Institute to conduct research and serve as a training base for professionals in the field of helping others. His training videos for volunteers, mentors, and parents are used by the Big Brothers Big Sisters agencies nationally as well as internationally. Among his 15 best-selling books are *The Wonder of Boys* (1997), *A Fine Young Man* (1999), *Boys and Girls Learn Differently* (2001), *The Wonder of Girls* (2001), and *The Soul of a Child* (2002). His latest work, *The Miracle*, will be released in 2003.

Deborah Knight-Kerr

The Commonwealth Fund/Johns Hopkins Hospital Youth Mentoring Program

Deborah Knight-Kerr is renowned for her sustaining contributions to the field of mentoring and community service. She has been nationally cited for the quality of her public service in this area, particularly her work as the executive director of the Community and Education Projects at Johns Hopkins University's Department of Human Resources and Organizational Effectiveness. In that capacity, Knight-Kerr serves as the leader of an exemplary youth mentoring project, the Commonwealth Fund/Johns Hopkins Hospital Youth Mentoring Program. A unique, innovative, and replicable project, the Commonwealth Fund/Johns Hopkins Hospital Youth Mentoring Program serves at-risk youth in 15 nationwide hospital-based mentoring programs. Knight-Kerr's program reaches out to disadvantaged youth, including those from single-parent and/or low-income families. One segment of the program mentors physically or mentally challenged youth. Youth in the program are offered work experience, job shadowing, and career guidance in addition to role modeling and mentoring. The program demonstrates the efficacy of mentoring in difficult circumstances and with a challenging population.

Debra Lambrecht

Caring About Kids

Debra Lambrecht is the founder and executive director of Caring About Kids, an organization dedicated to developing resilient youth and thriving communities. A strong advocate for youth mentoring, Lambrecht has developed a variety of training manuals for mentoring support, including *Caring About Kids' Elementary and High School Programs* and *Supporting Group Facilitation.* The Rotary International Service Club has selected Lambrecht's program, Caring About Kids, as its international service to youth program, with full implementation in cities across the world. Since 1997, Caring About Kids mentors have spent more than 40,000 hours supporting local children and helping them succeed in life.

Eugene Lang

"I Have a Dream"® *Foundation*

Eugene Lang has contributed to the field of youth mentoring by his example of inspiring at-risk youth to dream and work hard to reach important goals. In 1981, Lang, a prominent New York businessman and multi-millionaire, returned to his former elementary school, Public School 121 in East Harlem, New York, intending to give a speech on the importance of hard work for success in life. When Lang learned of the startlingly low high school graduation rate for students at this school, he made a spontaneous promise to the 61 children that he would provide partial college scholarships if they graduated from high school. This was the beginning of his involvement in the field of child and youth mentoring and support. Later, Lang strengthened the potential impact of his promise to P.S. 121 students by implementing a process of sustained intervention. Initially, tutoring and SAT preparation courses were the components of Lang's invitation for students to drop by his office on Saturdays if they wanted to talk or "get help." In 1986, a formal "I Have a Dream" (IHAD) foundation was created, leading to the implementation of the program in other city schools and, ultimately, the replication of the innovation nationwide. Lang's example not only marked him as an inspirational leader in the youth mentoring field, it also led to tangible results for his original group of students: Of the original P.S. 121 "dreamers," 90 percent graduated from high school or received a GED. Sixty percent went on to college or vocational training. There are currently 175 "I Have a Dream" projects in 62 cities and 26 states, serving more than 13,000 disadvantaged youth.

Stephen Menchini

MENTORING USA

Stephan Menchini, former director of the International Year of the Child for UNICEF and the executive director of MENTORING USA, a New York City mentoring program, has been honored by many states and organizations throughout the country for his efforts on behalf of children. His work on the New York State Mentoring Program, a position to which he was appointed by the state governor, developed his expertise in the field of mentoring children and youth. Menchini's contributions to mentoring include mentoring program and curriculum development, along with mentor volunteer recruitment, training, and support. An innovator, Menchini currently heads an initiative to provide musical instruments and musical technical support to at-risk children attending inner-city schools in the New York–New Jersey area. Menchini is the principal at Stephen J. Menchini & Associates, a consulting group that focuses on implementing mentoring and other programs for at-risk youth. His clients include Communities in Schools New York and the New York City Department of Juvenile Justice.

David Moen

e-Mentoring

David Moen is a leader in the area of technological mentoring. Moen created the "e-Mentoring" program model in 1995 to increase the number of corporate adult volunteer mentors matched with Minneapolis, Minnesota, public school students. As the e-Mentoring program model concept has grown into its current structure, more than 1,400 corporate volunteers are matched with Minnesota middle school youth. The program has been widely replicated, and numerous corporations such as General Mills and IBM have created partnerships to use and expand this model. The e-Mentoring model received a 2000 National Partners in Education Technology award.

A presenter at regional and national conferences, Moen is currently the director of the Youth Leadership for Vital Communities Initiative. His education includes a B.S. and an M.S. from the University of Wisconsin–Madison. Acknowledged nationally as an expert in mentoring and e-Mentoring, Moen authored *e-Mentoring: A Model and Guide for a New Concept in Mentoring,* published by Youth Trust (1999).

Moen is listed as a consulting expert with The Mentoring Partnership, a national mentoring resource nonprofit organization. Moen's professional experience includes the coordination of a 32-member mentoring collaboration. He possesses expertise in increasing mentoring awareness, creating standards for quality mentoring programs, providing training for nonprofit mentoring programs, engaging strategies to recruit mentors, and creating a mentor recruitment initiative targeted at African American males.

David Neils

International Telementor Program

David Neils, an innovator in the field of electronic mentoring, is the founder and director of the International Telementor Program (ITP).

Springing from a pilot project in 1993, ITP (originally entitled the HP Telementoring Program) has evolved from a corporation-based mentor program (where all of the mentors were HP employees) to an independent nonprofit program mentoring youth from nine different countries. Currently the mentors come from many nations and are all employees of ITP's business sponsors.

David Neils is a good match for electronic mentoring. With degrees from state universities in both Montana and Colorado and high standards for both himself and those around him, Neils has set the standard for project based-mentoring. His program is the largest academic/project-based mentoring program in the world, with 15,000 students being mentored from 1995–2003. Unlike most programs, with 3,000 trained professionals signed up to participate, Neils has a surplus of mentors waiting for youth to tutor. Due to the nature of the mentoring relationship (virtually rather than in person), mentor-mentee matches can be made in minutes rather than in months, as would be required by traditional programs.

Neils attributed much of his own success to being encouraged and mentored as a child, having learned early on that, in the eyes of his mentor, his own thoughts had value and importance. Neils has sought to use the same approach of encouragement to positively influence others through the ITP. The International Telementor Program is based in Fort Collins, Colorado, where Neils resides with his wife and five-year-old son.

Mrs. John G. O'Keefe and Mrs. Willard Parker Jr.

First Big Sisters

Youth mentoring folklore recognizes Mrs. John G. O'Keefe as the very first "Big Sister." O'Keefe developed the Catholic Big Sisters of New York program, the first mentoring organization for girls in the United States. The concept of the Catholic Big Sisters was based on the organizational structure of the New York Big Brothers Association. Subsequently, Mrs. Willard Parker Jr., the director of an orphans' home in New York City, discovered that no Big Sister services were available for Protestant girls. Her contributions to the field of youth mentoring was to develop mentoring opportunities for girls of Protestant denominations, thus expanding the concept that mentoring benefits all children. Separate organizations, divided along religious lines and affiliations, existed for a number of years, but eventually all of the branches of the Big Sister movement merged to form a single organization.

Colin Powell

Secretary of State

Known internationally in many professional arenas, Colin Powell has been a major influence in the field of youth mentoring, becoming one of the highest-profile individuals in the country to actively advocate for mentoring as a form of positive youth intervention.

Powell served as a professional soldier for 35 years, including in a military advisory capacity under Presidents Reagan, Bush, and Clinton. His numerous distinguished posts include serving as the Commander in Chief of the U.S. Armed Forces Command, Chairman of the Joint Chiefs of Staff, and United States Secretary of State. Powell has garnered numerous military and civilian honors, including the Defense Distinguished Service Medal, the Army Distinguished Service Medal, the Bronze Star, the Purple Heart, two Presidential Medals of Freedom, the President's Citizens Medal, and the Congressional Gold Medal, among others. The governments of 18 other nations have also decorated him. Presently the Secretary of State, Powell continues to advocate for children, insisting that there is no credible future without making certain that youth have hope and support as they mature.

Since April 1997, when Powell chaired the Presidents' Summit for America's Future, he has served as the founding chairman of America's Promise—The Alliance for Youth. This national initiative seeks to bolster the competencies of America's youth. Powell also serves on the board of trustees at Howard University, the board of governors of the Boys and Girls Clubs of America, the board of directors of the United Negro College Fund, and the advisory board of the Children's Health Fund. Powell graduated with a B.S. in geology from City College of New York and an M.B.A. from George Washington University.

Jean E. Rhodes

Researcher, Author

Jean E. Rhodes has made significant contributions to child and youth mentoring in the course of her research and resulting publications, which focus on mentoring efforts in general and specifically on factors such as mentoring relationships. Currently an associate professor of psychology at the University of Massachusetts, Boston, Rhodes previously served as an associate professor of clinical/community psychology at the University of Illinois, Urbana-Champaign. Much of Rhodes's research concentrates on identifying factors that enhance positive adolescent development. A recent series of longitudinal studies explored the influence of nonparent adults and mentoring interventions on urban adolescents' academic, emotional, and social functioning. In her most recent book, *Stand By Me: The Risks and Rewards of Mentoring Today's Youth* (2002, Harvard University Press), Rhodes provides a synthesis of research on the topic of youth mentoring, highlighting both the benefits and risks associated with mentoring relationships. Rhodes received her Ph.D. in clinical/community psychology from DePaul University and completed a clinical internship at the University of Chicago.

Anita M. Rogers

Temple University Center for Intergenerational Learning

Anita Rogers's leadership in the field of child and youth mentoring is particularly noted in the area of linking older individuals with school-aged individuals. Rogers is the project director at the Temple University Center for Intergenerational Learning and author of valuable mentoring resources such as *Linking Lifetimes Program Development Manual: Elders as Mentors* (video and guide), *The Mentoring Planner,* and *Elder Mentor Handbook.* Her Linking Lifetimes project, a four-year national mentoring effort, matches more than 500 children and youth with elder mentors. Rogers's expertise is in the area of both organizational and program development. She regularly trains personnel from universities, nonprofit organizations, and businesses on how to envision, develop, and implement mentor programs. Rogers has a Ph.D. in educational psychology.

Shayne Schneider

Mentors Unlimited

Shayne Schneider is a nationally recognized leader in the field of both school-based mentoring and workplace mentoring. Since 1994 she has served as the president of Mentors Unlimited, a mentor consulting organization. Schneider is also the founder of Mentors, Inc., a nonprofit organization serving children in the Washington, D.C., public schools. In the mentoring field, Schneider uses her personal hands-on knowledge of mentoring children and youth in schools to help others develop mentoring programs. Schneider serves as a consultant on program design and training for both workplace and school-based programs. She works with corporations, government agencies, nonprofit organizations, universities, school systems, and service organizations. Schneider is a member of Leadership Washington and has served as board member and program chair for that organization. Schneider has developed training for mentees and speaks widely on the necessity of preparing youth to be successful in a mentoring relationship. She currently writes an online article for mentors on the Web site of the National Mentoring Partnership (www. mentoring.org). She is active in community affairs, serving on the board of directors of the Environmentors Project and the Hyattstown Mill Arts Program, and on the advisory boards of the Holocaust Museum Education Outreach Program and Women of Washington. A graduate of the University of Wisconsin, Schneider also holds a master of education degree from the University of Washington in Seattle.

Jerry Sherk

Counselor, Consultant

Jerry Sherk is well known for his efforts on behalf of children and youth. A former National Football League (NFL) defensive tackle star and for 12 years the most decorated Cleveland Browns player (1970s), Sherk has spent his second career helping at-risk youth attain success. He is the founder of the Professional United Mentoring Program (PUMP), a school-based program in which mentors use sports as a model to teach students how to reach goals in academics and other areas of their lives. Sherk is also a mentoring consultant to alcohol and drug programs. He continues to hold leadership roles in the NFL Players Association of San Diego. In that capacity, Sherk promotes the Players Association's mission statement, which supports mentoring programs in the greater San Diego area. Sherk has a master's degree in counseling psychology and is a consultant and technical assistant for children and youth mentoring programs. He is currently the president of Mentor Management Systems located in Encinitas, California.

Jay Smink

National Dropout Prevention Center

Jay Smink's work with preventative strategies to empower at-risk youth has marked him a leader in the area of child and youth mentoring programs, alternative educational strategies, and formal mentor program development and training.

Since 1988, Smink has been the executive director of the National Dropout Prevention Center at Clemson University. The National Dropout Prevention Center has a membership of more than 3,000 key leaders from the community, business, and education. Smink's experience ranges from teaching at the local school level to research at the university level, and much of his research and writing focuses on mentoring. He consults regularly in a variety of capacities and serves on several boards across the nation. Smink holds a doctorate in education (Ed.D.) in educational administration from Pennsylvania State University.

Mary Williamson Strasser

One to One/The Greater Philadelphia Mentoring Partnership

Mary Williamson Strasser, executive director of One to One/The Greater Philadelphia Mentoring Partnership, has more than 20 years of successful experience with youth-serving organizations. Strasser has modeled community collaboration and partnership development in the service of youth. As One to One/The Greater Philadelphia Mentoring Partnership's first leader, Strasser developed and expanded mentoring initiatives with religious/faith-based organizations. She has also developed a nationally accepted and replicated school-to-career youth mentoring model. Her expertise has contributed significantly to the field of child and youth mentoring, particularly in the area of mentor program design and development, mentor volunteer recruitment and training, and mentor curriculum development.

Judy Strother

Two by Two Mentoring

Judy Strother is known for developing innovative approaches to sustaining youth mentoring programs. Strother is a specialist in the field of youth development, youth mentoring, delinquency prevention, juvenile justice, and alternative health care. Her experience ranges from direct service delivery at the community level to policy development at the White House. She is the creator of the Two by Two mentoring model, used by many mentoring programs nationwide. Strother has more than

30 years' experience in service delivery, treatment, training, and technical assistance in initiatives sponsored by the U.S. Departments of Justice, Labor, and Health and Human Services. She has directed national initiatives for numerous federal agencies, including the Office of Juvenile Justice and Delinquency Prevention, the Bureau of Prisons, and the Agency for International Development.

Susan G. Weinberger

Norwalk Mentor Program

Susan Weinberger is known for her work in developing a highly successful and nationally replicated child and youth mentoring project, the Norwalk Mentor Program. The Norwalk Mentor Program is a school-based program that matches volunteers from corporations, civic and social organizations, and the community with disadvantaged youth in kindergarten through grade 12. In addition to directing the Norwalk Mentor Program, Weinberger consults in the areas of mentoring program development and management, mentor program training, mentoring curriculum development, mentor recruitment and retention, parental involvement in mentoring, evaluation of mentor programs, and fundraising activities for mentoring efforts.

Irvin F. Westheimer (1879–1980)

Big Brothers

Like Ernest Coulter, Irvin Westheimer is recognized as an originator of the Big Brother concept. He spearheaded the foundation of an initial Big Brothers agency in 1910. As the story has been retold over the years, the then 23-year-old businessman (Westheimer) was working at his office on July 4, 1903, when he looked out his window and witnessed a boy scavenging through garbage in search of food. Feeling compassion, Westheimer went out and introduced himself to the boy and learned that the boy came from a poor, fatherless family with five children. Westheimer took the child out for a meal and later met his family. He maintained contact with the boy, taking him to a ball game, giving simple gifts and treats, and providing understanding companionship. Subsequently, Westheimer urged his friends and business associates to befriend other troubled and disadvantaged youth and to offer them similar support and encouragement. According to mentoring folklore, one of these boys referred to his adult mentor as "my big brother," and the term stuck. (For more information, see the section on Big Brothers Big Sisters of America.)

Kathy Witkowicki

Stand By Me Mentoring Program

Kathy Witkowicki has received numerous honors for her work in developing grassroots school-based mentoring programs. Witkowicki is the cofounder of the Stand By Me mentoring program and is the executive director of the Sonoma Valley Mentoring Alliance. The alliance is a nonprofit corporation formed by local community members to support mentoring efforts and to expand the program and mentoring services in the community. The award-winning Stand By Me Children and Youth Mentoring Program, established in 1996, is a stellar example of a grassroots organization, assisted by grant funding and community support, with documented evidence of positive outcomes for hundreds of children and youth involved in one-on-one school-based mentoring. The Stand By Me mentoring program serves 10 schools in the Sonoma Valley Unified School District of rural Northern California. As a result of her exemplary leadership and the example of effective mentoring program development and expansion, Witkowicki has been an invited presenter at both the California State and the National Mentoring Summits.

A lifelong community activist, Witkowicki's interest in supporting at-risk youth was piqued via volunteer work in the public schools where she saw, firsthand, the needs of children struggling academically. A grant writer and public speaker in the area of mentoring, Witkowicki has been the recipient of numerous local, county, state, and national awards for her work on behalf of children, including two Spirit of Mentoring awards by the California State Mentor Initiative at the California State Annual Mentoring Summit Conference.

THE FACES OF MENTORING

The following descriptions are drawn from conversations with two mentors and their mentees. The conversations are supplemented by access to nonconfidential files regarding the mentors and their mentees, specifically verifying length of relationship and the form of mentoring—site-based or community-based. To protect the privacy of the individuals, the names of all participants have been changed.

John and Salvador

John, age 45, and Salvador, age 13, have been in a mentoring relationship for five years, paired by a school-based mentoring organization in the southern part of the United States. Salvador was initially referred to his elementary school mentoring program because of a lack of academic success. Sal had also exhibited signs of an anger management problem. John had been recruited into the mentoring program by a school-based mentor program coordinator. The coordinator was tenacious in approaching community members to become involved in mentoring. Salvador was fluent in Spanish and was an English language learner. John was fluent in both languages.

Relationship building in the first year following the initial match was slow. Salvador was quiet and John was reticent to push a relationship. Although the focus of the school-based program was academics, John soon realized that academic tutoring was not the best bridge to building trust with his mentee, and he introduced sports into the relationship. John and Salvador would work together each week on math or reading for 40 minutes, but would spend the last 20 minutes of their hour together shooting hoops on the school playground. The introduction of sports changed the relationship from one of distance and shy hellos to one of eager anticipation on both parts.

John has increasingly played a significant role in Salvador's educational life. He attends all school conferences, at the request of both Salvador and his parents. He also serves as a communication link between Salvador's parents and the English-speaking school environment. With the mentor's encouragement, Salvador's parents followed through on their suspicion that a learning problem might be getting in the way of Salvador succeeding in school. The parents and the mentor requested a special education evaluation. The testing proved that although Salvador had an above-average IQ, there was a marked discrepancy between his ability and his performance due to a learning disability. Salvador improved in all areas of academics following his qualification for special education; however, he continued to be challenged, in general, by his learning differences. A bright and charismatic young man, he continues to compensate for his lack of academic success by acting out in school situations. This is an area Salvador is working on with his mentor. John continues to meet with Salvador weekly during the school year and sees him less frequently during the summer months. John is encouraged by the progress his mentee has made over the years.

Melinda and Carrie

Melinda, age 62 and a retired teacher, and Carrie, age 10, have been in a formal East Coast community-based mentoring relationship for the last two years. They have actually known each other for five years, as Melinda was Carrie's first grade teacher. Their match was serendipitous, but finding out that the match was "someone from the past" was a surprise and delight to both of them. Thus, the pair started their relationship at a higher affective level than most beginning mentor-mentee matches.

Although a positive mentoring relationship was established from the start, their familiarity created some interesting challenges. It was six months before Carrie felt comfortable calling her old teacher anything but Mrs. Anderson. On Melinda's part, as a mentor, she had anticipated that the mentoring relationship would consist of providing academic support for her mentee. Melinda needed to drop her expectations for that significant tutorial component, because it became immediately evident that Carrie's primary challenges were more social and personal than academic. Fortunately, both parties were committed to the relationship and they worked at modifying and adjusting expectations until there was mutual satisfaction. They did spend time talking about school "stuff," but more time was spent discussing the social and emotional problems Carrie faced. In reflection, they agreed that it would have been less frustrating had they been able to voice their expectations about the relationship to one another from the start of the match. Both express the desire to be in a mentoring relationship for a long time and to be friends for even longer. As Carrie said, "Being with Melinda is important to me. I am glad that she cares enough about me to want me to have a lot of good choices when I grow up."

PROGRAMMATIC AND ORGANIZATIONAL LEADERS IN THE FIELD OF MENTORING CHILDREN AND YOUTH

This section describes select organizations and programs that have made enduring and significant contributions to the mentoring of children and youth. Although the list is not exhaustive in terms of importance to the field, the organizations and programs in this section have proven track records of success and represent both best practices and promising, innovative programs.

100 Black Men of America, Inc.
141 Auburn Avenue
Atlanta, GA 30303
Phone: (404) 688-5100 or (800) 598-3411
Fax: (404) 688-1024
Web: www.100blackmen.org

Begun originally in 1963 as the 100 Black Men of New York, 100 Black Men of America, Inc., is a national alliance of men of African descent from all professional areas of work who have made a formal, public commitment to mentor one million African American children and youth. A volunteer organization, the mission of the mentoring program is to empower young people by giving them confidence and skills to be competitive in today's society. The program's emphasis is on the nurturing of academic achievement, social responsibility, and creativity on the part of youth.

In 1976, Dr. William Hayling founded the 100 Black Men organization in New Jersey. In 1986, the individual chapters of New Jersey, Los Angeles, Indianapolis, St. Louis, Pittsburgh, Atlanta, Bay Area, Nassau/Saffol, and Sacramento merged to form a national organization called the 100 Black Men of America, Inc., with Dr. Hayling as the founding president. On May 27, 1987, in Atlanta, Georgia, this newly formed organization introduced itself to the nation during its first national conference.

With a mission to improve the quality of life and enhance educational opportunities for African Americans, members of the 100 seek to serve as a strong force for overcoming the societal and financial obstacles that have limited the achievements of African American youth, particularly males. The organization highlights the societal role African Americans play in corporate and community leadership. The 100 has also demonstrated that the training and support provided for thousands of youth each year improves opportunities to stabilize their learning environment and become self-supportive and empowered to control their own destinies.

Across Ages Mentoring Program
Temple University Center of Intergenerational Learning
1601 N. Broad Street, Room 206

Philadelphia, PA 19122
Phone: (215) 204-6708
Fax: (215) 204-6733
Web: www.temple.edu/cil/acrossageshome.htm

The Across Ages program is an elder-youth mentoring program that seeks to help at-risk youth become productive and self-reliant members of society. Established in 1991, the program is considered to embody the best practices in the mentoring field, not only because of its innovative linking of elders with youth, but also because of its comprehensive program design. In Across Ages, mentors undergo 8 to 10 hours of preservice training in areas related to mentoring, such as adolescent development, communication skills, and problem-solving techniques. Youth and families receive orientation about the program requirements, and the informed consent of the youth, parents, or guardian is obtained. The minimum specified time for one-to-one contact is generally between two and six hours a week, and mentors are expected to make a commitment of at least one year. Matching mentors with more than one youth is allowed only if minimum required contact hours are maintained.

The Across Ages mentoring program has the general goals of promoting social competence, productivity, and self-reliance, but the specific mentoring activities and objectives are decided by each matched pair, with an expectation that the activities will be tailored to the needs of the youth. The Across Ages match receives ongoing support, and mentors receive stipends and/or expense reimbursement. Across Ages received an Exemplary Substance Abuse Prevention Award from the National Center for Substance Abuse Prevention in 1999. The Across Ages program model is integrated into regular agency services, which differentiates it from traditional school-based mentoring models. Originally, the program was developed as a school-based program to address substance abuse prevention. The program focus was expanded in recent years to address multiple risk/protective factors for children and youth.

Big Brothers Big Sisters of America
230 N. 13th Street
Philadelphia, PA 19107
Phone: (215) 567-7000
Fax: (215) 567-0394
Web: www.bbbsa.org

Founded in 1904 and with a century of experience in facilitating meaningful, long-lasting adult-youth relationships, Big Brothers Big Sisters of America (BBBS) is the oldest, most established mentoring program in the country. Begun as the Big Brothers organization by concerned men in the community, the movement was duplicated by community women wanting to offer similar opportunities for girls. In 1977, the Big Brothers and Big Sisters organizations united into the Big Brothers Big Sisters of America, with the national headquarters of the organization established in Philadelphia.

The BBBS model pairs unrelated adult volunteers (mentors) with youth, typically from single-parent families. The Big Brothers Big Sisters operational philosophy is that the matched relationships will help youth transition from childhood and adolescence to adulthood. Following the BBBS model, the mentor functions as a source of support to the mentee. The BBBS program does not specifically set out to change a young person's nature or characteristics, but research shows that significant positive outcomes are possible for mentored children and youth, especially in terms of the prevention of substance abuse, improved school attendance, decreased aggression, and increased trustworthiness.

BBBS's national office develops and publishes standards and operating procedures that regulate participant screening, orientation, and training, and outline strategy for the creation and monitoring of matches. These standards and procedures are widely adopted by youth mentoring organizations worldwide.

BBBS is recognized as the leader in the field in terms of risk management and precautions in assessing potential mentors. Volunteers for BBBS are among the most carefully screened of any mentoring organization, and, as such, the matching process may take a month or more. Additionally, involvement in the BBBS program requires a substantial time commitment from both the volunteer mentor and the youth. The mentor-mentee matches are expected to meet two to four times per month for at least one year. Guidelines suggest that each visit last three to four hours.

Likewise, youth participants and their families are carefully screened. This process involves completion of a written application, as well as youth and parent interviews and a home assessment. BBBS programs target youth between the ages of 5 and 18 years who live in single-parent homes. Typically, these youth are screened for a minimum level of social skills and motivation for the program. Consent of both the young person and a parent or guardian is required for participation.

The "I Have a Dream"® Program
The "I Have a Dream" Foundation
330 Seventh Avenue, 20th Floor
New York, NY 10001
Phone: (212) 293-5480
Fax: (212) 293-5478
Web: www.ihad.org

With 180 projects in 64 cities across 27 states, the "I Have a Dream"® program (IHAD) has served more than 13,000 students in the past 20 years. Established as a national foundation in 1986 by businessman Eugene Lang, IHAD developed from a commitment that Lang made in 1981 to financially help sixth-grade students at New York City's Public School 121 to go to college. Financial support for college was not the only promise; Lang also committed to monitor the students' progress over the years and to stay in touch. The "dreamers," as his protégés became known, accepted the challenge and at least 60 percent of the original students went on to two or more years of higher education. The "I Have a Dream" organization challenges mentors/supporters to encourage youth to complete their high school education and to enter and graduate from college.

The International Telementor Program
3919 Benthaven Drive
Fort Collins, CO 80526
Phone: (970) 206-9352 or (800) 376-8053
Web: www.telementor.org

The International Telementor Program (ITP), one of the world's largest telementoring programs, was established in 1995 to facilitate electronic mentoring for students worldwide. Since its formation, more than 15,000 students have been served in at least nine countries, receiving support, encouragement, and professional guidance. The International Telementor Program creates mentor-mentee matches between industry professionals from ITP sponsor companies and students (kindergarten through college) targeting specific communities around the world. Students are matched only with professional individuals employed by the ITP sponsor organizations. Those organizations include Hewlett-Packard, the original sponsor of the innovation. ITP has evolved from a Hewlett-Packard-based program to a stand-alone non-profit organization based in Colorado.

Former Hewlett-Packard employee David Neils, who is currently ITP's director, conceived the idea for this form of electronic mentoring. The ITP program creates project-based online mentoring support for students and teachers in classrooms and home environments with a focus on serving a diverse student population. Telementoring is described as a process that combines the proven practice of mentoring with the speed and ease of electronic communication, enabling busy professionals to make significant contributions to the academic lives of students. Through mentoring by industry professionals, a corporation helps students develop the skills and foundation to pursue their interests successfully and operate at their potential. ITP points out that, although research shows that face-to-face mentoring programs can have a variety of positive impacts, many top professionals believe they simply don't have the time to make that kind of commitment. By spending about 30–45 minutes per week, it is anticipated that mentors can help students achieve academic excellence and explore career and educational futures.

JUMP/The Office of Juvenile Justice and Delinquency Prevention

Office of Juvenile Justice and Delinquency Prevention
810 Seventh Street N.W.
Washington, DC 20531
Phone: (202) 307-5914
Fax: (202) 514-6382
Web: www.ojjdp.ncjrs.org/jump/index.htm

The Juvenile Mentoring Program (JUMP) supports one-on-one mentoring programs for youth at risk of failing in school, dropping out of school, or becoming involved in delinquent behavior, including gang activity and/or substance abuse. An amended part of the Juvenile Justice and Delinquency Act of 1974 (Section G) authorizes the Department of Justice to provide seed money to develop juvenile mentoring programs. The United States Congress funds such programs, and, as of 2001, Congress had apportioned more than $56 million for such efforts.

The federal Office of Juvenile Justice and Delinquency Prevention (OJJDP) has sponsored more than 9,200 at-risk children and youth (in kindergarten through grade 12) in mentoring relationships through JUMP. Located in 47 states, these mentoring programs target at-risk male and female youth of all ethnicities and special populations, including immigrant, court-involved, and abused and neglected youth; children of incarcerated parents; and youth with disabilities. The term at-risk youth refers to a youth who is exposed to high levels of risk in his or her family, home, community, and social environment, to a degree that may lead to educational failure, dropping out of school, or involvement in juvenile delinquency, including gang-related delinquent activity. Mentors have been recruited from both the public and private sectors, including faith-based institutions, community-based organizations, schools, police and fire departments, hospitals, and banks and local businesses.

JUMP was developed to support three goals: (1) the improvement of academic performance, (2) the reduction of school drop-out rates, and (3) the prevention of delinquent behavior. JUMP's objectives are to (1) provide general guidance and support to at-risk youth, (2) promote personal and social responsibility among at-risk youth, (3) increase participation of at-risk youth in elementary and secondary education and enhance their ability to benefit from this schooling, (4) discourage use of illegal drugs and firearms, involvement in violence, and other delinquent activity by at-risk youth, including involvement of at-risk youth in gangs, and (5) encourage participation in service and community activities by at-risk youth. A 1998 report to the U.S. Congress on the efficacy of JUMP noted that participating JUMP children and youth believed that their mentoring experience had helped them to improve their academic performance, have better relationships with their family and friends, and avoid the use of tobacco and other drugs.

To strengthen the mentoring capability of JUMP grantees, OJJDP additionally funds the National Mentoring Center in Portland, Oregon. That center—a collaborative effort between the Northwest Regional Educational Laboratory, Big Brothers Big Sisters of America, and Public/Private Ventures—provides training and technical assistance, produces and distributes bulletins, and conducts regional training programs throughout the United States. Additional information about the center may be found online at www.nwrel.org/mentoring.

MENTORING USA

113 E. 13th Street
New York, NY, 10003
Phone: (212) 253-1194
Fax: (212) 253-1267
Web: www.mentoringusa.org

Mentoring USA is a nationally replicable mentoring program whose mission is to provide early intervention and support to at-risk children.

Trained adult mentors provide the support in the form of early, consistent, and frequent positive attention. Mentoring USA has developed a curriculum package that is replicable as a site-based mentoring program. The program provides structured one-to-one mentoring to particularly at-risk populations such as young children who are already experiencing difficulty or failure in school, children in foster care, and children who have become homeless. Mentoring USA offers communities and schools the opportunity to start local programs using already developed print materials (manuals, brochures, guides, etc.), videotapes, training sessions, workshops (including problem-solving and evaluation issues), and technical assistance. The Mentoring USA program is a proven early-intervention school- or community-based program to address present or future school drop-out. By focusing on academic success and *connectedness* to school, the program encourages each mentored child to reach his or her potential. The program uses volunteer adults as mentors. By offering the fee-based replicable program and programmatic materials, Mentoring USA takes away the necessity for new start-up programs to reinvent the wheel, allowing new program developers to focus their energy on serving children and youth.

Project RAISE
Baltimore Mentoring Institute
605 N. Eutaw Street
Baltimore, MD 21201
Phone: (410) 685-8316
Fax: (410) 752-5016

Initiated in 1988, the Project RAISE mentoring program began with seven community sponsors who made a seven-year commitment to offer support to 60 at-risk students per sponsor. The programmatic design of the mentoring program involved sponsoring these students from 6th grade through 12th grade. The strategy involved providing caring adult-youth connections to promote self-esteem and positive school-related behaviors and progress, as well as curbing high-risk behaviors. The RAISE model includes a full-time director and a complement of support staff responsible for overall program development and administration, along with paid school-based advocates for each sponsor. Administration of the program is located in the Baltimore Mentoring Institute. The advocates monitor the students assigned to each sponsor and keep track of attendance, grades, and behavior, while developing trusting relationships with each student.

The program goal includes the use of volunteers to provide one-to-one mentoring for each student. The model calls for a substantial commitment in terms of time and energy from volunteers, with a minimum expectation of one year of weekly contacts and biweekly face-to-face meetings. Volunteer mentors receive orientation and ongoing training. Project RAISE is funded by grants, along with annual contributions for the sponsors.

Stand By Me Mentoring Program
17860 Sonoma Highway
Sonoma, CA 95476
Phone: (707) 996-6843
Fax: (707) 935-8136
Web: www.sonomamentoring.org

The Stand By Me mentoring program demonstrates how matching at-risk children with caring adults can make a difference, not just in the lives of those two people, but also in the life of an entire community. The mentoring program was envisioned in the spring of 1996 and, with the help of a grant from the California State Office of the Secretary of Education Academic Volunteer Mentoring and Tutoring Mentor Program, commenced that fall. Stand By Me began with hope, minimal funding, and little else but a dynamic program coordinator. The start-up year was difficult. Mentors had no dedicated space to meet with their mentees, and sessions were held under narrow walkway eaves during the rainy Northern California winter.

By 2000, proven success and demonstrated outcomes (reading levels raised, school safer, attendance at school increasing) from the program solidified community support, turning Sonoma Valley into a community of mentors. After starting at one school with a fledging program in 1996, by 2003 ten schools and more than 300 children and youth in need of academic and/or social and emotional support were being mentored one-on-one in school-based programs scattered throughout the school district. Mentors and mentees are no longer meeting in the rain; currently most of the school sites have their own separate mentor building, equipped with study aids, computers, reading material, sports equipment, art projects, and (at some sites) even an outdoor garden. The program goal is to have mentoring taking place at every district school by the year 2004. Overwhelming community support and the establishment of a nonprofit community corporation to sustain the program make the Stand By Me mentoring program model a youth mentoring program that should be replicated.

The Tutor/Mentor Connection
Cabrini Connections
800 W. Huron
Chicago, IL 60622
Phone: (312) 492-9614
Fax: (312) 492-9795
Web: www.tutormentroconnection.org

The Tutor/Mentor Connection (T/MC) was established in 1993 by Chicago-based Cabrini Connections to develop a tutor/mentor program based on best practices, one that would serve as a model across the nation. Among the goals of the Tutor/Mentor Connection are to increase the: (1) awareness of tutor/mentor programs nationally, (2) flow of resources for any city in need, and (3) provision of support and direction to the youth of the greater Chicago area, especially through comprehensive one-on-one, group, and other forms of mentoring programs.

T/MC has created a comprehensive network of Chicago-area mentoring programs, but the benefits offered by this program extend beyond Chicago. T/MC's Web site, for example, contains valuable information related to establishing and maintaining effective mentoring programs, including an extensive array of online training documents for volunteers and leaders of mentor programs. T/MC also hosts topic-focused online discussions and features a "Best Practices" section that serves as a model for mentoring networks throughout the country.

As a leader in the field of youth mentoring activities, T/MC has hosted 16 leadership conferences on children and youth support and has published a report entitled *A Collaborative Study of Chicago's Youth Services Programs: A Look at 272 Youth Services Programs in the Community.*

The Village Project
Village Project Volunteer Mentor Program
Third District Juvenile Court
450 S. State, 2nd Floor
P.O. Box 140431

Salt Lake City, UT 84114-0431
Phone: (801) 238-7700
Web: www.utcourts.gov/specproj/mentors/village/index.htm

An example of a promising practice with the potential for replication in other communities, the Village Project is an exemplary volunteer mentor program sponsored by the Third District Juvenile Court in Salt Lake City. The project serves only court-involved youth, pairing them with volunteer adult mentors from the community who are willing and coached to work with troubled and discouraged youth, thereby making a difference in their lives. Mentees are court-involved for a variety of reasons, including being delinquent, dependent, abused, or neglected. Mentors in this project are matched with youth based on location and common interests. Each mentor meets with his or her mentee (who may be at the elementary, middle, or high school level) for one to three hours per week. The project sponsors regular evening and weekend activities that are voluntary in nature but allow the mentors-mentees to participate with the greater community. Both mentors and mentees are provided ongoing support and training by project staff.

Youth Connect
National Indian Youth Leadership Project
P.O. Box 2140
Gallup, NM 87301-4711
Phone: (505) 722-9176
Fax: (505) 722-9794
Web: www.niylp.org

Founded by McClellan Hall, a Cherokee/Pawnee youth advocate and activist, the National Indian Youth Leadership Project (NIYLP) is a program committed to the development of all Native American youth. The mission of the National Indian Youth Leadership Project is to prepare Native youth for healthy, productive lives while honoring the Native American culture and engaging Native youth positively in their communities and schools. The Youth Connect mentoring program is one of five key programs developed to meet the NIYLP goals.

Youth Connect is a mentoring program focusing on sixth-grade Native American students. Sixth graders are targeted for Youth Connect mentoring due to their unique developmental issues. Based in both school and nonschool settings in the Gallup, New Mexico, area, the program uses both one-on-one and group mentoring to help Native youth reach mutually set goals. Native culture awareness/appreciation and outdoor activity are a part of the weekly group meetings. Service to the immediate community is a key element of the program.

The overarching goal of Youth Connect and NIYLP is to empower Native youth for positive futures. Using culturally appropriate, experiential service learning and out-of-the-classroom experience as an instructional strategy, the NIYLP has developed exemplary programs (Youth Connect, Project Venture, Al Chini Ba, A+, and Native Youth Corps) to enhance youth leadership qualities and to reduce substance abuse among Native American youth.

4

Facts and Data

Everyone needs someone special in their life.... like a big sister or a mentor. Mentoring is the best thing that ever happened to me. My mentor helps me out with my homework when it is too hard. At first it was scary when I met my mentor because I was shy. By going out with my big sister, I grew out of my shyness.

Amanda, 15 years old

Despite mentoring's long tradition, efforts to gather related data and research are relatively new. This chapter provides information on important sources of mentoring data, as well as an overview of research in the area of mentoring efficacy. In addition, the chapter includes an interview with a prominent figure in mentoring, examples of federal and state mentoring proclamations, and a sample of youth mentoring legislation.

DATA SOURCES

Big Brothers Big Sisters of America

Web: www.bbbsa.org

Big Brothers Big Sisters of America is the oldest, most established mentoring program in the country. The national office develops and publishes standards and operating procedures that regulate participant screening, orientation, and training, and outline how to create and monitor matches.

National Mentoring Center

Web: www.nwrel.org/mentoring

The Northwest Regional Educational Laboratory's National Mentoring Center, funded by the Office of Juvenile Justice and Delinquency Prevention (OJJDP), offers training and technical assistance to mentoring programs. Its services include conducting research as well as providing training and technical assistance to education, government, community agencies, business, and labor. The Web site includes information on training (events, a listserv, and online learning opportunities) and resources (publications, a lending library, and Web resources).

The National Mentoring Partnership

Web: www.mentoring.org

This partnership promotes the growth of mentoring nationwide and serves as a resource for mentors and mentoring initiatives. The partnership is headquartered in Alexandria, Virginia, and works with a national network of 30 state and local partnerships. The National Mentoring Partnership Web site offers advice on becoming a mentor, improving mentoring skills, and finding a mentor. The site also provides information related to running a mentoring program. Useful mentoring resources are described, and the "Research Corner" provides recent news in the field of mentoring.

Public/Private Ventures

Web: www.ppv.org

Public/Private Ventures is a national nonprofit action-based research, public policy, and program development organization. The organization's mission is to advance social policies, programs, and community initiatives serving youth and young adults. P/PV works in partnership with philanthropies, the public and business sectors, and nonprofit organizations. P/PV makes significant contributions in the area of program evaluation and development, and has conducted extensive research evaluating mentoring programs. The organization's Web site contains invaluable resources for those interested in mentoring research and state-of-the-art mentoring practices. The Web site lists a variety of downloadable mentoring-related publications.

Temple University Center for Intergenerational Learning

Web: www.temple.edu/cil

Since 1979, the Center for Intergenerational Learning (CIL) at Temple University has worked to strengthen communities using intergenerational programming. The CIL is a national resource for programs seeking to improve the lives of individuals and families by creating opportunities for youth and elders to contribute to their communities and promoting partnerships among organizations serving young people, families, and older adults. The center advocates for intergenerational strategies and works to educate and assist in the development of intergenerational programs. The CIL generates and supports a variety of intergenerational programs, such as Across Ages, while also engaging in materials development, research, and evaluation. The CIL also provides extensive training and technical assistance to agencies interested in developing intergenerational programs. Interested individuals should consult the Web site for further access to these resources.

BENEFITS OF MENTORING

The concept of mentoring is centuries old and has consistently been met with great popular support. The popularity of a program or strategy, however, even one as widely accepted as mentoring, does not always correspond with significant outcomes. In this case, research tends to support the efficacy of the mentoring relationship and suggests that mentoring is an effective means of fostering child and youth development.

What follows in this section is an overview of current research regarding the effectiveness of mentoring in general and in terms of specific areas of school achievement and social and emotional benefits for mentees/protégés. Research regarding benefits gained by the mentors is also presented.

Mentoring Effectiveness in General

- Researchers have linked mentor support to improvements in at-risk adolescents' psychological, social, academic, and career functioning (Munch & Blyth, 1993; Rhodes & Davis, 1996).
- In an evaluation of youth development programs, Roth and colleagues (Roth, Brooks-Gunn, Murray, & Foster, 1998) concluded that caring adult-adolescent relationships were key to program success.
- It appears that young people value mentoring and seek respectful relationships with caring adults (Carnegie Council on Adolescent Development, 1992; Philip & Hendry, 1996).
- Overall, mentoring appears to be moderately effective at improving the general well-being of children and youth (Flaxman, Ascher, & Harrington, 1988; Freedman, 1993).
- One of the most extensive studies of mentoring to date, an evaluation of Big Brothers Big Sisters programs, concluded that significant evidence exists that mentoring relationships between youth and nonrelative adults are associated with a variety of discernible benefits (Grossman & Tierney, 1998; Tierney, Grossman, & Resch, 1995).

Mentoring Offers Numerous Academic Benefits

Beginning in the 1990s, a steady stream of both research and general information regarding mentoring efficacy began to surface in professional journals and in popular magazines. The reports supported the concept of mentoring as potentially beneficial, academically, to children and youth. Mentoring programs appear to positively impact a variety of academically related behaviors, in addition to improving academic performance. Table 4.1 outlines specific academic benefits and supporting research studies.

Mentoring Promotes Social and Emotional Development

Mentoring and mentoring programs appear to positively impact a variety of youth behaviors in addition to improving academic performance. Research regarding youth mentoring supports the concept that mentoring leads to identifiable beneficial effects on the social and emotional

Table 4.1
Academic Impact of Mentoring

Area of Positive Impact	Data Sources
Attitudes about school, including: •Confidence •Optimism •Enthusiasm •Receptivity •Feelings of belonging to the school community	Curtis and Hansen-Schwoebel, 1999 Grossman and Tierney, 1998 Henkin, Rogers, and Lyons, 1992 Newman, Morris, and Streetman, 1999 Pringle et al., 1993 Taylor et al., 1999 Tierney et al., 1995
High school drop-out rate	Dondero, 1997
Attendance	Curtis and Hansen-Schwoebel, 1999 Grossman and Tierney, 1998 McPartland and Nettles, 1991 Pringle et al., 1993 Tierney et al., 1995
Test scores and grades	Curtis and Hansen-Schwoebel, 1999 Grossman and Tierney, 1998 McPartland and Nettles, 1991 Pringle et al., 1993 Tierney et al., 1995
Completion of schoolwork	Newman et al., 1999 Pringle et al., 1993
Study and organizational skills	Pringle et al., 1993
Disciplinary referrals	Pringle et al., 1993
Adjustment to college	Soucy and Larose, 2000
Retention	Curtis and Hansen-Schwoebel, 1999

development of youth. Table 4.2 details specific socioemotional benefits and associated research studies.

Mentoring Benefits Mentors

Mentoring programs do more than benefit the child or adolescent. They also enable the mentors, including older adults, to maintain active roles in their communities. Youth in mentoring positions—those who serve as peer tutors/mentors—may improve their own academic performance, particularly if they simultaneously receive mentoring, intensive training, or monitoring (Pringle, Anderson, Rubenstein, & Russo, 1993). Teaching others reinforces the student mentor's own learning while providing him or her with internalized teaching strategies.

Table 4.2
Social and Emotional Impact of Mentoring

Area of Positive Impact	Data Sources
Drug and alcohol attitudes and usage	Grossman and Tierney, 1998 Taylor et al., 1999 Tierney et al., 1995
Aggressive behavior	Grossman and Tierney, 1998 Jackson, 2002 Tierney et al., 1995
Feelings of anxiety and/or improved ability to handle anxiety	Rogers and Taylor, 1997 Taylor et al., 1999 Turner and Scherman, 1996
Aspirations	Lee and Cramond, 1999
Relationships with family	Grossman and Tierney, 1998 Tierney et al., 1995
Self-confidence, self-concept, self-esteem, and positive attitudes toward personal attributes	Curtis and Hansen-Schwoebel, 1999 Henkin, Rogers, and Lyons, 1992 Turner and Scherman, 1996
Communication skills, including ability to express feelings	Curtis and Hansen-Schwoebel, 1999 Henkin et al., 1992
Conduct and attention problems	Jackson, 2002
Self-management and peer relationship skills	Curtis and Hansen-Schwoebel, 1999 Newman et al., 1999
Attitudes about elders	Rogers and Taylor, 1997
Relationships with adults	Curtis and Hansen-Schwoebel, 1999
Susceptibility to parental rejection	Santiago, Achille, and Lachance, 1998
Engagement in at-risk behaviors (carrying weapons, drug use, smoking, sexual activity)	Beier, Rosenfeld, Spitalny, Zansky, and Bontempo, 2000

Adults who mentor report that they gain a great deal from the experience, and some describe how mentoring gave them the motivation to address unresolved issues in their own lives (Yancey, 1998). Involvement in mentoring has been found to improve employees' work attitudes (Weinberger, 2000). Mentoring allows elder citizens to pass on to others valuable life experience. Interactions with young people offer an opportunity to decrease the loneliness and isolation many elders experience. When elder adults feel valuable and needed, they may experience a renewed sense of purpose (Newman, Vasudev, & Onawola, 1985). Senior citizens who mentor describe feeling better about themselves and experiencing improved health. They find mentoring enjoyable, productive, and rewarding, and view it as an opportunity to learn new skills (Newman & Larimer, 1995; Newman, Morris, & Streetman, 1999).

Limitations of Mentoring

Youth mentoring, despite all of its positive attributes, is not a cure-all for youth problems. It is unrealistic to expect that a single mentoring relationship, or other relationship, could make up for the multiple challenges that may face any given young person (Freedman, 1993; Rhodes et al., 1996). A mentor's "job" is to support and assist his or her protégé/mentee; mentors, ideally, should not be compensating for unsatisfactory parental relationships but rather acting as supplemental support resources that allow youth to "elicit and appreciate the positive aspects of their social support networks and more effectively cope with relationship problems" (Rhodes et al., p. 218).

There is growing recognition that mentoring, while offering many benefits, also has some inherent risks. In her book *Stand by Me: The Risks and Rewards of Mentoring Today's Youth* (2002), Jean Rhodes synthesizes existing mentoring research and cautions that many questions related to mentoring remain unanswered. She also addresses the potentially harmful effects of relationships that fail to deliver consistent support. According to Rhodes, because a personal connection serves as the crux of a mentoring relationship, young mentees are vulnerable to the effects of inconsistency or disappointment in their relationships with mentors. This is, in part, due to the fact that young people often incorporate acceptance or rejection from significant adults into their sense of self. Mentoring programs need to attend to issues such as orientation, training, and mentor support to increase match success, while giving careful consideration to the steps taken when mentoring relationships fail. Interested readers are referred to chapter 2 in this book for more information on mentoring program infrastructure and support.

Assessing mentoring outcomes is particularly difficult in light of the various components of a mentoring relationship, such as a mentor's perceived role and the quality of the mentoring relationship (Beier, Rosenfeld, Spitalny, Zansky, & Bontempo, 2000). Research on the effectiveness of mentoring interventions as a whole exists, but more research is needed that is tailored to discerning when and how mentoring is most effective. Future research needs to:

- specify clear mentoring program goals
- identify well-defined interventions
- consider the unique contributions of various elements of typical mentoring "packages," such as the ones that Flaxman and colleagues (1988) suggest
- focus on the long-term impact of youth mentoring
- consider elements of effective mentoring relationships
- explore why mentoring works; that is, clarify the mechanisms by which mentoring has its impact

Research Regarding the Mentoring Process

Public/Private Ventures has conducted extensive research on mentoring. One notable source of information on mentoring is the Public/Private Ventures article synthesizing the organization's research between the years of 1988 and 1995 (Sipe, 1996). Participants in Big Brothers Big Sisters of America served as the sample for this research. At the time this research was conducted, BBBS annually matched 75,000 youth and adults. For the Public/Private Ventures BBBS research, a majority of research participants fell between the ages of 11 and 14 years.

Public/Private Ventures found that, over a six-month period, the eight agencies selected for study received a combined 2,500 inquiries from potential mentors. The demographic makeup of these prospective mentors reflected the following characteristics:

- 74 percent Caucasian
- 58 percent female
- 66 percent under 30 years of age
- 71 percent attended or completed college (10 percent attended graduate school)

The creation of a mentoring match required a prolonged process that resulted in a significantly smaller pool of potential mentors than presented by the 2,500 individuals making the initial inquiries. Forty-three percent of those inquiring made a formal application to the program.

Research by Roaf and colleagues (Roaf, Tierney, & Hunt, 1994) indicated that three to nine months following the initial inquiry:

- 35 percent of the applicants were matched or in line for a match (with a match for minority females and Caucasian males most likely)
- 30 percent had withdrawn their application or were rejected due to screening
- 35 percent of applications remained in process

Public/Private Ventures research indicates that, once a match is made in the BBBS organization:

- On average, matches last 1.5 years (Furano, Roaf, Styles, & Branch, 1993)
- 45 percent form successful relationships (Tierney & Branch, 1992)
- 25–67 percent form sustained relationships (Furano et al., 1993; Mecartney, Styles, & Morrow, 1994; Styles & Morrow, 1992; Tierney et al., 1992)

IS ELECTRONIC MENTORING PART OF THE FUTURE OF YOUTH MENTORING?

In a 2002 interview with the National Mentoring Center, David Neils, founder and director of the International Telementor Program, wrote of the present and the future of electronic mentoring. The author has granted permission to include this portion of that e-article.

Telementoring

David Neils (http://www.telementor.org/)

The potential for telementoring is incredible. Although ITP has served over 11,000 students throughout nine countries since 1995 I consider that reach a drop in the bucket when you consider the gap telementoring is trying to fill. For example, in Silicon Valley alone there are 19,000 fifth grade students and over 325,000 K–12 students. Mentoring is a powerful medium. Nobody would argue the benefits of mentoring. Unfortunately our youth wait an average of one year to two years before being matched in a traditional mentoring program (Big Brothers and

Sisters, etc.). At ITP the average wait time for a match is measured in minutes. How do we reach more individuals with the benefits of tele-mentoring? We'll need to create or find healthy learning environments, train qualified staff, eliminate technology and access issues, and work to close the human potential gap. I consider these three to be the most important issues.

CREATING AND FINDING HEALTHY LEARNING ENVIRONMENTS

Our public schools are not, on average, healthy places for students to learn. It is a rare school classroom where students are developing the skills and confidence to pursue their unique interests successfully. During your next visit to a classroom ask these questions:

1. Can you define academic success without using grades, GPA, or standardized test results? This question is appropriate for teachers, students, principals, and parents.
2. How many of you have heard an adult, including your parents, speak positively about his or her work in the last month? You'll find the role models are nonexistent. Laughter is the most common response.
3. How many of you have ever in your lifetime heard an adult, including your parents, speak positively about his or her work? A few hands will go up. Now you have their attention.
4. Do you know what it takes to pursue a dream successfully? Can you identify one person you know who is pursuing a dream successfully?

At ITP, we are working hard to help students answer these questions. If we want students to operate at their potential today and long into the future we must help them develop the skills and foundation to pursue their interests successfully. It's not okay to watch thousands of high school students graduate every year without a primary interest to pursue or a plan to pursue it. In a healthy learning environment there would be a negative visceral reaction from parents, teachers, administrators, and even students if this was the case. Our high school graduation ceremonies today celebrate the fact that my son or daughter was warehoused successfully for the past thirteen years and I hope, with a wing and a prayer, that they will be successful down the road.

Today we are not alarmed by this. I hope to see a radical change in the future. As a society we have gotten hung up on the big question, "So Johnny and Susie, what do you plan to do with your life?" as if we knew the answer at eighteen years of age. A more appropriate question would be, "What are you excited about today?" Let's focus on helping students, beginning in the elementary grades, create plans, communicate those plans to the right people, and finally, ask those individuals to invest in the student and his or her plan. Confidence soars based on tangible results that the student can be proud of.

So what does a healthy learning environment look like? How can telementoring support this environment? A healthy learning environment allows the student to exist at the center of this environment. Teachers act as facilitators rather than topic gurus (which is rarely the case anyway) or classroom cops. Students, when asked about academic success, begin the conversation talking about primary interests followed by how they are leveraging resources at school and beyond to pursue those interests. They can articulate the connection between dreams and time spent throughout the day. For example, a student who is interested in thunderstorms will seek to understand the connection between what's happening in math class and thunderstorms. This becomes the focal point for the student rather than what's on the next test. Grades, GPA, and bubble test results become by-products. They are no longer the focal point. We have a long way to go before our classrooms can be defined in this way.

Fortunately, we are witnessing more and more after school environments where the benefits of telementoring will stick and provide a platform for success (as defined by the youth being served). These environments include the Boys and Girls Club, 21st Century Learning Centers, MESA programs, and many others. In these environments the staff supporting the students do not have the standardized test requirements hanging over their head. They are not pulled in so many negative directions as the average teacher in the classroom is swayed. We need to leverage these environments for telementoring.

QUALIFIED STAFF AND RICH PARENTAL SUPPORT

Teachers in today's public schools are caught between ridiculous requirements at the local, state, and national level and a knowing of what really works for students. I hesitate to mention this, as it tends to paint teachers into a victim position. There are no victims in this scenario. Teachers can begin to provide individual support for students through telementoring and other mediums where the student is treated like a human being rather than another cow or sheep in the K12 chute. ITP teachers are learning how to provide support for students to pursue their interests while meeting these external requirements. A wave of transformation can occur when an entire school district or community supports the ITP goals. Students know they can take advantage of telementoring year after year. This is in contrast to the student who enjoys telementoring in the fifth grade but then finds out his or her middle school doesn't support the program.

Teachers need support from administrators, parents, governors, presidents to help their students in this way. We have a long road to travel before the standardized test regime crumbles because it fails to produce what our economy and communities need.

A few years ago I was asked to hold Proactive Learning Workshops for parents of students in the local school district. The focus of the workshops was to provide some new strategies for parents to support their kids to develop the critical skills, confidence, and foundation necessary to pursue interests successfully. Moving way beyond, "How did school go today?" and replacing that question with these questions:

1. What are you excited about today?
2. What did you do at school today to pursue this interest?
3. What is the connection between every class, teacher, principal, librarian, book, computer, janitor and your interest? (One at a time)
4. What can we do together to pursue this interest outside of school?
5. What do you want to learn and how long do you want to spend on this topic?

These questions may result in a blank stare from the child at first but over time the conversations will be rich and productive. Few parents were ever asked these questions when then were young. It takes awareness and support before we start witnessing these conversations between parents and their children. But it's worth it.

ACCESS TO TECHNOLOGY AND THE INTERNET

We've made great gains in this country regarding technology in our schools. What limits telementoring today is the amount of time per week that students have access to the technology. ITP competes with many other activities and priorities. Fortunately, it won't be long before all students have secure, wireless connections that they carry with them throughout the day. Computer labs will become museum artifacts. There is nothing personal about the personal computers in a computer lab. Students will create demand for better ways to use and access technology.

There are thousands of students who have sufficient access now that we aren't serving yet. Focusing on the barriers to serve these students should be our priority. The technology issue will take care of itself over time.

ADDRESSING AND CLOSING THE HUMAN POTENTIAL GAP

It is impossible for a human being to operate at his or her potential without the ability and confidence to pursue unique interests successfully. Young children, before entering our reactive, brain deadening public school systems are full of life and can be very articulate regarding how they want to spend the next five minutes or the entire day. Ask your average seventh grader how he or she wants to spend a chunk of time that involves personal creativity and the answer is typically, "Huh, I dunno." The system has squeezed the lifeblood and spark out of most students by the seventh grade. "Gifted" students are simply those students whose spark hasn't been completely doused by their education and home environments. The other "average" kids didn't survive the onslaught.

Every child should have the opportunity to pursue his or her interests successfully (as a child and as an adult!). For this to happen we need teachers, parents, friends, pastors, coaches, administrators, and most importantly, kids to redefine success as a human being. Telementoring, if done correctly, can have an incredible impact on students. This is what one enlightened teacher from Topeka had to say about her students and this year:

Telementoring offers students the opportunity to participate in real world workplace communications. They learn how to approach mentors in a business like manner. They learn how to write asking for specific help and aid.

What amazes me most is there are people working in corporate America who are willing to commit to an 8 week project working with young people they have never, and probably will never meet. These mentors become an extension of our classroom and offer one-on-one instruction. It's like having another teacher in the room.

Telementoring has taken my students from "Waz Up" note writing typical of middle school students to a higher level of technical writing. When your students begin to imitate the writing style of career professionals, I know they are learning in a better way than worksheets can provide. One of my students now routinely ends her e-mails with "Best Regards," and her name. She's learned that from her mentor.

We have many star teachers in the program who are bucking the reactive public education system and grabbing the telementoring bull by the horns. We need to work together to figure out the best way to support and reward these teachers. They are closing the human potential gap.

EXCITING ADVANCES

Fortunately, through the work of organizations like Con-nect, George Lucas Education Foundation, and others there is a new focus on project-based learning. Telementoring fits under the project-based learning environment perfectly. All student/mentor communication at ITP is project-based. This allows our students, teachers, and mentors to leverage a growing number of resources in this field. Project-based learning also moves the entire education system away from drill and kill and toward learning that means something to the students.

At ITP we've created an internal messaging system that is completely secure and avoids the problems associated with e-mail systems on the school side of the telementoring equation. Rather than spending time securing and maintaining student e-mail accounts teachers can now focus more attention on the telementoring project and the help each student needs. Everybody wins. ITP staff can also support individual relationships more effectively as the entire student/mentor conversation exists on a single Web page. Students can now communicate with an ITP mentor from school, home, library, or any place Web access is available. The security remains constant regardless of the access point.

STATE AND NATIONAL SUPPORT OF YOUTH MENTORING

Many states across the nation have developed mentoring initiatives, most under the auspices of the office of the governor. Many have likewise designated a Mentoring Month or Mentoring Week for the state in acknowledgment of the importance of mentoring children and adolescents. The president of the United States declared January 2003 as National Mentoring Month. That proclamation and two state proclamations (Maine and Texas) follow.

NATIONAL MENTORING MONTH

On January 2, 2003, President George W. Bush issued a Proclamation designating January 2003 as

National Mentoring Month, 2003
By the President of the United States of America
A Proclamation

Across our great Nation, many Americans are responding to the call to service by mentoring a child in need. By offering love, guidance, and encouragement, mentors put hope in children's hearts, and help ensure that young people realize their full potential. During National Mentoring Month, we recognize the vital contributions of dedicated mentors, and we encourage more Americans to make a difference in the hearts and souls of our communities by volunteering their time to meet the needs of America's youth.

Volunteers provide friendship and support to young people who are facing challenging situations, serve as positive role models, and help to instill important values, goals, and skills. Mentors help young Americans build confidence, gain knowledge, and develop the character necessary to make the right choices and achieve their dreams. Statistics show that at-risk children with mentors demonstrate improved academic performance and are less likely to be involved in destructive activities such as drugs, alcohol, and violence.

During these extraordinary times, we are experiencing a growing culture of service, citizenship, and compassion in our country, with millions of Americans sacrificing for causes greater than self. Dedicated individuals are getting involved in mentoring through faith-based and community organizations, corporate initiatives, school-based programs, and many other outlets for kindness. By dedicating their time and their talents to offer a child a quality relationship with a caring adult, mentors strengthen our families and our communities and reflect the true spirit of America.

Many Americans can point to individuals who influenced their lives and helped to shape them into who they are today. Whether they were teachers, coaches, relatives, clergy, or other community leaders, these positive role models have been critical to our healthy development and helped to instill purpose in our lives. As we honor these everyday heroes, we also recognize that there is a great need for more mentors in America. Too many children in our Nation are growing up without enough support and guidance in their lives, and we must work to ensure that no child is left behind.

This month, I encourage all Americans to become a mentor and change the life of a child in need. In July, the National Mentoring Partnership helped establish the USA Freedom Corps Volunteer Network—the largest system in the Nation for matching individuals with volunteer opportunities. I am proud of this partnership and ask individuals to go online at www.usafreedomcorps.gov or call 1-877-USACORPS to find millions of ways to help children in their neighborhoods. Together, we can reaffirm the promise of America and point the way to a brighter future for all of our children.

NOW, THEREFORE, I, GEORGE W. BUSH, President of the United States of America, by virtue of the authority vested in me by the Constitution and laws of the United States, do hereby proclaim January 2003 as National Mentoring Month. I call upon the people of the United States to recognize the importance of being role models for our youth, to look for mentoring opportunities in their communities, and to celebrate this month with appropriate ceremonies, activities, and programs.

IN WITNESS WHEREOF, I have hereunto set my hand this second day of January, in the year of our Lord two thousand three, and of the Independence of the United States of America the two hundred and twenty-seventh.

GEORGE W. BUSH

STATE OF MAINE MENTORING PROCLAMATION

Proclamation Regarding Maine Mentoring Day

WHEREAS, mentoring is a caring, committed, formal, long-term, personal relationship between a young person and an older person that fosters the development of individuals to fulfill their potential; and

WHEREAS, mentoring is important because the difference one individual can make in the life of another is powerful beyond measure; and

WHEREAS, teachers report students who are mentored improve academically, have better attitudes toward school, have more productive relationships with authority figures, and have better school attendance; and

WHEREAS, parents report children who are mentored are affected positively and would like to have their mentoring continue; and

WHEREAS, Maine Mentoring Partnership was created to promote, advocate, foster and support mentoring for Maine's 300,000 children and youth; and

WHEREAS, the goal of Maine Mentoring Partnership is to increase the number of mentoring relationships to 35,000 by December 2005 because Maine's mentoring programs believe that young people's needs are best met within the context of family and community relationships; and

WHEREAS, Maine's mentoring programs are making outstanding efforts toward creating increased numbers of effective and safe mentoring relationships for young people by utilizing nationally recognized standards for mentoring; and

WHEREAS, that with mentors young people will be encouraged to continue their education as well as their personal and professional growth and development; and

WHEREAS, the 3rd Annual Maine Mentoring Day recognizes those who are mentored along with the programs, mentors, businesses and organizations that make mentoring a success in Maine.

NOW, THEREFORE, I, John E. Baldacci, Governor of the State of Maine, do hereby proclaim March 17, 2003 as

MAINE MENTORING DAY
THROUGHOUT THE STATE OF MAINE, AND URGE ALL
CITIZENS TO RECOGNIZE THE IMPORTANCE AND POTEN-
TIAL OF MENTORING, TO BECOME INVOLVED IN MENTOR-
ING YOUTH, AND TO SUPPORT LOCAL MENTORING
PROGRAMS IN THEIR COMMUNITIES.

In testimony whereof, I have caused
the Great Seal of the State to be
hereunto affixed GIVEN under my
hand at Augusta this fourteenth
day of March in the Year of our
Lord Two Thousand and Three.
John E. Baldacci
Governor
Dan A. Gwadosky
Secretary of State

STATE OF TEXAS MENTORING PROCLAMATION

State of Texas
Office of the Governor

Children are our state's most precious resource, and mentoring is a proven, effective strategy for helping to set young Texans on the path to success. Research has shown that caring relationships with adults can be beneficial in preventing young people from engaging in negative behaviors, while also encouraging them to develop good social skills and positive self-esteem. The guidance and stability offered through mentoring can help young people function responsibly in the world around them, encouraging them to make healthy, fulfilling life choices.

In the United States, 17.6 million youngsters want or need mentors to help them reach their full potential. However, just 2.5 million youngsters are in formal mentoring relationships. During January, a month-long campaign will be conducted to emphasize the positive impacts of mentoring, and to recruit volunteer mentors for young people who are at risk of not achieving their full potential.

Through guidance, encouragement, and friendship, mentors make a difference in the lives of young Texans. I therefore encourage Texans across the Lone Star State to recognize the many benefits associated with mentoring youths, and to explore the possibility of becoming mentors. It is through such positive efforts that we will continue to lay the groundwork for a future of success for tomorrow's leaders.

Therefore, I, Rick Perry, Governor of Texas, do hereby proclaim January 2003 Mentoring Month in Texas, and urge the appropriate recognition whereof.

In official recognition whereof, I hereby affix my signature this the 1st day of January, 2003.

RICK PERRY
Governor of Texas

LEGISLATION

In January 2001, H.R. 17, the Younger Americans Act was introduced to Congress. The Younger Americans Act outlines a national youth policy to assure that all youth have access to essential resources that will promote positive development. The proposed act mirrored the principles of America's Promise in asserting that youth in the United States are entitled to: (1) ongoing relationships with caring adults; (2) safe places with structured activities in which to grow and learn; (3) services that promote healthy lifestyles, including those designed to improve physical and mental health; (4) opportunities to acquire marketable skills and competencies; and (5) opportunities for community service and civic participation.

The bill was to have created, in the Executive Office of the President, an Office of National Youth Policy and a 12-member Council on Youth Policy charged with setting national priorities for youth programs, coordinating federal youth programs, and assisting the states in implementing those programs. Funds were to have also been allotted to serve the needs of Native American organizations, as well as high-risk youth such as those youth in correctional and other out-of-home settings, high poverty areas, and rural areas. The act would have authorized bestowal of grants and contracts to eligible entities for specified evaluation, education and training, research, and dissemination activities.

This particular legislation was presented to the 107th Congress, just as similar legislation had been previously submitted to the 106th Congress. A variety of youth- and mentoring-related organizations supported the legislation, including Big Brothers Big Sisters of America, the Child Welfare League, the Coalition for Juvenile Justice, the Boy Scouts and Girl Scouts of the USA, the National Crime Prevention Council, the Urban League, Save the Children, the United Way, and the YMCA/YWCA of the USA. The act was referred to the Subcommittee on Education Reform, where it eventually expired.

One piece of legislation particularly akin to mentoring efforts did successfully pass through the 107th Congress, however, the *No Child Left Behind* (NCLB) Act. The NCLB act was signed into federal law on January 8, 2002. This law reauthorized the Elementary and Secondary Education Act of 1965, establishing the federal framework for the provision of public education, nationwide. The *No Child Left Behind* legislation was built upon the original framework of 1965 but added four additional philosophic pillars to ensure that every child, regardless of their need, would receive a quality education. Those pillars were: (1)flexibility for states, communities, and districts in their use of funding; (2) accountability, with an emphasis on results; (3) use of research-proven effective materials and curriculum; and (4) emphasis on parental involvement, with information, influence, and choice for all parents.

Efforts to establish a National Youth policy were still ongoing in the 108th Congress as of the publication of this book. In 2003 an amendment to the No Child Left Behind Act of 2002, sections of which pertain to the very tenets of the youth mentoring movement, were introduced in both the House (H.R. 936) and the U. S. Senate (S. 448). Sections from the U. S. House of Representatives version of the proposed amendment (H.R. 936) follow in this chapter. H.R. 936 tackles topics such as Enhancing Healthy Emotional Development in Young Children (Title VII, Subtitle F, Section 8501), Youth Development (Title IX, Chapter 1), Grants for State and Community Programs *(supporting youth development)* (Title IX, Chapter 2), Coordination of a National Youth Policy (Title IX, Subtitle E), and Youth Programs (Title IX, Subtitle B).

Both proposed amendments have universal endorsement and have been sent to their respective committees for further review. Whatever the immediate outcome, it is evident that a National Youth Policy is an important piece of legislation, and attempts to have such a policy enacted into law will be ongoing until those efforts are successful.

H.R. 936

LEAVE NO CHILD BEHIND ACT OF 2003 (INTRODUCED IN THE HOUSE)

TITLE IX—SUCCESSFUL TRANSITION TO ADULTHOOD

SUBTITLE A—YOUTH DEVELOPMENT

CHAPTER 1—SHORT TITLE; POLICY; DEFINITIONS

SEC. 9001. SHORT TITLE.

This subtitle may be cited as the "Younger Americans Act."

SEC. 9002. A NATIONAL YOUTH POLICY.

It is the policy of the United States, in keeping with the traditional United States concept that youth are the Nation's most valuable resource, that youth of the Nation need, and it is the joint and several duty and responsibility of governments of the United States, of the several States and political subdivisions, and of Indian tribes, to ensure that all youth have access to and participate in the full array of core resources needed to fully prepare youth to become healthy and productive adults and effective citizens, including—

(1) ongoing relationships with caring adults;

(2) safe places with structured activities;

(3) services that promote healthy lifestyles, including services designed to improve physical and mental health;

(4) opportunities to acquire marketable skills and competencies; and

(5) opportunities for community service and civic participation.

SEC. 9003. DEFINITIONS.

In this Subtitle:

(1) AREA PLAN—The term "area plan" means an area youth development plan described in section 9108.

(2) ASSOCIATE COMMISSIONER—The term "Associate Commissioner" means the Associate Commissioner of the Family and Youth Services Bureau of the Administration on Children, Youth, and Families of the Administration for Children and Families of the Department of Health and Human Services.

(3) COMMUNITY-BASED—The term "community-based," used with respect to an organization, means an organization that—

    (A) is representative of a community or significant segment of a community; and

    (B) is engaged in providing services to the community.

(4) CONSORTIUM—The term "consortium" means a youth development consortium established in accordance with section 9107(a).

(5) CONVENING COMMUNITY-BASED AGENCY—The term "convening community-based agency" means an organization that—

    (A) is directed by a board with wide representation from a community;

    (B) generates and distributes charitable funds for diverse health and human service programs and coordinates the efforts of multiple agencies as needed or requested;

    (C) does not itself provide direct services to children, youth, or their families; and

    (D) operates within the geographic boundaries of the youth development area for which it exercises its convening duty.

(6) CONVENING UNIT OF GENERAL PURPOSE LOCAL GOVERNMENT—The term "convening unit of general purpose local government" means the unit of general purpose local government with the greatest number of youth residing within the geographic boundaries of the youth development area for which it exercises its convening duty.

(7) COUNCIL—The term "Council" means the Coordinating Council for National Youth Policy.

(8) INDIAN—The term "Indian" has the meaning given the term in section 4(d) of the Indian Self-Determination and Education Assistance Act (25 U.S.C. 450b(d)).

(9) LIBRARY—The term "library" has the meaning given the term in section 213(2) of the Museum and Library Services Act of 1996.

(10) NATIVE AMERICAN ORGANIZATION—The term "Native American organization" means—

   (A) a tribal organization, as defined in section 4(l) of the Indian Self-Determination and Education Assistance Act (25 U.S.C. 450b(l));

   (B) a Native Hawaiian Organization, as defined in section 4009(4) of the Augustus F. Hawkins-Robert T. Stafford Elementary and Secondary School Improvement Amendments of 1988 (20 U.S.C. 4909(4)) (as in effect on the day before the date of enactment of the Improving America's Schools Act of 1994);

   (C) an Alaska Native Village Corporation or Regional Corporation as defined in or established pursuant to the Alaskan Native Claims Settlement Act (43 U.S.C. 1601 et seq.); or

   (D) a private nonprofit organization established for the purpose of serving youth who are Indians or Native Hawaiians.

(11) NATIVE HAWAIIAN—The term "Native Hawaiian" has the meaning given the term in section 4009(1) of the Augustus F. Hawkins-Robert T. Stafford Elementary and Secondary School Improvement Amendments of 1988 (20 U.S.C. 4909(1)) (as in effect on the day before the date of enactment of the Improving America's Schools Act of 1994).

(12) OUTLYING AREA—The term "outlying area" means the United States Virgin Islands, Guam, American Samoa, and the Commonwealth of the Northern Mariana Islands.

(13) STATE—The term "State" means each of the several States of the United States, the District of Columbia, and the Commonwealth of Puerto Rico.

(14) STATE PLAN—The term "State plan" means a State youth development plan described in section 9105.

(15) UNIT OF GENERAL PURPOSE LOCAL GOVERNMENT—The term "unit of general purpose local government" means—

(A) A political subdivision of a State whose authority is general and not limited to only 1 function or combination of related functions; or

(B) a Native American organization.

(16) YOUTH—The term "youth" means an individual who is not younger than age 10 and not older than age 19.

(17) YOUTH DEVELOPMENT AREA—The term "youth development area" means a geographic area designated by the State youth development agency in accordance with section 9104(a)(1)(E).

(18) YOUTH DEVELOPMENT ORGANIZATION—The term "youth development organization" means a public or private youth-serving organization with a major emphasis on providing youth development programs.

(19) YOUTH DEVELOPMENT PROGRAMS—The term "youth development programs" means programs, services, supports, opportunities, and activities that prepare youth to contribute to their communities and to meet the challenges of adolescence and adulthood through a structured, progressive series of activities and experiences (in contrast to deficit-based approaches that focus solely on youth problems) that—

(A) help the youth obtain social, emotional, ethical, physical, and cognitive competencies; and

(B) address the broader developmental resources all children and youth need, such as the core resources described in section 9002.

(20) YOUTH-SERVING ORGANIZATION—The term "youth-serving organization" means a public or private organization with a primary focus on providing youth development programs, or health, mental health, fitness, education, workforce preparation, substance abuse prevention, child welfare, evaluation and assessment, parenting, arts and cultural engagement, recreation, teen pregnancy prevention, rehabilitative, or residential services to youth.

CHAPTER 2—GRANTS FOR STATE AND COMMUNITY PROGRAMS

SEC. 9101. PURPOSE.

The purpose of this chapter is to encourage and assist States and youth development consortia in mobilizing and supporting communities in planning, implementing, and being accountable for strategies that link community-based organizations, local government, volunteer centers, schools, community colleges, colleges, universities, faith-based organizations, businesses, parks and recreation agencies, libraries and museums, arts and cultural organizations, other youth-serving organizations, and other segments of the community to ensure that all youth have access to, and participate in, the full array of core resources described in section 9002.

SEC. 9102. AUTHORIZATION OF APPROPRIATIONS.

There are authorized to be appropriated to carry out this chapter $500,000,000 for fiscal year 2004, $750,000,000 for fiscal year 2005, $1,000,000,000 for fiscal year 2006, $1,500,000,000 for fiscal year 2007, and $2,000,000,000 for fiscal year 2008.

SEC. 9103. ALLOTMENTS TO STATES.

(a) RESERVATIONS—From sums appropriated under section 9102 for each fiscal year, the Associate Commissioner shall reserve—

 (1) 94 percent of the sums for allotments to States to enable the States to make allocations to youth development consortia and to perform State activities;

 (2) 1 percent of the sums for grants to Native American organizations to carry out activities consistent with the objectives of this chapter;

 (3) 1 percent of the sums for grants to outlying areas to carry out activities consistent with the objectives of this chapter;

 (4) 3 percent of the sums for Federal competitive grant programs aimed at demonstrating ways to respond, through programs that meet the requirements of subsection (b), to the special developmental needs of youth—

(A) in areas with high concentrations of poverty;

(B) in rural areas;

(C) in situations in which the youth are at higher risk due to abuse, neglect, disconnection from family, disconnection from school, or another community risk factor;

(D) in alternative educational settings or who have been expelled or suspended from school;

(E) in correctional facilities and other out-of-home residential settings;

(F) with disabilities; and

(G) coming from homes where the primary languages spoken are not English; and

(5) 1 percent of the sums for the Associate Commissioner to carry out planning, policy development, administration, and accountability duties and activities under this chapter and under chapter 3 of this subtitle.

(b) USE OF FUNDS—For each fiscal year for which a State receives a State allotment, the State shall ensure that funds made available through the allotment, and used by the State or a youth development consortium in the State to fund youth development programs, shall be used for the purpose of conducting community-based youth development programs that—

(1) recognize the primary role of the family in youth development in order to strengthen families;

(2) promote the involvement of youth (including program participants), parents, grandparents, and guardians, and other community members in the planning and implementation of the youth development programs;

(3) coordinate services with other entities providing youth and family services in the community;

(4) eliminate barriers, such as a lack of transportation, cost, and service delivery location, to the accessibility of youth development services;

(5) provide, directly or through a written contract, a broad variety of accessible youth development programs for youth that are designed to assist youth in acquiring skills, competen-

cies, and connections that are necessary to make a successful transition from childhood to adulthood;

(6) incorporate activities that foster relationships between positive adult role models and youth, provide age-appropriate activities, and provide activities that engage youth in, and promote youth development, including activities such as—

(A) youth clubs, character development activities, mentoring, community service, civic engagement, leadership development, community action, recreation, and literacy and educational tutoring;

(B) sports, workforce readiness activities, peer counseling, and fine and performing arts; and

(C) camping and environmental or science education, arts and cultural engagement, risk avoidance programs, academic enrichment, and participant-defined special interest group activities, courses, or clubs; and

(7) employ strong outreach efforts to engage the participation of a wide range of youth, families, and service providers.

(c) ALLOTMENTS—[See bill for this section at http://thomas. loc.gov/.]

(d) WITHHOLDING—[See bill for this section at http:// thomas.loc.gov/.]

(e) REALLOTMENTS—[See bill for this section at http:// thomas.loc.gov/.]

SEC. 9104. STATE YOUTH DEVELOPMENT AGENCIES AND YOUTH DEVELOPMENT AREAS.

(a) STATE YOUTH DEVELOPMENT AGENCIES—In order for a State to be eligible to receive a State allotment under this chapter—

(1) the State shall, in accordance with regulations issued by the Associate Commissioner, designate a State agency as the sole State agency to—

(A) be primarily responsible for the planning, policy development, administration, coordination, priority setting, accountability, and evaluation of all State activities related to the objectives of this subtitle;

(B) coordinate its activities with other State, local, and private agencies, offices, and programs, including—

(i) State Commissions on National and Community Service established under section 178 of the National and Community Service Act of 1990 (42 U.S.C. 12638);

(ii) entities carrying out programs under the Runaway and Homeless Youth Act (42 U.S.C. 5701 et seq.) and other programs under the Juvenile Justice and Delinquency Prevention Act of 1974 (42 U.S.C. 5601 et seq.);

(iii) entities carrying out independent living programs;

(iv) entities carrying out child welfare programs;

(v) youth councils established under section 117(h) of the Workforce Investment Act of 1998 (29 U.S.C. 2832(h));

(vi) entities carrying out related activities under the Elementary and Secondary Education Act of 1965 (20 U.S.C. 6301 et seq.); and

(vii) entities carrying out literacy activities under the Museum and Library Services Act of 1996 (20 U.S.C. 9101 et seq.);

(C) develop a State youth development plan to be submitted to the Associate Commissioner for approval pursuant to section 9105;

(D) provide assurances that the State will solicit and take into account, with regard to general policy related to the development and the administration of the State plan for any fiscal year, the views of youth who are the targeted and actual recipients of services provided for in the plan;

(E) administer the State plan;

(F) develop and disseminate a uniform format for use by youth development consortia in developing area plans;

(G) divide the State into distinct youth development areas, after considering the views offered by units of general purpose local government and appropriate public or private agencies and organizations in the State, in accordance with regulations issued by the Associate Commissioner;

(H) ensure that each unit of general purpose local government of the State is included in a youth development area;

(I) in accordance with guidelines issued by the Associate Commissioner, make allocations to youth development consortia pursuant to section 9106(b);

(J) provide assurances that Federal funds made available under this chapter for the State for any period will be used to supplement, and not supplant, the State, local, and other funds that would in the absence of such Federal funds be made available for the youth development programs described in this chapter;

(K) compile reports from youth development consortia, including outcome and utilization data developed under section 9301(1) and evaluation information regarding youth development programs funded under this chapter and provide an annual report based on the compilation to the Associate Commissioner;

(L) serve as an effective and visible advocate for youth in the State government, by actively reviewing and commenting on all State plans, policies, and programs affecting youth;

(M) public forums for discussion on issues regarding youth, publicize the core resources youth need, and obtain information relating to ensuring all youth have access to, and participate in, the full array of core resources described in section 9002, by conducting public hearings, and by conducting or sponsoring conferences, workshops, and other similar meetings;

(N) develop mechanisms to foster collaboration and resolve administrative and programmatic conflicts between State programs that would be barriers to parents, grandparents, and guardians, community-based, youth-serving, and youth development organizations, local government entities, State government entities, tribes, older adult organizations, faith-based organizations, and organizations supporting youth involved in community service and civic participation, related to the coordination of services and funding for programs promoting access to, and participating in, the full array of core resources described in section 9002; and

(O) consult with and assist local governments and community-based organizations with respect to barriers the governments encounter related to the coordination of services and funding for youth development and youth services programs.

(b) YOUTH DEVELOPMENT AREA—

   (1) UNIT OF GENERAL PURPOSE LOCAL GOVERNMENT—

      (A) CRITERIA—In carrying out subsection (a)(1), the State agency may designate as a youth development area any unit of general purpose local government.

      (B) HEARING—In any case in which a unit of general purpose local government applies to the State agency to be designated as a youth development area under this paragraph, the State agency shall, upon request, provide an opportunity for a hearing to such unit of general purpose local government.

   (2) REGION—The State agency may designate as a youth development area under subsection (a)(1) any region in the State that includes 1 or more units of general purpose local government if the State agency determines that the designation of such a regional youth development area is necessary for, and will enhance, the effective administration of the youth development programs authorized by this chapter.

   (3) ADDITIONAL AREAS—The State agency may include in any youth development area designated under subsection (a)(1) such additional areas, adjacent to a unit of general purpose local government, as the State agency determines are necessary for, and will enhance, the effective administra-

tion of the youth development programs authorized by this chapter.

(4) INDIAN RESERVATIONS—The State agency, in carrying out subsection (a)(1), shall to the extent practicable include all portions of an Indian reservation in a single youth development area.

SEC. 9105. STATE YOUTH DEVELOPMENT PLANS.

(a) IN GENERAL—To be eligible to receive a State allotment under this title, a State shall develop, prepare, and submit to the Associate Commissioner a State youth development plan, for a 2- or 3-year period, at such time, in such manner, and meeting such criteria as the Associate Commissioner may by regulation prescribe, and shall make such annual revisions as may be necessary to the plan.

(b) CONTENTS—Each such State plan shall contain assurances that the plan is based on area youth development plans developed under section 9108 by youth development consortia in the State and describes the State's intended use of its allotment for State discretionary grants authorized in section 9106(a)(1)(C).

SEC. 9106. DISTRIBUTION OF FUNDS FOR STATE ACTIVITIES AND AREA ALLOCATIONS.

(a) IN GENERAL—From a State allotment made under this chapter for any fiscal year—

(1)

(A) the State agency may use such amount as the State agency determines to be appropriate, but not more than 7 percent, for the purposes of subparagraphs (B) and (C);

(B) the State agency may use such amount as the State agency determines to be appropriate, but not more than 4 percent of the State allotment, for paying the cost of—

(i) reviewing area youth development plans and distributing funds to youth development consortia;

(ii) assisting youth development consortia in carrying out activities under this chapter; and

(iii) monitoring and evaluating activities funded through this subtitle by youth development consortia; and

(C) the State agency may use such amount as the State agency determines to be appropriate, but not less than 3 percent and not more than 7 percent of the State allotment, for making State discretionary grants to respond to the special developmental needs of youth—

(i) in areas with high concentrations of poverty;

(ii) in rural areas;

(iii) in situations in which the youth are at greater risk due to abuse, neglect, disconnection from family, disconnection from school, or another community risk factor;

(iv) in alternative educational settings or who have been expelled or suspended from school;

(v) in correctional facilities and other out-of-home residential settings;

(vi) with disabilities; and

(vii) coming from homes where the primary languages spoken are not English; and

(2) the State agency shall use the remainder of such allotment to make allocations under subsection (b) to youth development consortia to pay for the cost of youth development programs under this chapter that are specified in area youth development plans that—

(A) are developed through a comprehensive and coordinated system of planning;

(B) have been approved by the consortia involved;

(C) are submitted by the consortia for their respective youth development areas; and

(D) have been approved by the State agency.

(b) ALLOCATIONS AND COMPETITIVE GRANTS—

(1) ALLOCATIONS—Except as provided in paragraph (2), from the remainder of the State allotment described in subsection (a)(2), the State agency, using the best available data,

shall allocate for each youth development area in the State the sum of—

(A) an amount that bears the same ratio to 1/2 of the remainder as the number of individuals who are not younger than age 10 and not older than age 19 in the youth development area bears to the number of such individuals in the State; and

(B) an amount that bears the same ratio to 1/2 of the remainder as the number of youth in poverty as measured by the most recent decennial and annual demographic program data available from the Bureau of the Census in the youth development area bears to the number of such youth in the State.

(2) COMPETITIVE GRANTS—

(A) IN GENERAL—For any fiscal year for which the amount appropriated to carry out this subtitle is less than $150,000,000, the State agency shall use the remainder of the State allotment described in subsection (a)(2) to make competitive grants to consortia.

(B) RESPONSIBILITIES—A consortium that receives such a grant shall be considered to have received an allocation under this subsection, and shall comply with the requirements of this subtitle relating to funds received through such an allocation. A State that makes such grants shall be considered to have complied with the requirements of this subsection relating to making allocations.

(c) NON-FEDERAL SHARE—A State that uses Federal funds provided under this chapter to carry out the activities described in section 9106(a)(1)(B) shall make available (directly or through donations from public or private entities) non-Federal contributions in cash in an amount equal to not less than $1 for every $1 of the Federal funds.

(d) REALLOTMENTS—If the State agency does not receive from a youth development consortium a letter of intent declaring the consortium's intention to submit an area youth development plan to the State agency, within 120 days of the State agency's announcement of the availability of allocations under subsection (b) to youth development areas to pay for the cost of youth development programs under this chapter, the State agency shall determine that any amount allotted to the youth development area for a fiscal year under this section will not be used by such area for carrying out the purpose for which the allotment was made and shall make such amount available for carrying out such purpose to 1 or more other youth development areas to the extent the State agency determines that such other areas will be able to use such amount for carrying out such purpose.

SEC. 9107. YOUTH DEVELOPMENT CONSORTIA.

(a) YOUTH DEVELOPMENT CONSORTIA—

   (1) CONVENED—

      (A) CONVENING UNITS OF GENERAL PURPOSE LOCAL GOVERNMENT AND CONVENING COMMUNITY-BASED AGENCIES—Except as otherwise provided in this paragraph, in order to receive funds from a State pursuant to this chapter, a youth development area shall have a youth development consortium convened jointly by the chief executive officer of a convening community-based agency in the area and the chief executive officer of the convening unit of general purpose local government in the area.

      (B) PRIVATE AGENCIES AND LOCAL GOVERNMENTS—In the event that a convening community-based agency is not represented in the youth development area, or the chief executive officer of a convening community-based agency in the area is unwilling or unable to participate in jointly convening the consortium, the State agency, after consideration of the views offered by units of general purpose local government and by nonprofit agencies and organizations in such area, shall designate a private nonprofit agency or organization in the area to convene the consortium jointly with the chief executive officer of the convening unit of general purpose local government in the area.

(C) LOCAL FUNDING AND COORDINATING AGEN-
CIES AND PUBLIC ENTITIES—In the event that a
chief executive officer of the convening unit of general
purpose local government in the youth development
area is unwilling or unable to participate in jointly convening the consortium, the State agency, after consideration of the views offered by units of general purpose
local government and by youth-serving agencies and
organizations in such area, shall designate an executive
official of a public entity in the area to convene the consortium jointly with the chief executive officer of a convening community-based agency and any other chief
executive officers of units of general purpose local government in the area.

(D) EXISTING ENTITY—An existing entity in the youth
development area may serve as the consortium if—

(i) such entity's membership meets the requirements
for a consortium or is adapted to meet such requirements; and

(ii) such entity is approved by the State agency.

(E) PUBLIC NOTICE—A consortium may not be convened under this paragraph before the expiration of the
30-day period beginning on the date the particular convening authorities described in this paragraph provide
such reasonable public notice of the date and time of
the first convening of the consortium as is sufficient to
inform all units of local general purpose government,
and nonprofit youth-serving and youth development
agencies, of such first convening.

(2) CHAIRPERSONS—The consortium shall elect 2 chairpersons from among its membership. One chairperson shall be
an officer or official of a general unit of local purpose government and 1 chairperson shall be an officer or official
from a nonprofit youth-serving and youth development
agency.

(3) COMPOSITION—A consortium shall consist of an equal
number of local representatives from each of the following 3
groups:

(A) A group comprised of individuals under age 20 at the time of service on the consortium.

(B) A group comprised of representatives of—

   (i) private youth-serving and youth development organizations;

  (ii) public youth-serving and youth development organizations;

 (iii) organizations supporting youth involved in community service and civic participation; and

 (iv) organizations providing or operating local youth correctional programs or facilities and local law enforcement agencies.

(C) A group comprised of representatives of—

    (i) local elected officials;

   (ii) educational entities, including local elementary and secondary schools, community colleges, colleges, and universities;

  (iii) libraries and museums;

  (iv) parks and recreation agencies;

   (v) volunteer centers;

  (vi) philanthropic organizations, including community foundations;

 (vii) businesses and employee organizations;

(viii) faith-based organizations;

  (ix) health and mental health agencies;

   (x) parents, grandparents, and guardians, including at least 1 parent, grandparent, or guardian of a youth who has participated in an activity described in section 9112(b) within the 3-year period preceding service on the consortium;

  (xi) if a military installation is located in the youth development area, personnel of the installation; and

 (xii) arts and cultural organizations.

(4) RESPONSIBILITIES—Each consortium in each youth development area shall—

(A) submit to the State agency within 120 days of the State agency's announcement of the availability of allocations under section 9106(b) to youth development areas to pay for the cost of youth development programs under this chapter, a letter of intent declaring the consortium's intention to submit an area youth development plan to the State agency;

(B) prepare, submit, implement, and evaluate the area plan described in section 9108;

(C) designate for the youth development area a fiscal agent that agrees not to seek an award of a grant, or to enter into a contract, to carry out youth development programs under the area plan; and

(D) compile reports from entities carrying out youth development programs approved by the consortium for funding under this subtitle, including outcome and utilization data developed under section 9301(1) and evaluation information regarding youth development programs funded under this chapter, and provide an annual report based on the compilation to the State agency.

(b) COMMUNITY MOBILIZATION EXPENSES—The fiscal agent and other entities as determined appropriate by the consortium may use such amount as the consortium determines to be appropriate, but not more than 8 percent of the area allotment, for paying the cost of—

(1) generating additional commitments of cash and in-kind resources;

(2) administration;

(3) planning;

(4) monitoring;

(5) evaluation;

(6) training; and

(7) technical assistance.

SEC. 9108. AREA YOUTH DEVELOPMENT PLANS.

(a) IN GENERAL—Each consortium for a youth development area shall, in order to be approved by the State agency and receive an allocation under this chapter, develop, prepare, and submit to the State agency a single area youth development plan, approved by the consortium, for the youth development area, at such time, in such manner, and meeting such criteria as the State agency may prescribe. Such plan shall be for a 2- or 3-year period with such annual revisions as may be necessary. Each such plan shall be based upon a uniform format for area plans in the State prepared in accordance with section 9105(b).

(b) CONTENTS—Each such plan shall—

   (1) provide specific outcome objectives for youth development programs to be carried out in the youth development area, based on an assessment of needs and resources, sufficient to ensure that all youth in the area have access and participate through a comprehensive and coordinated system to the full array of core resources described in section 9002;

   (2) provide an assurance that, in awarding grants and contracts to entities to implement the area plan to provide youth with access to core resources described in section 9002 through youth development programs, the agency will give priority to entities as described in section 9110(b);

   (3) provide that not less than 30 percent of the funds allocated under this chapter for the youth development area will be used for youth development programs that respond to the special developmental needs of youth—

      (A) in areas with high concentrations of poverty;

      (B) in rural areas;

      (C) in situations in which the youth are at higher risk due to abuse, neglect, disconnection from family, disconnection from school, or another community risk factor;

      (D) in alternative educational settings or who have been expelled or suspended from school;

      (E) in correctional facilities and other out-of-home residential settings;

      (F) with disabilities; and

    (G) coming from homes where the primary languages spoken are not English;

(4) provide assurances that youth engaged in youth development programs carried out under the area plan will be treated equitably;

(5) contain strategies for mobilizing and coordinating community resources to meet the outcome objectives;

(6) describe activities for which funds made available through the allocation will be used to fill gaps between unmet needs and available resources;

(7) describe the inclusive process used by the consortium to engage all segments of the communities in the youth development area in developing the area plan;

(8) provide measures of program effectiveness to be used in evaluating the progress of the youth development programs approved by the consortium in the area in ensuring access for all youth to the full array of core resources described in section 9002, including specific measures for providing access to such resources for youth with special developmental needs, and including specific measures of the participation of youth;

(9) describe how local requirements for providing matching funds will be met, how resources will be leveraged, and the uses to which matching funds and leveraged resources will be applied, in carrying out the area plan;

(10) provide for the establishment and maintenance of outreach sufficient to ensure that youth and their families in the youth development area are aware of youth development programs providing access to the core resources described in section 9002, and to ensure that the participation of youth is sustained;

(11) provide that the consortium will—

    (A) conduct periodic evaluations of, and public hearings on, activities carried out under the area plan;

    (B) furnish technical assistance to entities carrying out youth development programs under this title within the youth development area;

    (C) establish effective and efficient procedures for the coordination of—

        (i) entities carrying out youth development programs under this chapter within the youth development area; and

        (ii) entities carrying out other Federal, State, local, and private programs for youth within the youth development area; and

    (D) take into account in connection with matters of general policy arising in the development and administration of the area plan, the views of youth who have participated in youth development programs or who desire to participate in youth development programs pursuant to the plan; and

  (12) provide for the utilization of entities carrying out volunteer service centers and organizations supporting youth in community service and civic participation in the area to—

    (A) encourage and enlist the services of local volunteer groups to provide assistance and services appropriate to the unique developmental needs of youth in the youth development area;

    (B) encourage, organize, and promote youth to serve as volunteers to communities in the area; and

    (C) promote recognition of the contribution made by youth volunteers to youth development programs administered in the youth development area.

SEC. 9109. GRANTS AND CONTRACTS TO ELIGIBLE ENTITIES.

[See bill for this section at http://thomas.loc.gov/.]

SEC. 9110. ELIGIBLE ENTITIES.

[See bill for this section at http://thomas.loc.gov/.]

SEC. 9111. APPLICATIONS.

[See bill for this section at http://thomas.loc.gov/.]

SEC. 9112. YOUTH DEVELOPMENT PROGRAMS.

(a) ACCESS—An eligible entity that receives a grant or contract under section 9109 to carry out a youth development program shall implement a program that promotes, either directly, through a contract, or indirectly through collaboration with other community entities, access to the full array of core resources described in section 9002.

(b) ACTIVITIES—An eligible entity that receives a grant or contract under section 9109 to carry out a youth development program may include among eligible activities provided through the program, which are part of an effort to provide access to, and participation in, the full array of core resources described in section 9002—

   (1) character development and ethical enrichment activities;

   (2) mentoring activities, including one-to-one relationship building and tutoring;

   (3) provision and support of community youth centers and clubs;

   (4) nonschool hours, weekend, and summer programs and camps;

   (5) sports, recreation, and other activities promoting physical fitness and teamwork;

   (6) services that promote health and healthy development and behavior on the part of youth, including risk avoidance programs;

   (7) academic enrichment, peer counseling and teaching, and literacy activities;

   (8) camping, environmental, and science education;

   (9) arts and cultural engagement, including through music, fine and performing arts;

   (10) workforce preparation, youth entrepreneurship, and technological and vocational skill building;

   (11) opportunities for community service and community action aimed at involving youth in providing the full array of core resources described in section 9002 to other youth, including opportunities provided in conjunction with activities being performed by entities under the National and Community Service Act of 1990 (42 U.S.C. 12501 et seq.);

(12) opportunities that engage youth in civic participation and as leaders or partners in decisionmaking, especially opportunities with respect to programs and strategies that seek to offer access to, and participation in, the full array of core resources described in section 9002;

(13) special interest group activities or courses, including activities or courses regarding video production, cooking, gardening, pet care, photography, and other youth-identified interests;

(14) efforts focused on building the capacity of community-based youth workers, utilizing community colleges, colleges, and universities;

(15) public and private youth led programs, including such programs provided by youth-serving or youth development organizations;

(16) transportation services to foster the participation of youth in youth development programs in the community involved;

(17) subsidies for youth that meet the income eligibility guidelines for a free or reduced price lunch under section 9(b) of the Richard B. Russell National School Lunch Act (42 U.S.C. 1758(b)), if the provision of such a subsidy allows a youth to fully participate in a youth development program that is part of a strategy to promote access to, and participation in, the full array of core resources described in section 9002;

(18) training or group counseling to assist youth, by State certified counselors, psychologists, social workers, or other State licensed or certified mental health professionals who are qualified under State law to provide such services to youth; and

(19) referrals to State certified counselors, psychologists, social workers, or other State licensed or certified mental health professionals or health professionals who are qualified under State law to provide such services to youth.

(c) INFORMATION—An eligible entity that receives a grant or contract under section 9109 shall be considered to be a person directly connected with the administration of a Federal education program for purposes of section 9(b)(2)(C)(iii)(II)(aa) of the Richard B. Russell National School Lunch Act (7 U.S.C. 1758(b)(2)(C)(iii)(II)). A school serving youth who are receiving services under this chapter from the eligible entity shall provide information to the eligible entity on the income eligibility status of the youth who are children described in section 9(b)(2)(C)(iv) of such Act (7 U.S.C. 1758(b)(2)(C)(iv)), in accordance with that section, to enable the eligible entity to determine eligibility for subsidies under subsection (b)(17).

(d) PARTICIPATION IN PLANNING, DESIGN, AND IMPLEMENTATION—An eligible entity that receives a grant or contract under section 9109 shall actively engage parents, grandparents, guardians, and youth in the planning, design, and implementation of youth development programs supported by funds made available through the grant or contract, including using consumer feedback and evaluation mechanisms at least once a year.

CHAPTER 3—ACCOUNTABILITY

SEC. 9201. PURPOSES.

The purposes of this chapter are—
(1) to ensure that funds appropriated to carry out this subtitle are expended in compliance with this subtitle; and
(2) to establish mechanisms at the Federal, State, and local levels to monitor expenditures of the funds and respond to noncompliance with this subtitle.

SEC. 9202. FEDERAL LEVEL ACCOUNTABILITY.

[See bill for this section at http://thomas.loc.gov/.]

SEC. 9203. STATE LEVEL ACCOUNTABILITY.

[See bill for this section at http://thomas.loc.gov/.]

SEC. 9204. LOCAL LEVEL ACCOUNTABILITY.

[See bill for this section at http://thomas.loc.gov/.]

SEC. 9205. STATE AUDIT.

[See bill for this section at http://thomas.loc.gov/.]

CHAPTER 4—TRAINING, RESEARCH, AND EVALUATION

SEC. 9301. PURPOSE.

The purpose of this chapter is to expand the Nation's knowledge and understanding of youth, youth development programs, and community mobilization aimed at providing all youth with access to, and participation in, the full array of core resources described in section 9002 by—

(1) assisting States in evaluating the effectiveness of activities implemented under this subtitle (including evaluating the outcomes resulting from the activities alongside the activities' inputs and fidelity of these inputs), including assisting in the specification of a minimum set of quality, outcome, and utilization data to be collected, and development of common definitions to be used, by entities receiving funds under this subtitle;

(2) placing priority on the education and training of personnel, with respect to youth development programs, to work with youth, with a special emphasis on youth with special developmental needs;

(3) conducting research (that includes samples that are representative of broader populations; that is longitudinal; that can examine effects across multiple levels, such as the effects on youth, programs, and communities; and that addresses participation, selection, participant retention, and program reach) and identifying effective practices directly related to the field of youth development;

(4) disseminating widely information acquired through such research to national, State, and local youth development organizations and youth-serving organizations; and

(5) establishing a clearinghouse for the collection, dissemination, training, and technical assistance of youth development best practices, including quality, outcome, and performance measurements.

SEC. 9302. GRANTS AND CONTRACTS.

(a) IN GENERAL—The Associate Commissioner may award grants and contracts to eligible entities to carry out evaluation, education and training, and dissemination activities described in this section.

(b) EVALUATION—

[See bill for this section at http://thomas.loc.gov/.]

(c) EDUCATION AND TRAINING—The Associate Commissioner shall develop and establish a system for providing education and training of personnel of States and consortia to increase their capacity to work with youth, with a special emphasis on youth with special developmental needs, in carrying out quality youth development programs under this subtitle.

(d) IMPACT EVALUATION—

(1) BIENNIAL EVALUATION—

(A) IN GENERAL—The Associate Commissioner shall conduct an independent biennial evaluation of the impact of youth development programs assisted under this subtitle to promote positive youth development.

(B) CONTENTS—The evaluation shall report on—

(i) whether the entities carrying out the youth development programs—

(I) provided a thorough assessment of local resources and barriers to access to, and participation in, the full array of core resources;

(II) used objective data and the knowledge of a wide range of community members;

(III) developed measurable goals and objectives;

(IV) implemented research-based youth development programs that have been shown to be effective and meet identified needs; and

(V) conducted periodic evaluations to assess progress made toward achieving the goals and objectives and used evaluations to improve the goals and objectives, and the youth development programs;

(ii) whether the youth development programs have been designed and implemented in a manner that specifically targets, if relevant to the youth development programs—

(I) research-based variables that are predictive of healthy youth development;

(II) risk factors that are predictive of an increased likelihood that youth will use drugs, alcohol, or

tobacco, become sexually active, or engage in violence or drop out of school; or

(III) protective factors, buffers, or assets that are known
to protect youth from exposure to risk, either by
reducing the exposure to risk factors or by changing
the way a youth responds to risk, and to increase the
likelihood of positive youth development;

(iii) whether the entities carrying out the youth development programs have appreciably reduced individual risk-taking behavior and community risk
factors and increased either individual or community protective factors; and

(iv) whether the entities carrying out the youth development programs have incorporated effective
youth and parent involvement.

(2) BIENNIAL REPORT—Not later than January 1, 2006, and
every 2 years thereafter, the Associate Commissioner shall
submit to the President and Congress a report on the findings of the evaluation conducted under paragraph (1)
together with data available from other sources on the well-
being of youth.

(e) DISSEMINATION—The Associate Commissioner shall
develop a system to facilitate the broad dissemination of information acquired through research to States, youth development
consortia, and the public about successful and promising strategies for providing all youth with the full array of core resources
described in section 9002.

SEC. 9303. AUTHORIZATION OF
APPROPRIATIONS.

There are authorized to be appropriated to carry out this chapter
$7,000,000 for fiscal year 2004, and such sums as may be necessary for
each of fiscal years 2005, 2006, 2007, and 2008.

SUBTITLE E—COORDINATION OF NATIONAL YOUTH POLICY

SEC. 9401. COORDINATING COUNCIL FOR NATIONAL YOUTH POLICY.

(a) ESTABLISHMENT—There is established in the Executive Office of the President a Coordinating Council for National Youth Policy.

(b) ADMINISTRATION—The Assistant to the President for Domestic Policy within the Executive Office of the President shall oversee the functioning of the Council established under subsection (a).

(c) COMPOSITION—

  (1) NUMBER—The Council shall be composed of the following members:

   (A) The Attorney General.

   (B) The Secretary of Education.

   (C) The Secretary of Health and Human Services.

   (D) The Secretary of Housing and Urban Development.

   (E) The Secretary of Labor.

   (F) The Secretary of Transportation.

   (G) The Commissioner of Social Security.

   (H) The Chief Executive Officer of the Corporation for National and Community Service.

   (I) The heads of such other Federal departments and agencies as the Secretary considers appropriate.

   (J) 15 individuals who are neither officers nor employees of the United States.

  (2) QUALIFICATIONS OF NON-FEDERAL MEMBERS— The President shall appoint the members of the Council specified in paragraph (1)(J) from among—

   (A) individuals who have expertise in or experience with youth development or youth-serving programs, especially programs serving rural and inner-city urban youth and youth with special developmental needs;

(B) representatives of national organizations with an interest in youth development programs;

(C) representatives of business and faith communities;

(D) parents, grandparents, and guardians; and

(E) youth who have participated in local youth development programs or who desire to participate in local youth development programs.

(3) AGE OF NON-FEDERAL MEMBERS—At least 1/3 of the individuals appointed under paragraph (1)(J) shall be younger than 20 years of age at the time of appointment.

(d) APPOINTMENT AND TERMS OF NON-FEDERAL MEMBERS—

(1) TERMS—

(A) IN GENERAL—Except as otherwise provided in this section, a member of the Council appointed under subsection (c)(1)(J) shall serve for a term of 4 years.

(B) END OF TERM—The term shall end on March 31 regardless of the actual date of the appointment of such member.

(2) SERVICE—Members of the Council appointed under subsection (c)(1)(J) shall serve without regard to the provisions of title 5, United States Code.

(e) SERVICE DURING VACANCIES—Any member of the Council appointed under subsection (c)(1)(J) appointed to fill a vacancy occurring prior to the expiration of the term for which such public member's predecessor was appointed shall be appointed for the remainder of such term. Members of the Council appointed under subsection (c)(1)(J) shall be eligible for reappointment and may continue to serve after the expiration of their terms until their successors have taken office.

(f) VACANCIES—Any vacancy in the Council shall not affect the powers of the Council, but shall be filled in the same manner as the original appointment was made.

(g) CHAIRPERSON—The Secretary of Health and Human Services shall serve as Chairperson for the Council.

(h) MEETINGS—The Council shall meet at the call of the Chairperson at least twice a year.

(i) DUTIES—The Council shall—

(1) serve as an effective and visible advocate for youth in the Federal Government, by actively reviewing and commenting on all Federal policies affecting youth;

(2) advise and assist the President and the heads of Federal departments and agencies on matters regarding the core resources youth need and the capacity of youth to contribute to the Nation and their communities;

(3) make recommendations to the President and to Congress with respect to Federal policies regarding youth;

(4) provide public forums for discussion on issues regarding youth, publicize the core resources youth need, and obtain information relating to ensuring all youth access and participate in the full array of core resources described in section 9002, by conducting public hearings, and by conducting or sponsoring conferences, workshops, and other similar meetings;

(5) develop mechanisms to foster collaboration and resolve administrative and programmatic conflicts between Federal programs that would be barriers to parents, grandparents, and guardians, community-based, youth-serving, and youth development organizations, local government entities, State government entities, tribes, older adult organizations, parks and recreation agencies, libraries and museums, arts and cultural organizations, faith-based organizations, and organizations supporting youth involved in community service and civic participation, related to the coordination of services and funding for programs promoting access to, and participation in, the full array of core resources described in section 9002; and

(6) consult with and assist State and local governments with respect to barriers the governments encounter related to the coordination of services and funding for youth development and youth services programs.

(j) REPORTS—[See bill for this section at http://thomas.loc.gov/.]

(k) TRAVEL EXPENSES—[See bill for this section at http://thomas.loc.gov/.]

(l) PERMANENT COMMITTEE—[See bill for this section at http://thomas.loc.gov/.]

(m) AUTHORIZATION OF APPROPRIATIONS—There are authorized to be appropriated to carry out this section $500,000 for fiscal year 2004 and such sums as may be necessary for fiscal years 2005 through 2008.

SUBTITLE B—YOUTH PROGRAMS

SEC. 9201. AMERICORPS.

Section 501(a)(2)(A) of the National and Community Service Act of 1990 (42 U.S.C. 12681(a)(2)(A)) is amended by striking "$300,000,000" and all that follows and inserting "$500,000,000" for fiscal year 2004 and such sums as may be necessary for fiscal year 2005.

REFERENCES

Beier, S. R., Rosenfeld, W. D., Spitalny, K. C., Zansky, S. M., Bontempo, A. N. (2000). The potential role of an adult mentor in influencing high-risk behaviors in adolescents. *Archives of Pediatric Adolescent Medicine, 154,* 327–331.

Carnegie Council on Adolescent Development. (1992). *Consultation on evaluation of youth development programs: Report on the meeting.* Washington, DC: Author.

Curtis, T., & Hansen-Schwoebel, K. (1999). *Big Brothers Big Sisters school-based mentoring: Evaluation and summary of five pilot programs.* Philadelphia: Big Brothers Big Sisters of America.

Dondero, G. (1997). Mentors: Beacons of hope. *Adolescence, 32* (128), 881–886.

Flaxman, E., Ascher, C., & Harrington, C. (1988). *Youth mentoring: Programs and practices.* New York: ERIC Clearinghouse on Urban Education at Columbia University.

Freedman, M. (1993). *The kindness of strangers: Adult mentors, urban youth, and the new voluntarism.* New York: Cambridge University Press.

Furano, K., Roaf, P. A., Styles, M. B., & Branch, A. Y. (1993). *Big Brothers Big Sisters: A study of program practices.* Philadelphia: Public/Private Ventures.

Grossman, J. B., & Tierney, J. P. (1998). Does mentoring work? An impact study of the Big Brothers Big Sisters Program. *Evaluation Review, 22*(3), 403–426.

Henkin, N., Rogers, A., & Lyons, M. (1992). *Linking Lifetimes: A national mentoring initiative summary report.* Philadelphia: Center for Intergenerational Learning, Temple University.

Jackson, Y. (2002). Mentoring delinquent children: An outcome study with young adolescent children. *Journal of Youth and Adolescence, 31,* 115–122.

Lee, J., & Cramond, B. (1999). The positive effects of mentoring economically disadvantaged students. *Professional School Counseling, 2*(3), 172–178.

McPartland, J. M., & Nettles, S. M. (1991). "Using community adults as advocates or mentors for at-risk middle school students: A two-year evaluation of Project RAISE." *American Journal of Education, 99,* 568–586.

Mecartney, C. A., Styles, M. B., & Morrow, K. V. (1994). *Mentoring in the juvenile justice system: Findings from two pilot programs.* Philadelphia: Public/Private Ventures.

Munch, J., & Blyth, D. A. (1993). An analysis of the functional nature of adolescents' supportive relationships. *Journal of Early Adolescence, 13,* 132–153.

Newman, S., & Larimer, B. (1995). *Senior Citizen School Volunteers Program: Report on cumulative data, 1988–1995.* Pittsburgh: Generations Together.

Newman, S., Morris, G. A., & Streetman, H. (1999). Elder-child interaction analysis: An observation instrument for classrooms involving older adults as mentors, tutors, or resource persons. *Child and Youth Services, 20,* 129–145.

Newman, S., Vasudev, J., & Onawola, R. (1985). Older volunteers' perceptions of the impact of volunteering on their psychological well-being. *Journal of Applied Gerontology, 4*(2), 123–127.

Philip, K., & Hendry, L. B. (1996). Young people and mentoring: Towards a typology? *Journal of Adolescence, 19,* 189–201.

Pringle, B., Anderson, L. M., Rubenstein, M. C., & Russo, A. W. (1993). *Peer tutoring and mentoring services for disadvantaged secondary students: An evaluation of the secondary schools basic skills demonstration assistance program.* Washington, DC: Policy Studies, Inc. Sponsored by the U.S. Department of Education, Office of Policy and Planning.

Roaf, P. A., Tierney, J. P., & Hunte, D. E. I. (1994). *Big Brothers Big Sisters: A study of volunteer recruitment and screening.* Philadelphia: Public/Private Ventures.

Rhodes, J. E. (2002). *Stand by me: The risks and rewards of mentoring today's youth.* Cambridge, MA: Harvard University Press.

Rhodes, J. E., & Davis, A. B. (1996). Supportive ties between nonparent adults and urban adolescent girls. In B. J. R. Leadbeater & N. Way (Eds.), *Urban girls: Resisting stereotypes, creating identities* (pp. 213–225). New York: New York University Press.

Rogers, A. M., & Taylor, A. S. (1997). Intergenerational mentoring: A viable strategy for meeting the needs of vulnerable youth. *Journal of Gerontological Social Work, 28*(1–2), 125–1240.

Roth, J., Brooks-Gunn, J., Murray, L., & Foster, W. (1998). Promoting healthy adolescents: Synthesis of youth development program evaluations. *Journal of Research on Adolescence, 8*(4), 423–459.

Santiago, S., Achille, P. A., & Lachance, L. (1998). The influence of Big Brothers on the separation-individuation of adolescents from single-parent families. *Adolescence, 33,* 343–353.

Sipe, C. (1996). *Mentoring: A synthesis of P/PV's research: 1988–1995.* Philadelphia: Public/Private Ventures.

Soucy, N., & Larose, S. (2000). Attachment and control in family and mentoring contexts as determinants of adolescent adjustment to college. *Journal of Family Psychology, 14*(1), 125–143.

Styles, M. B., & Morrow, K. V. (1992). *Understanding how youth and elders form relationships: A study of four Linking Lifetimes programs.* Philadelphia: Public/Private Ventures.

Taylor, A. S., LoSciuto, L., Fox, M., Hilbert, S. M., & Sonkowsky, M. (1999). The mentoring factor: Evaluation of the Across Ages intergenerational approach to drug abuse prevention. *Child and Youth Services, 20,* 77–99.

Tierney, J. P., & Branch, A. Y. (1992). *College students as mentors for at-risk youth: A study of six Campus Partners in Learning programs.* Philadelphia: Public/Private Ventures.

Tierney, J. P., Grossman, J. B., & Resch, N. L. (1995). *Making a difference: An impact study of Big Brothers Big Sisters.* Philadelphia: Public/Private Ventures.

Turner, S., & Scherman, A. (1996). Big brothers: Impact on little brothers' self-concepts and behaviors. *Adolescence, 31*(124), 875–882.

Weinberger, S. (2000). *Allstate mentoring program.* Norfolk, CT: Mentoring Consulting Group.

Yancey, A. K. (1998). Building positive self-image in adolescents in foster care: The use of role models in an interactive group approach. *Adolescence, 33*(130), 253–267.

5

Directory of National, International and State Organizations and Agencies

> In terms of joy, I get as much out of this relationship as my mentee does. Maybe more. That is the most surprising part to me. I thought I was going to do the giving and that is not what happened.
>
> Thomas, adult mentor

Many organizations exist that promote and support mentoring of children and youth. This chapter presents a review of the national organizations and agencies with missions that contribute to the creation of youth-adult relationships in general, or mentoring in particular. Following the national listings are the listings for mentoring organizations in each state. This state listing is not comprehensive; rather, it seeks to be representative of the organizations that exist to support mentoring across the United States. The entries include contact information, including, where possible, World Wide Web sites and e-mail addresses. Entries were correct at the time this book went to press, but the nonprofit world may be changeable, due to economic uncertainties. If contact information becomes outdated, readers are encouraged to go to the National Mentoring Partnership Web site (www.mentoring.org) and consult the partnership's state by state listing.

NATIONAL PROGRAMS AND RESOURCE, EDUCATIONAL, AND SUPPORT ORGANIZATIONS RELATED TO MENTORING

America's Promise—The Alliance for Youth
909 N. Washington Street, Suite 400
Alexandria, VA 22314-1556
Phone: (703) 684-4500
Fax: (703) 535-3900
Web: www.americaspromise.org

Secretary of State General Colin Powell (USA-ret) is founding chairman of this organization, which supports a national effort to make youth a priority and to fulfill five promises to youth. These promises pronounce that every young person in this country is entitled to: (1) an ongoing relationship with caring adults (parents, mentors, tutors, coaches); (2) safe places with structured activities during nonschool hours; (3) a healthy start and future; (4) a marketable skill through effective education; and (5) opportunities to give back through community service.

America's Promise was founded after the Presidents' Summit for America's Future, April 27–29, 1997 in Philadelphia. The summit was attended by Presidents Clinton, Bush, Carter, and Ford, with former First Lady Nancy Reagan representing her husband, as well as nearly 30 governors, 100 mayors, 145 community delegations, dozens of prominent business leaders, and several thousand concerned citizens. The summit was cosponsored by the Points of Light Foundation and the Corporation for National Service.

America's Promise now consists of an alliance of nearly 500 national organizations, called partners, which make large-scale national commitments to fulfill one or more of the five promises. Partners work to expand existing youth programs or create new ones and to evaluate program progress. Partners may be corporations, not-for-profits, higher-education and faith-based groups, associations and federal agencies, or arts and culture organizations.

Community and state partners form grassroots coalitions among the public, private and not-for-profit sectors to bolster youth resources. Coalitions that seek to fulfill all Five Promises for youth are known as Communities of Promise.

Big Brothers Big Sisters of America
230 N. 13th Street
Philadelphia, PA 19107

Phone: (215) 567-7000
Fax: (215) 567-0394
Web: www.bbbsa.org
E-mail: National@bbbsa.org

Big Brothers Big Sisters of America is the oldest, most established mentoring program in the country. The BBBS model pairs unrelated adult volunteers with youth between the ages of 5 and 18 who live in single-parent homes. The mentor functions as a source of support, and the program does not seek to change specific youth characteristics. BBBS has a national office, as well as programs in each of the 50 states. The national office develops and publishes standards and operating procedures that regulate participant screening, orientation, and training, and outline how to create and monitor matches. The BBBS Web site provides a complete listing of state affiliates.

Boys and Girls Clubs of America

National Headquarters
1230 W. Peachtree Street, N.W.
Atlanta, GA 30309
Phone: (404) 487-5700
Web: www.bgca.org

The Boys and Girls Club offers young people resources for connecting with caring adults. Local Boys and Girls Clubs are housed in neighborhood-based buildings designed exclusively for youth programs and activities, and include full-time, trained youth development professionals and volunteer support personnel. The mission is to inspire and enable all young people, especially those from disadvantaged circumstances, to reach their full potential as productive, responsible, and caring citizens.

Child Welfare League of America

440 First Street, N.W., 3rd Floor
Washington, DC 20001-2085
Phone: (202) 638-2952
Fax: (202) 638-4004
Web: www.cwla.org
E-mail: webweaver@cwla.org

This alliance of more than 1,000 public and nonprofit agencies is committed to the prevention and treatment of child abuse and neglect, while offering a variety of services such as kinship care, family foster care, adoption, youth development programs, residential group care, child care, family-centered practice, and programs for pregnant and parenting teens. In 1998 the Child Welfare League, in collaboration with Generations United, launched the Foster Grandparent Program, which promotes supportive mentoring relationships between disadvantaged youth and seniors.

Communities In Schools, Inc.
National Office
277 S. Washington Street, Suite 210
Alexandria, VA 22314
Phone: (800) CIS-4KIDS
Fax : (703) 519-7537
Web: www.cisnet.org

Communities In Schools (CIS) is a leading community-based organization helping kids succeed in school and prepare for life. Communities In Schools champions the connection of needed community resources with schools to help young people learn and grow. By bringing resources, services, parents and volunteers into schools, CIS creates a community of caring adults who work hand in hand with educators. Teachers are free to teach, and students can concentrate on learning. CIS programs now operate in more than 2,300 education sites in 33 states. More than 1.4 million young people have access to services through CIS. CIS programs benefit from approximately 1,500 repositioned agency staff and more than 800 reassigned school staff members. More than 40,000 volunteers contribute their time to helping young people through CIS.

Corporation for National Community Service
AmeriCorps and Senior Corps
1201 New York Avenue, N.W.
Washington, DC 20525
Phone: (202) 606-5000
Web: www.AmeriCorps.org and www.nationalservice.org
E-mail: webmaster@cns.gov

The Corporation for National Community Service provides volunteer opportunities for adults, senior citizens and children. AmeriCorps and Senior Corps are two organizations affiliated with the Corporation for

National Service that provide, among other things, volunteer opportunities related to mentoring.

AmeriCorps is a domestic Peace Corps that seeks to strengthen communities by providing intensive, results-driven service to people in need across the country. AmeriCorps members train volunteers, tutor and mentor at-risk youth, build housing, clean up rivers and streams, help seniors live independently, provide emergency and long-term assistance to victims of natural disasters, and meet other community needs. At the completion of their term of service, members receive education awards that provide college-related financial assistance. Many AmeriCorps members serve within existing projects, such as Habitat for Humanity, the American Red Cross, and Boys and Girls Clubs. Others work in AmeriCorps°VISTA (Volunteers in Service to America) and AmeriCorps°NCCC (the National Civilian Community Corps). The AmeriCorps Web site includes information about starting a program, as well as a state-by-state listing of AmeriCorps projects. Many of the AmeriCorps-affiliated projects related to mentoring are listed below in the state mentoring directory.

In the past 30 years, the Senior Corps has linked more than 450,000 older Americans to volunteer opportunities in their communities. There are three main Senior Corps programs: the Foster Grandparent Program, Retired and Senior Volunteer Program (RSVP), Seniors in Schools and Senior Companion Program. Each program creates an opportunity for interested older Americans to find challenging and rewarding local service placements.

Foster Grandparents is the nation's second largest mentoring program. Foster grandparents offer emotional support to children and adolescents who are at risk or have special needs. Eligible volunteers are 60 years of age or older and serve 20 hours a week, providing one-on-one assistance to children.

The Retired and Senior Volunteer Program engages volunteers 55 years of age and older in a variety of community services, including tutoring or mentoring.

4-H Council
7100 Connecticut Avenue
Chevy Chase, MD 20815-4999
Phone: (301) 961-2983
Fax: (301) 961-2984
Web: www.fourhcouncil.edu

National 4-H Headquarters
Cooperative State Research, Education, and Extension Service
US Department of Agriculture
1400 Independence Avenue, S.W.—MS 2225
Washington, DC 20250-2225
Phone: (202) 690-1568
Web: www.national4-hheadquarters.gov

4-H (Head, Heart, Hands, Health) is dedicated to promoting youth development through experiential learning and lifeskill growth. 4-H is the youth education branch of the Cooperative Extension Service, a program of the United States Department of Agriculture. Participants range in age from 5 to 21 years. Adults and young people spend time together engaged in a variety of activities. For 100 years, 4-H has served youth nationwide, with a 4-H program available in every county in the nation. There are numerous levels of 4-H engagement, including club, county, district, state, national and international. Currently, 6.8 million young people, from both urban and rural communities, participate in 4-H programs.

The National 4-H Council is the national, private sector nonprofit partner of 4-H and the Cooperative Extension Service which partners with 4-H at all levels (national, state and local). The council offers training, support, and curriculum development, and facilitates connections within the 4-H partnership.

GEAR UP
Gaining Early Awareness and Readiness for Undergraduate Programs
Office of Postsecondary Education
Department of Education
1990 K Street, N.W.
Washington, DC 20006-8524
Phone: (202) 502-7676
Web: www.ed.gov/gearup
E-mail: gearup@ed.gov

This federal program is sponsored by the U.S. Department of Education. It funds partnerships among high-poverty middle schools, colleges and universities, community organizations, and businesses to create college opportunities for at-risk students. The partnerships provide tutoring, mentoring, information on college preparation and financial aid, an emphasis on core academic preparation, and, in some cases, scholarships. GEAR UP seeks to engage students early in their academic career and follow them through high school graduation. The mentoring students receive is long-term, covering a period of six years or more.

The Hospital Youth Mentoring Program: Career Exploration
The Johns Hopkins Hospital, Phipps 454
600 N. Wolfe Street
Baltimore, MD 21287-1454
Phone: (410) 955-1488
Fax: (410) 955-9803
Web: www.mentor.jhmi.edu

Since June 1993, the Hospital Youth Mentoring Program (HYMP), administered by the Johns Hopkins Hospital and funded by the Commonwealth Fund until 1997, has supported youth mentoring projects at 15 hospitals. Twelve of the 15 hospitals have institutionalized their programs. By involving hospitals with youth from their communities, the program has not only helped youth but has also encouraged the hospitals to take a more active role in addressing local community needs and educating their future workforce.

The HYMP model is flexible. Each of the programs is differently organized, but all share the following elements: (a) a mentoring relationship between a student (preferably from grade 9 or 10) and a hospital staff member who meet at the hospital or elsewhere twice a month in person and twice a month on the phone; (b) career development activities, such as career days, college or employment guidance, paid work experience, organized career exploration, job shadowing, speakers and tours of the hospital; (c) administration by a designated person at the school and at the hospital; and (d) social, athletic, and career exploration activities at the hospital. Sites have had the most success with C-average students who, though at risk of not finishing high school on time, indicate an interest in their future. They appear most able to develop a relationship with a mentor and to be motivated by a mentoring program.

Participating hospitals include Albert Einstein Medical Center, Philadelphia, Pa.; Barnes-Jewish Hospital, St. Louis, Mo.; Beth Israel Medical Center, N.Y.; Cedars-Sinai Medical Center, Los Angeles, Calif., Duke University Medical Center, Durham, N.C.; Iowa Health System, Des Moines, Iowa; Johns Hopkins Hospital, Baltimore, Md.; Maine Medical Center, Portland, Maine; University of Michigan, Ann Arbor, Mich.; Mount Sinai Medical Center, N.Y.; Vanderbilt University Medical

Center, Nashville, Tenn.; and Washington Hospital Center, Washington, D.C.

Hospitality Business Alliance

175 W. Jackson Boulevard, Suite 1500
Chicago, IL 60604
Phone: (800) 765-2122 ext. 340
Fax: (312) 466-1596
Web: www.nraef.org/hba

The Hospitality Business Alliance (HBA) initiative is an educational partnership formed by the National Restaurant Association and the American Hotel & Lodging Association to create a nationwide system of high school hospitality courses linked with mentored work-site experiences.

The mission of the Hospitality Business Alliance is to encourage young people to enter the hospitality industry. In order to meet this goal, the Alliance helps create and support high school hospitality school-to-career programs and industry mentoring programs that lead to an industry-recognized national certification. The Hospitality Business Alliance hopes to have partnerships in all U.S. states by the year 2005. The organization currently has partnerships in 35 states and Washington D.C., including Alaska, Arizona, Arkansas, California, Colorado, Florida, Georgia, Hawaii, Illinois, Indiana, Iowa, Kansas, Louisiana, Maryland, Massachusetts, Michigan, Mississippi, Nebraska, New Jersey, New Mexico, New York, Ohio, Oklahoma, Oregon, Pennsylvania, Rhode Island, South Carolina, Texas, Utah, Vermont, Virginia, Washington, West Virginia, Wisconsin, and Wyoming. A complete listing of state programs is available on the Web site.

HOSTS (Help One Student To Succeed) Corporation

222 N.E. Park Plaza Drive, Suite 230
Vancouver, WA 98684-3402
Phone: (800) 833-4678
Web: www.hosts.com
E-mail: info@hostscorp.com

The Help One Student To Succeed (HOSTS) program, the nation's largest and oldest structured academic mentoring program, links at-risk students with community volunteers, business partners, and student mentors in order to promote learning in a variety of areas, such as reading, language arts, Spanish language arts, and math. The mentoring component of the comprehensive, research-based HOSTS program is called HOSTSLink™. This component supports the affective and academic needs of HOSTS students as they work to master academic skills.

"I Have a Dream" Foundation
330 Seventh Avenue, 20th Floor
New York, NY 10001
Phone: (212) 293-5480
Fax: (212) 293-5478
Web: www.ihad.org

The "I Have a Dream" (IHAD) Foundation is a nationwide network of projects that encourage children to stay in school, graduate, and go to college or obtain meaningful employment. The national foundation assists in the launching of new local projects and provides information and support to existing projects. Individual "I Have a Dream" foundations exist in 64 cities across the United States, each supporting one or several projects. A project consists of one "dreamer" class, a group of disadvantaged children "adopted" by a sponsor and provided with a year-round program of tutoring, mentoring, and social and cultural activities, plus college tuition assistance. Projects exist in Arizona, California, Colorado, Connecticut, Delaware, the District of Columbia, Florida, Georgia, Illinois, Indiana, Kentucky, Maryland, Massachusetts, Michigan, Missouri, Nevada, New Jersey, New Mexico, New York, Ohio, Oregon, Pennsylvania, South Carolina, Texas, Virginia and Washington.

KIDS HOPE USA
P.O. Box 2517
Holland, MI 49422-2517
Phone: (616) 546-3580
Fax: (616) 546-3586
Web: http://community.gospelcom.net/Brix?pageID=420

KIDS HOPE USA began in 1993, with three pilot programs initiated in February 1995. This program teaches churches to recruit, screen, train, match, and supervise their own members for one-to-one relationships with at-risk public elementary school children. Programs are housed in a local church, which is matched with a neighborhood school.

The church provides the trained mentors and behind-the-scenes prayer partner for each child. Participating churches seek to offer one prayer partner for each mentor-mentee relationship. Mentors meet weekly with a child in an effort to promote values, self-esteem, and academic skills. KIDS HOPE USA has assisted over 200 churches of varying dominations, including those in urban, suburban, and rural communities. The program is now active in 26 states. KIDS HOPE USA received a Daily Presidential Points of Light Award and has been named a lead church-based partner by America's Promise.

National Association of Partners in Education

901 N. Pitt Street, Suite 320
Alexandria, VA 22314
Phone: (703) 836-4880
Fax: (703) 836-6941
Web: www.napehq.org
E-mail: napehq@napehq.org

The National Association of Partners in Education offers leadership in the development and maintenance of effective school volunteer, intergenerational, community service, and business partnership programs that empower students to succeed. It is the only national membership organization devoted solely to providing leadership in the field of education partnership development.

Partners in Education seeks to increase the number, quality, and scope of effective partnerships; increase the resources to support effective partnerships; increase awareness about the importance of partnerships for promoting youth success; and promote the importance of effective partnerships to policymakers. Partners in Education provides training and technical assistance, research and materials development, and a national member network. The organization's Web site includes descriptions of numerous helpful publications related to partnership development and evaluation.

National Kinship Affiliate Network

3210 Oliver Avenue N.
Minneapolis, MN 55412
Phone: (612) 588-4655
Fax: (612) 588-4680

Web: www.kinship.org
E-mail: mail@kinship.org

Founded in 1954, Kinship is an interdenominational Christian-based mentoring program targeting children 5 to 15 years of age. The organization seeks to provide children with long-term (minimum one-year) connections with individuals, couples and families. Kinship has 40 national affiliates.

National Mentoring Center
Northwest Regional Education Laboratory (NWREL)
101 S.W. Main Street, Suite 500
Portland, OR 97204
Phone: (800) 547-6339 ext. 135 or (503) 275-9500
Web: www.nwrel.org/mentoring
E-mail: mentorcenter@nwrel.org

Created and funded by the Office of Juvenile Justice and Delinquency Prevention (OJJDP), the National Mentoring Center strives to foster educational achievement for children, youth and adults. Its services include conducting research, as well as providing training and technical assistance to education, government, community agencies, business, and labor. NWREL's primary service area is the Northwest states of Alaska, Idaho, Montana, Oregon, and Washington.

The National Mentoring Partnership
1600 Duke Street, Suite 300
Alexandria, VA 22314
Phone: (703) 224-2200
Fax: (703) 226-2581
Web: www.mentoring.org

This partnership promotes the growth of mentoring nationwide and serves as a resource for mentors and mentoring initiatives. The partnership is headquartered in Alexandria, Virginia and works with a national network of 30 state and local partnerships. State/Local partnerships exist in Arizona, California, Connecticut, Delaware, Florida, Kansas/ Missouri, Maine, Maryland, Massachusetts, Minnesota, Mississippi, Nebraska, New Jersey, New York, North Carolina, Ohio, Oregon, Pennsylvania, Texas, Utah, and Virginia.

The National School and Community Corps
684 Whitehead Road
Lawrenceville NJ 08648
Tel: (609) 392-6662
Fax: (609) 392-6211
Web: http://198.139.224.157/index.htm

The National School and Community Corps (NSCC), an AmeriCorps national service program, has more than 300 members currently serving in inner-city schools. The goals of the NSCC are to enhance the capacity of urban schools to serve students, their families, and the community. NSCC is a dynamic part of school restructuring, joining national service with urban school reform. It brings a vision, activities, services, and resources to schools and neighborhoods. NSCC members enrich the school environment and extend the school day, week and year to benefit students, their parents, and the community as a whole. Students participating in NSCC build relationships with caring adults, do better in school, discover new skills and ideas, and develop confidence in themselves and their future. The NSCC offers services related to literacy, arts, and service learning to children and adults, as well as mentoring, homework help, club activities, youth leadership, conflict resolution, and other programs.

Office of Juvenile Justice and Delinquency Prevention (OJJDP)
Juvenile Mentoring Program (JUMP)
810 Seventh Street, N.W.
Washington, DC 20531
Phone: (202) 307-5911
Fax: (202) 307-2093
Web: http://ojjdp.ncjrs.org

The OJJDP provides national leadership, coordination, and resources to develop, implement, and support effective methods to prevent juvenile victimization and respond appropriately to juvenile delinquency. The OJJDP implements its mission through prevention programs and a juvenile justice system that protects the public safety, holds juvenile offenders accountable, and provides individually tailored treatment and rehabilitative services.

Funded by Congress, the Juvenile Mentoring Program (JUMP) supports one-to-one mentoring programs for youth at risk for educational failure, dropping out of school, or involvement in delinquent activities, including gangs and drug abuse. In particular, the program focuses on the issues of poor school performance and dropping out of school. This program, which seeks to provide youth with support and structure, emphasizes the importance of school collaboration in mentoring programs. Funding is provided for collaborative efforts between local educational agencies and public/private nonprofit organizations or tribal nations to support development of effective mentoring programs for at-risk youth. Projects tend to use adult mentors and target only at-risk youth in high crime areas where 60 percent or more of the youth in the participating school are approved to receive Chapter I funds (Free and Reduced Lunch Program) under the Elementary and Secondary Education Act of 1965 and where a considerable number of youth drop out of school each year.

100 Black Men of America, Inc.
141 Auburn Avenue
Atlanta, GA 30303
Phone: (404) 688-5100 or (800) 598-3411
Fax: (404) 688-1024
Web: www.100blackmen.org

Founded in 1963, this national alliance of leading African American men of business, industry, public affairs and government is designed to improve the quality of life for African Americans and other minorities. The organization provides mentoring, education, health and wellness, and economic development programs, with the aim of promoting creativity, academic achievement, and social responsibility.

Public/Private Ventures
2000 Market Street, Suite 600
Philadelphia, PA 19103
Phone: (215) 557-4400
Fax: (215) 557-4469
Web: www.ppv.org
E-mail: webmaster@ppv.org

Public/Private Ventures is a national nonprofit action-based research, public policy, and program development organization. The organization's mission is to advance social policies, programs, and community initiatives, serving youth and young adults. P/PV works in partnership with philanthropies, the public and business sectors, and nonprofit organizations. P/PV makes significant contributions in the area of program evaluation and development and has conducted extensive research evaluating mentoring programs. The organization's Web site lists a variety of valuable mentoring-related publications, many of which can be downloaded directly from the Web site.

Student 2 Student
Skills USA National Staff
P.O. Box 3000
Leesburg, VA 20177-0300
Phone: (703) 777-8810
Fax: (703) 777-8999
Web: www.skillsusa.org

Student 2 Student was created as a vehicle for SkillsUSA members to participate in America's Promise—The Alliance for Youth. The program connects a service project with career awareness and professional development. In the program, high school students function as mentors to younger middle or elementary school students, with a focus on increasing knowledge of career options. Local business and industry may also be involved.

Temple University Center for Intergenerational Learning
1601 N. Broad Street, Room 206
Philadelphia, PA 19122
Phone: (215) 204-6970
Fax: (215) 204-3195
Web: www.temple.edu/cil
E-mail: intergnerationallearning@yahoo.com

Since 1979, the Center for Intergenerational Learning at Temple University has worked to strengthen communities using intergenerational programming. The CIL is a national resource for programs seeking to improve the lives of individuals and families by creating opportunities for youth and elders to contribute to their communities and by promoting partnerships among organizations serving young people, families, and older adults. The center is an advocate for intergenerational strategies, and works to educate and assist in the development of intergenerational programs. The Center for Intergenerational Learning has created a variety of intergenerational programs, such as Across Ages, a mentor program linking older adults and youth ages 9 to 15. The CIL is involved in materials development, research, and evaluation, and also provides extensive training and technical assistance to agencies interested in developing intergenerational programs.

Young Men's Christian Association (YMCA) of the USA
101 N. Wacker Drive
Chicago, IL 60606
Phone: (312) 977-0031
Fax: (312) 977-9063
Web: www.ymca.net
E-mail: webmaster@ymca.net

This 150-year-old organization began as a Christian men's group and has grown into the largest not-for-profit community service organization in America. Currently there are 2,400 YMCAs nationwide, as well as YMCAs in more than 120 countries worldwide. The organization seeks to address the health and social service needs of 18 million men, women and children across the country. YMCAs welcome individuals of diverse backgrounds, regardless of ability to pay. Each local branch of the YMCA provides unique services, targeted to the community it serves. The national YMCA Web site allows visitors to search for local YMCA branches.

YMCAs provide young people with a safe place staffed by caring, dedicated adults who listen to them and help them cope effectively with the stresses, changes, and choices that come with adolescence. In serving the needs of young people, YMCAs run a variety of programs including: mentoring, tutoring, social events, fitness programs, after-school programs, and youth employment programs.

Young Women's Christian Association (YWCA) of the USA
1015 18th Street, N.W., Suite 1100
Washington, DC 20036
Phone: (202) 467-0801
Fax: (202) 467-0802 or (800) YWCAUS1
Web: www.ywca.org

The YWCA organization incorporates Christian principles to achieve its vision of building strong kids, strong families and strong communities, promoting the core values of caring, honesty, respect, and responsibility. The mission includes empowering women and girls by offering a wide range of services and programs that enrich and transform their lives, including the YWCA TechGYRLS™ Clubs and the YWCA/NIKE Sports Program. Women are encouraged to exercise their political clout at the Institute for Public Leadership. The YWCA promotes social justice by annually presenting the YWCA Week Without Violence® and the YWCA National Day of Commitment to Eliminate Racism. There are nearly 100 locations worldwide.

INTERNATIONAL ORGANIZATIONS

Big Brothers Big Sisters International
1315 Walnut Street, Suite 704
Philadelphia, PA 19107
Phone: (215) 717-5130
Fax: (215) 717-5134
Web: www.bbbsi.org
E-mail: bbbsi@bbbsi.org

This extension of BBBSA includes volunteer activities in numerous countries, including: Antigua and Barbuda, Australia, Barbados, Bermuda, Bulgaria, Canada, Cayman Islands, Croatia, the Czech Republic, Denmark, Estonia, Georgia, Germany, Ghana, Grenada, Guyana, Ireland, Israel, Japan, Kyrgyzstan, Latvia, Lithuania, Macedonia, Moldova, the Netherlands, New Zealand, Poland, Romania, Russia, Serbia and Montenegro, Singapore, Slovakia, South Africa, Turkey, Ukraine, United Kingdom and the United States.

STATE ORGANIZATIONS

What follows is a selected list of mentoring programs, with representative mentoring efforts from each of the 50 states, as well as Puerto Rico and the District of Columbia.

Alabama

Lighthouse Mentor Program
Lighthouse Counseling Center
1415 E. South Boulevard
Montgomery, AL 36117
Phone: (334) 286-5980

Fax: (334) 286-5993
Web: www.lighthousehelp.com

The Lighthouse is one of only two formal mentoring programs in the state of Alabama serving adolescents in the foster care system. Started in 1998, the program serves approximately 50 adolescents each year. Most mentoring activities take place in the community. Therefore, each qualified volunteer must be at least 21 years of age and have a clean criminal background, valid driver's license, and current automobile insurance. The Lighthouse is an outreach program of the Lighthouse Counseling Center, which has a 30-year history in the city of Montgomery. One-on-one mentoring is the heart of the Lighthouse mentoring program, but other forms, including group mentoring, have also been utilized when the number of eligible foster children has exceeded the available mentors. Mentors commit a minimum of 10 hours per month to their mentee, and most extend their commitment far beyond the required one year.

Links-Up Mentoring
Camp Fire USA
Central Alabama Council
3600 8th Avenue S., Suite 502
Birmingham, AL 35222
Phone: (205) 324-2434
Fax: (205) 322-7988
Web: www.campfire-al.org/programs.htm#linksup

Links-Up Mentoring is an award-winning peer mentoring program conducted in central Alabama schools and community facilities by Camp Fire USA. Serving children ages 5–18 in group and team configurations, Links-Up is staffed by trained volunteers who function under the supervision of a professional counselor. It is one of a series of Camp Fire USA programs that offer career and employment skill development, mentoring, tutoring, camps, and weekly club activities. In Links-Up, school principals and counselors select potential mentees based on behaviors that place those children at risk for drug use, dropping out, teen pregnancy, or violence. Links-Up is designed to make a difference in the lives of those mentees by teaching them alternate behavior patterns and to enhance their educational experiences and their awareness of themselves and others.

Mentor Alabama
The Attorney General's Mentoring Initiative
11 S. Union Street, 3rd Floor
Montgomery, AL 36130
Phone: (334) 242-7300
Fax: (334) 242-7458
Web: www. ago.state.al.us/mentor/

Mentor Alabama is the Attorney General of the state of Alabama's Mentoring Initiative. Founded in 2000, this program promotes mentoring as a strategy for fighting juvenile crime by involving caring, appropriate adults in the lives of youth as mentors and role models. Mentor Alabama maintains a complete statewide network and database of existing mentoring organizations. Both school- and community-based mentoring opportunities are available. The program also recruits adults to become involved with existing school- and community-based mentoring. Mentor Alabama includes the faith community in its outreach efforts.

UAB Science Education Program
University of Alabama at Birmingham
1530 3rd Avenue S.
Birmingham, AL 35294-1150
Phone: (205) 934-8804 or (205) 934-7995
Fax: (205) 975-2497
Web: http://main.uab.edu

The UAB Science Education Program set the standard for cross age career mentoring in biomedical research when it established the Science Education Program. The program gives high school juniors and seniors a chance to experience firsthand the challenges and rewards of biomedical research. Included is the completion of a university laboratory orientation course by the high school mentees, as well as several scientific seminars and educational workshops. Mentees spend seven weeks working side-by-side with a UAB biomedical scientist or graduate student who serve as mentors and role models. Eligibility requirements for the high school students include a 3.00 or better grade point average and completion of algebra 1, geometry, and at least one year of biology, chemistry, or physics.

Alaska

School to Work
Juneau-Douglas High School
10014 Crazy Horse Drive
Juneau, AK 99801-8529
Phone: (907) 463-1900
Fax: (907) 463–1919

The school-to-work mentoring program at Alaska's Juneau-Douglas High School targets young women. This career-linked mentoring initiative connects local high school students with the Juneau Women's Network. The collaborative program provides mentoring and role modeling for girls in grades 9 through 12. Potential candidates for the mentoring program are young women who possess a defined subject/career interest and who have the motivation to explore that career area with a mentor. Young women and girls who have not yet defined a career interest are also eligible for the mentoring program.

Wisdom Keeper's Program, Tribal Youth Program
Ketchikan Indian Corporation
2960 Tongass Avenue
Ketchikan, AK 99950
Phone: (07) 225-5758
Fax (907) 247-0429
Web: www.kictribe.com

Wisdom Keeper is an innovative youth mentoring program developed by the Tribal Youth Program (TYP) of Ketchikan, Alaska. Designed for American Indian and Alaska Native at-risk youth, Wisdom Keeper is a mentoring program focused on preserving native traditions, values, and skills. The Ketchikan Indian Corporation administers the program and provides additional services to the Alaska Native and American Indian people of Ketchikan. The TYP provides additional prevention services for at-risk youth and also intervention services for court-involved youth. Prevention activities include workshops on dating violence and anger management, and a juvenile offender tracking program. A TYP tracking program follows court-referred, high-risk youth for 6 months, providing case management, referrals, and the monitoring of recidivism. In addition to the mentoring, prevention component of the youth services, interventions include substance abuse assessments, referrals, counseling, parenting workshops, and substance abuse education activities for teens.

Arizona

Mesa Mentoring Project
207 N. Mesa Drive
Mesa, AZ 85201
Phone: (480) 969-7601
Web: www.ci.mesa.az.us/police/mentoring.asp

The Mesa Mentoring Project (MMP)–Elementary Connection reflects a collaboration between the Mesa Family YMCA, the city of Mesa, Mesa Police Department, and the Mesa Public Schools to provide mentoring services to children in need of such services. The school-based program matches volunteer adult mentors with grades 4–6 children for a minimum one-year relationship. Students in grades 7–9 are also mentored, but not during the school day. The older youth participate in the MMP after school and on weekends. Children are chosen for inclusion in the program based on criteria indicating that they are likely to benefit from having a mentor in their lives.

Volunteer Center of Southern Arizona
The Mentoring Partnership
924 N. Alvernon Way
Tucson, AZ 85711
Phone: (520) 881-3300
Fax: (520) 881-3366
Web: www.volunteertucson.org

The Mentoring Partnership seeks to expand existing youth-adult mentor connections in the Tucson area by creating mentoring collaboratives. Services include volunteer recruitment and training for partner organizations. Tutoring and mentoring services are provided to at-risk youth.

Youth Volunteer Corps
Youth in Action AmeriCorps
Northern Arizona University
Riles Building 15, Room 204
P.O. Box 6025

Flagstaff, AZ 86011
Phone: (928) 523-9043
Fax: (928) 523-6395
Web: www4.nau.edu/AmeriCorps/SiteAgencies.htm

Flagstaff's Youth in Action AmeriCorps has worked with 34 different community agencies across Northern Arizona. In its Youth Volunteer Corps (YVC) program, AmeriCorps adult volunteers directly mentor middle and high school students. The mentored youth attend club meetings, projects, and YVC activities. The mentees are offered training and guidance in the service-learning process and in the art of volunteering. As part of the project goals, both the mentors and the mentees work closely with AmeriCorps staff on program development. This form of mentoring promotes civic responsibility through the act of volunteerism. It actively involves youth in community problem solving through volunteer service.

Arkansas

Big Brothers Big Sisters of Central Arkansas
628 W. Broadway, Suite 102
North Little Rock, AR 72114
Phone: (501) 374-6661
Fax: (501) 375-0906
Web: www.bbbsca.org

Big Brothers Big Sisters of Central Arkansas (BBBSCA) is the local branch of the national association, Big Brothers Big Sisters of America. The Central Arkansas branch provides one-on-one mentoring to children from largely single-parent homes. In the 2002–2003 school year, 750 children were involved in mentoring relationships, either in the community or at a school site. BBBSCA became an affiliate of Big Brothers Big Sisters of America in 1968. Their mission is to make a positive influence on each child's life through a professionally supported, one-on-one relationship with a caring adult. The BBBSCA staff provides active training, counseling, and ongoing support to their adult mentors.

Big Brothers Big Sisters of North Central Arkansas
P.O. Box 153
Conway, AR 72033
Phone: (501) 336-9505

Fax : (501) 329-1745
Web: www.bbbsnca.com

Big Brothers Big Sisters of North Central Arkansas (BBBSNCA) is a branch of the national association, the Big Brothers Big Sisters of America. The North Central BBBS organization offers two basic programs, both serving children 6 to 15 years of age. One such program is school-based. Screened and trained adult volunteer mentors (the "Bigs") visit their mentees (the "Littles") at the youth's school for an hour per week. The second program is community-based. There the adult volunteer mentors spend four to six hours per week, outside the school day, with their Littles in community-based activities.

California

Boys to Men Mentoring Network
9587 Tropico Drive
La Mesa, CA 91941
Phone: (619) 469-9599
Fax: (619) 463-8521
Web: www.mkpsd.org
E-mail: boystomen@home.com

Boys to Men supports boys between the ages of 12 and 16 by pairing them with responsible adult males. The goal of these mentoring relationships is to encourage the development of positive life skills and life goals. Mentor-Mentee pairs meet once a week for one hour, and also participate in twice monthly group meetings. The latter involves the boys meeting with a group facilitator to discuss current concerns while mentors meet with one another. Following the group meetings, the entire group comes together for an informal event. Boys to Men has also developed an intensive eight hour mentor training program and a weekend responsibility building initiation experience for participating boys.

Caring About Kids
1141 High Street
Auburn, CA 95603
Phone: (530) 889-2401 or (916) 789-0992 or (530) 546-5855
Fax: (530) 889-2430

Web: www.caringaboutkids.org
E-mail: info@caringaboutkids.org

This organization began in 1981 to provide student assistance programs and youth development training. In 1996 the Community Building Mentor Program emerged. The program provides recruitment, training, screening, and certification of mentors. Mentor-youth relationships are fostered throughout Placer County. The Caring About Kids mentoring model is distinct in that it asks initially only for a five hour commitment. Yet, on average, mentoring relationships average seven to nine months. Mentors initially meet with young people at designated community sites, such as schools, churches, or youth clubs. As the relationship develops, mentoring activities may move off site. In addition, Caring About Kids facilitates the creation of county partnerships and community networking.

California Mentor Foundation
100 Main Street
Tiburon, CA 94920
Phone: (415) 789-1007
Fax: (415) 789-1008
Web: www.calmentor.org

Developed to encourage the involvement of Californians in mentoring, the California Mentor Foundation (CMF) collaborates with mentoring programs all over California. In partnership with the California Mentoring Initiative, the foundation seeks to expand and improve linkages between public and private sector investment, as well as to recruit new mentors. An important mission of the CMF is to reengineer existing state and federal prevention investments to incorporate mentoring as a key strategy to reduce alcohol abuse, drug use, teen pregnancy, academic failure, gang participation, and violence. The CMF not only supports quality mentoring in California but also assists other states' efforts to launch mentor initiatives. The Web site provides a "tip of the day" and a listing of the members of the California Mentor Coalition.

California Mentor Initiative
Mentor Resource Center
1700 K Street
Sacramento, CA 95814

Phone: (916) 323-6589 (outside Calif.) or (800) 444-3066 (in Calif.)
Fax: (916) 323-1270
Web: www.calmentor.org

The California Mentor Initiative was created in 1995, representing California's commitment to mentoring as a vehicle for promoting the optimal development of young people. The initiative currently has the goal of recruiting, training and matching quality mentors for 1 million young people by 2005. The CMI partners with many community-based mentoring programs to enhance the quality and availability of mentoring programs available for California youth.

Community Services and Employment Training, Inc. (C-SET)
Mentors Matter
P.O. Box 1350
Visalia, CA 93279-1350
Phone: (559) 732-4194
Web: www.cset.org

C-SET is a community action agency that works to strengthen youth, families, and communities (through multiple approaches, including mentoring) by helping build self-reliant lives and caring communities. Mentors Matter is a successful collaborative effort designed to provide direct mentoring services to children in Tulare County as well as to create and sustain a unified leadership for mentoring service providers. The collaborative provides no-cost training, screening, support, and follow-up for mentors of Tulare County children.

Create Now!
2007 Wilshire Boulevard, Suite 919
Los Angeles, CA 90057
Phone: (213) 484-8500
Fax: (213) 484-8555
Web: www.createnow.org

The Create Now! program serves youth ages 5 to 21 living in court-ordered residential care facilities in the Los Angeles area. Founded in 1996, Create Now! provides an array of mentoring programs, all of which involve various types of writing. Other Create Now! sponsored activities include painting, music, dance, and video production, with an emphasis on the crafts of the film and TV industry.

Fighting Back School-Based Mentoring Program

232 E. Canon Perdido Street
Santa Barbara, CA 93101
Phone: (805) 963-1433
Fax: (805) 963-4099
Web: www.fighting-back.org/

Santa Barbara's Fighting Back Collaborative is a community-wide effort to build a safer, healthier, and drug-free community by reducing the demand for alcohol and other drugs. The mentoring program involves mentors meeting with their protégés for one hour a week during the school day. The program serves students in grades 4 to 8 (up to age 17) identified as being at risk for low self-esteem, poor academic performance, and other problems.

Friends for Youth Mentoring Institute

1741 Broadway
Redwood City, CA 94063
Phone: (650) 368-4464 or (650) 368-4444
Fax: (650) 368-4475
Web: www.friendsforyouth.org
E-mail: info@mentoringinstitute.org

The mission of Friends for Youth Mentoring Institute is to encourage the utilization and effective application of mentoring as an intervention to help individuals succeed. The institute offers an array of services, including the gathering and dissemination of mentoring information, promotion of academic research about mentoring effectiveness, and the creation of ongoing mentoring awareness campaigns. The institute's technical assistance training assists new or existing mentoring efforts by providing assessment of project needs, as well as training covering topics such as structure of a successful mentoring program, staff training for program management, volunteer mentor training, and program strategies for successful mentoring relationships.

Greater Sacramento Mentoring Coalition

Communities in Schools
930 Alhambra Boulevard, Suite 292
Sacramento, CA 98519
Phone: (916) 447-2477

Fax: (916) 447-2507
Web: www.cis-sacramento.org

In May 1999 the United Way California Capitol Region and the Greater Sonoma Mentoring Coalition created a partnership designed to enhance area mentoring programs. The partnership was designed to lend mutual support to mentoring efforts and to reduce duplication of services. Coalition members include school-based, community-based, tutoring, lunch hour and social mentoring programs. The lead agency for the mentoring coalition changes periodically. In 2003, Communities in Schools was the lead organization for the Greater Sacramento Mentoring Coalition.

Los Angeles Mentoring Partnership/Los Angeles Mentoring Coalition
5670 Wilshire Boulevard, 2nd Floor
Los Angeles, CA 90036
Phone: (213) 634-4157
Fax: (323) 634–4295

The goal of the Los Angeles Mentoring Partnership is to provide every Los Angeles child with the chance for a productive future. The strategy to meet this goal is to give every child access to proven program and mentoring relationships that guide, empower, and encourage children to stay in school and develop marketable skills. The partnership brings together diverse community elements (businesses, government and services agencies, adult volunteers) to create integrated approaches that keep Los Angeles youth in school. Adults and youth are united in mentoring relationships through a wide variety of mentoring programs. The coalition/partnership serves as both cohesion and support to its mentoring partners.

San Francisco Mentoring Coalition
Volunteer Center of San Francisco
425 Jackson Street
San Francisco, CA 94111
Phone: (415) 982-8999
Fax: (415) 982-0890
Web: www.vcsf.org

This coalition is located in the Volunteer Center of San Francisco, which provides a wealth of community-based volunteer options to interested persons. The San Francisco Mentoring Coalition seeks to enlist adult volunteers in mentoring activities and to improve the quality of mentoring programs. The organization creates opportunities for networking and staff training.

Sonoma County Mentoring Partnership
Operation Getting It Together
500 N. Main Street
Sebastopol, CA 95472
Phone: (707) 823-6967
Fax: (707) 823–4335
Web: http://home.earthlink.net/~jbelter/ogit/ogit_index.html.

This community- and church-sponsored nonprofit organization has served at-risk youth and their families throughout Sonoma County for more than 20 years. In the one-on-one mentoring program, youth outreach workers/mentors are young adults primarily between the ages of 16 and 24. These individuals are matched with young people ages 8 to 14, and commit to spending at least four hours per week, for one full year, with their mentees. This organization provides a modest monthly activity allowance for its volunteers, as well as the possibility of scholarships, and school or college credit. The organization also supports academic mentoring programs in several area middle schools and a Young Men as Fathers mentoring program for teenage fathers. In addition to mentoring, the organization also provides anger management classes, family guidance and encouragement, crisis intervention, and referrals for additional services.

The Mentoring Center
1221 Preservation Park Way, Suite 200
Oakland, CA 94612
Phone: (510) 891-0427
Fax: (510) 891-0492
Web: www.mentor.org

The Mentoring Center (TMC) is recognized nationally as a leader in the field of mentoring. The mission of TMC is to enhance mentoring effectiveness and to promote mentoring as a means to promote positive development for all young people. TMC works to develop and provide innovative mentoring concepts and models, while offering technical assistance and training to mentoring agencies. TMC also conducts field testing and evaluation of technical assistance and training best-practice curriculums, tools, and materials.

Yolo County Youth Connections Mentor Coalition
327 College Street, Suite 100
Woodland, CA 95695
Phone: (530) 669-3285
Fax: (530) 669-3295
Web: www.yoloconnections.org

Yolo Connections is a nonprofit agency with a mission to promote mentoring, volunteerism, and community partnerships in Yolo County. The agency seeks to build healthy, strong families by providing family support, resource referrals, volunteer mentors, and wholesome youth and family activities. Among its many programs is the Cal Mentor Program, which provides one-on-one and group mentoring, life-skills classes, youth and family support, and referrals. As part of this program, special activities are planned including monthly family nights and youth activities that support the mentor-youth relationship and provide the youth with a variety of experiences.

Colorado

Colorado Mentoring!
Governor's Commission on Community Service
1391 N. Speer Boulevard, Suite 600
Denver, CO 80204
Phone: (303) 595-1541
Fax: (720) 904-9738
Web: www.gcncs.cccoes.edu

The relatively new Colorado Mentoring! program supports a collaborative partnership among the members of Colorado's mentoring community, working to encourage the development of new mentoring programs and to build a statewide network of mentoring agencies. The program seeks to facilitate communication, collaboration, and training between mentoring organizations and bolster public awareness of, and participation in, mentoring. Services include recruitment, matching, training and technical assistance.

Colorado Mountain College
Community Collaboration Team
P.O. Box 10001
Glenwood Springs, CO 81602
Phone: (970) 947-8375
Fax: (970) 947-8324
Web: www.coloradomtn.edu/AmeriCorps/

AmeriCorps members serve the young people in the rural mountain communities of western Colorado. In school-based placements, members provide tutoring and mentoring with the goal of enhancing social and academic skills. In social and human service agencies, members assist victims of child neglect, substance abuse, and domestic violence. In youth centers and recreation departments, members serve as positive role models for youth and do after-school programming, as well as weekend and summer activities.

Denver Kids, Inc.
1330 Fox Street
Denver, CO 80204
Phone: (303) 405-8266
Fax: (303) 405-8264
Web: www.denverkidsinc.org

Denver Kids, Inc., founded in 1993, is a preventive counseling and mentoring program for at-risk youth ages 5 to 18 in the Denver Public Schools. Students being referred for the program are often described by school personnel as being at-risk and needing support and guidance beyond that which is provided in school. There are approximately 700 Denver Boys and Denver Girls in the program and many of them are matched on a one-to-one basis with a volunteer from the community who commits his or her time and energy to serve as a volunteer Friend for one year. The volunteer Friend receives training and guidance and serves as a positive adult role model in the youngster's life. Each year, volunteers contribute over 30,000 hours to Denver Kids, Inc.

Mesa State College
The BIG Literacy Corps
1175 Texas Avenue
Grand Junction, CO 81502-2647

Phone: (970) 248-1874
Fax: (970) 248-1157

AmeriCorps members from Mesa State College mentor and tutor 300 at-risk youth with academic difficulties at alternative school sites, as well as youth in out-of-home placements for the BIG Literacy Corps. The Corps seeks to improve academic and life skills for youth while simultaneously involving youth in community service projects. The program also offers services at schools, both during the school day and in-school and after-school programs that offer positive alternative activities for elementary, middle and high school students.

Partners Mentoring Association
2222 S. Albion Street, Suite 150
Denver, CO 80222
Phone: (303) 831-7872
Fax: (303) 759-3376
Web: www.partnersmentoring.org

The largest mentoring organization in Colorado, Partners Mentoring Association develops and supports mentoring programs in mobilizing adult volunteers to serve as role models, advocates and friends to at-risk youth. Partners Mentoring Association and its 12 affiliates lead the field in mentoring youth in need from all types of communities—rural, urban and suburban. For more than three decades, Partners has offered highly structured mentoring services with the goal of helping at-risk youth learn central life skills while providing them with the emotional support needed to grow to become productive adults and good citizens.

Summit County Mountain Mentors
P.O. Box 4326
Frisco, CO 80443
Phone: (970) 668-4153
Fax: (970) 668-4148
Web: http://www.summitfoundation.org/nListing.php

Summit County Mountain Mentors is a year-round youth mentoring program offered to Summit County youth ages 6 to 13. Participating boys and girls are linked with adult volunteer role models for one year. The program offers several recreational, educational, and life-skill activities.

University of Denver
Colorado Campus Compact AmeriCorps Program
2199 S. University Boulevard
Mary Reed Building, 4th Floor
Denver, CO 80208
Phone: (303) 871-3706
Fax: (303) 871–3708

Colorado Campus Compact AmeriCorps members from the University of Denver are placed in community-based settings to serve as tutors and mentors to children in grades K–8 in nine communities. The mentoring program's focus is on enhancing academic performance and school attendance.

Y.E.S. (You're Extra Special) Pals
1290 Williams Street
Denver, CO 80218
Phone: (303) 355-3052
Fax: (303) 399-0727
Web:
    http://www.coloradoyouth.org/ProgramDetail.cfm?YouthID=146

The Y.E.S. (You're Extra Special) Pals Mentoring Program serves young people in the Capitol Hill community of Denver. Students ages 8 to 18 engage in a mentoring relationship with a caring, responsible adult volunteer mentor consisting of at least one face-to-face contact each month. Y.E.S. is a division of the Colorado Youth Resource Directory.

Connecticut

City SERVE! AmeriCorps
165 Miller Street
Meriden, CT 06450
Phone: (203) 630-4208
Fax: (203) 639-0039
Web: http://www.cityofmeriden.org/services/human/AmeriCorps.asp

City SERVE! of Meriden, Connecticut places its AmeriCorps members into youth-serving organizations to focus on the school readiness and school success of youth. City SERVE!'s impact on youth has been evaluated by an independent evaluator, by school principals, teachers, day care directors, and youth programming specialists. All find that the AmeriCorps members have a strong and positive impact on students, particularly their achievement in school, their behavior in class, and desire to succeed academically. Hundreds of youth are served each year by AmeriCorps members in schools and community organizations. AmeriCorps members offer schools and community organizations the ability to reach out to clients who otherwise may have been underserved. The city's mentoring program targets elementary and middle school children. AmeriCorps members offer in-class support (such as individual tutoring in reading and writing) as well as after-school services (enrichment activities, tutoring and mentoring). The program works to improve academic achievement, heighten youth interest in school, and decrease behavior problems.

Good Friend
185 Main Street
Danbury, CT 06810
Phone: (203) 790-0032
Fax: (203) 790-6411
Web: www.good-friend.org

Good Friends is a mentoring program that seeks to connect children and families to positive relationships with caring adults with the goal of fostering confidence, competence and caring. A stable and solid program, Good Friends has served children since 1975. A core of approximately 50 children are served directly each year with an additional 50 children receiving services such as general support and referral, camperships, holiday gifts, and involvement in after-school programs. Children are matched with mentors from ages 7–14. However, once matched, the formal relationship can continue until the youth reaches the age of 18.

The Governor's Prevention Partnership
30 Arbor Street
Hartford, CT 06106
Phone: (860) 523-8042
Fax: (860) 236-9412
Web: www.preventionworksct.org/mentor.html

This public-private partnership is aimed at increasing the number of mentors and mentoring organizations in Connecticut, as well as promoting standards for effective mentoring programs. The organization provides services in the areas of recruitment, matching, training, and technical assistance, as well as public awareness campaigns. Programs and special initiatives include the Mentoring Showcase and Awards Ceremony, a resource center, a toll-free referral line, a faith-based mentoring initiative, a school-business mentoring alliance, and an intergenerational mentoring initiative. There are two types of no-cost memberships in this partnership. The Basic Membership provides training and technical assistance, Web site access, research and newsletters, and participation in regional retreats. The Databank Membership offers all of the Basic Membership services, along with a toll-free referral service.

Leadership, Education, and Athletics in Partnership
31 Jefferson Street
New Haven, CT 06511
Phone: (203) 773-0770
Fax: (203) 773-1695
Web: www.leapforkids.org

Leadership, Education and Athletics in Partnership features AmeriCorps members who tutor and mentor 1,300 economically at-risk children, ages 7 to 14, after school and in the summer. Their mentoring and tutoring interventions positively impact reading, computer literacy, and overall academic performance. The program also seeks to enhance the communication skills, self-esteem and motivation, conflict resolution skills, and overall prosocial behavior of participating young people. Established in 1992, the mentoring component of the program is year-round while most of the tutoring takes place during the school year.

Delaware

Creative Mentoring
2126 W. Newport Pike
Suite 203
Wilmington, DE 19804
Phone: (877) 202-9050
Fax: (302) 633-1334
Web: www.creativementoring.org

Creative Mentoring supports in-school mentoring programs in 48 schools in the New Castle, Kent, and Sussex Counties of Delaware and also assists schools across the country in designing and implementing in-school mentoring programs. The program specializes in training volunteer in-school mentors and publishes the award-winning *Elements of Effective Mentoring* training manual. Training is available to volunteers throughout Delaware, regardless of program affiliation, at no charge. Interested individuals outside of Delaware may participate in the three-and-a-half hour training program for a fee. Creative Mentors work one-to-one with one to four children, with the goal of enhancing self-esteem, self-confidence, interpersonal communication skills, social values, aspirations, and scholastic achievement. Their Web site includes an online application for those interested in becoming mentors.

Delaware Mentoring Council
321 S. College Avenue, Suite 207
University of Delaware
Newark, DE 19716
Phone: (302) 831-0520 or (866) DEM-ENTOR
Fax: (302) 831-0523
Web: www.delawarementoring.org

Established in 1998, the Delaware Mentoring Council advocates for the mentoring of Delaware children. While not providing direct mentoring services, the organization works with 40 community-based mentoring programs and all of the school-based mentor programs throughout the state. The Delaware Mentoring Council provides support in the areas of recruitment, matching, training, and technical assistance, as well as public awareness campaigns. The Delaware Mentoring Council provides print and Web-based resources related to mentoring. The organization hosts mentoring events, such as the Delaware Mentoring Summit 2000 and Building Partnerships for Youth.

Delaware's Promise
1901 N. DuPont Highway
Charles E. Debnam Building
New Castle, DE 19720
Phone: (302) 577-4965 ext. 254
Fax: (302) 577-4972
Web: http://www.delawarementoring.org/mentoring_programs.htm

Delaware's Promise is designed to foster collaboration between the state's reform efforts, mentoring, and school-based/community-based mentoring initiatives. Delaware's Promise helps to coordinate and facilitate the needs of the community with the resources therein. In regards to the mentoring programs, youth are trained to mentor peers by AmeriCorps members, who also serve in a year-round family mentoring program.

University of Delaware
First State Service Corps
015 Willard Hall
Newark, DE 19716
Phone: (302) 831-0883
Fax: (302) 831-0523
Web: www.udel.edu

AmeriCorps members, primarily graduate students at the University of Delaware, have been providing mentoring services to Delaware students since 1997 with the aim of improving social and behavioral skills. In 2003 the federal budget cuts forced a reduction in the direct mentoring hours and redirected the effort into a focus of building a spirit and ethic of community service.

District of Columbia

Friends of the Children
The Friends Program
2909 Pennsylvania Avenue, S.E.
Washington, DC 20020
Phone: (202) 575-3337
Fax: (202) 575-2909
E-mail: sewhouse@aol.com

Friends of the Children is a quiet organization that has produced dramatic results. In existence since 1995 and serving approximately 120 students per year, Friends of the Children operates a mentoring program in one of the most underserved areas in the District of Columbia. Faith-based, Friends of the Children functions more as a community-based organization, although some of the mentoring activities can take place on the school site. Beginning in the first grade, Friends of the Children begins to mentor the most at-risk children. Most of these children commit to a mentor relationship through high school.

Heads Up AmeriCorps Youth Program
645 Pennsylvania Avenue, S.E.
Suite 300
Washington, DC 20003
Phone: (202) 544-4468
Fax: (202) 544-4437
Web: www.headsup-dc.org

Heads Up is a neighborhood initiative where AmeriCorps members provide year-round tutoring and mentoring to D.C. youth in grades 1 through 6. Interventions take place during an intensive summer session and in after-school sessions throughout the academic year.

Florida

Florida International University
Urban Services Corps
College of Education
University Park Campus, 343A
Miami, FL 33199
Phone: (305) 348-2087
Fax: (305) 348-2086
Web: www.flu.edu

Florida International University's Urban Services Corps AmeriCorps members are trained to be tutors, mentors, and teachers. Working with the local public schools, AmeriCorps members assist in classrooms and provide after-school and summer mentoring and tutoring.

Florida Mentoring Foundation
Governor's Mentoring Initiative
401 S. Monroe Street
Tallahassee, FL 32301
Phone: (850) 410-0697 or (800) 825-3786
Fax: (850) 487-1866
Web: www.flamentoring.org

The Florida Mentoring Foundation, also known as the Governor's Mentoring Initiative, promotes collaboration among state agencies, businesses, and nonprofit organizations. The Foundation dispenses grant funds statewide to both community- and school-based mentoring programs. The foundation supports mentor recruitment and matching services, and offers training statewide in the area of mentoring, especially children and youth. The foundation also includes a public awareness campaign, and technical assistance and training.

The Legacy Project
Legacy Foundation
934 N. Magnolia Avenue
Orlando, FL 32803
Phone: (407) 884-2999
Fax: (407) 814-7760
Web: www.nhf.org and
    http://elderaffairs.state.fl.us/doea/english/intergenerational.html

The Legacy Project serves communities in Orange County, Florida. This intergenerational project encourages a mentoring matching of senior citizens and youth. Students participating in the program receive tutoring assistance related to reading and math skills. Volunteers dedicate two hours per week as mentors in the mayor's Neighbors Helping Schools program.

The Mentor Center of Palm Beach County
311 S. Dixie Highway, Suite 217
West Palm Beach, FL 33405
Phone: (561) 655-8887
Fax: (561) 655-3395
Web: www.mentorcenterpbc.org
E-mail: mentor@mentorcenterpbc.org

The Mentor Center of Palm Beach County, established in 1999, is a collaborative of nearly two dozen nonprofit organizations providing youth mentoring programs. The Mentor Center serves as a recruitment and referral source for volunteer mentors, while striving to increase public awareness of the value of mentoring. The Mentor Center also provides training and technical assistance opportunities for participating programs.

The Mentor Connection of Tampa
1000 N. Ashley Drive
Suite 800
Tampa, FL 33602
Phone: (813) 274-0932

Fax: (813) 228-9549
Web: www.unitedwayhc.org

The Mentor Connection of Tampa is a component of the Volunteer Connection, a division of the United Way of Hillsborough County. This program actively supports mentoring, recruiting potential mentors, and hosting a mentor training institute.

Youth Volunteer Corps of Vero Beach
Volunteer Action Center–Boys and Girls Club
P.O. Box 5383
1756 33rd Avenue
Vero Beach, FL 32960
Phone: (561) 581-3997
Fax: (561) 778-1226
http://www.yvca.org/map.html

The Youth Volunteer Corps of America (YVCA) creates and increases volunteer opportunities to enrich America's youth, address community needs, and develop a lifetime commitment to service. In this YVCA branch, AmeriCorps members function as service learning coordinators and provide mentoring, tutoring, and reading support. Members also recruit, lead, and supervise volunteers in youth-generated service projects.

Georgia

Carroll County School Systems
Temple AmeriCorps Program
95 Otis Street
Carrolton, GA 30179
Phone: (770) 832-3076
Fax: (770) 562-0135
Web: www.AmeriCorps.org

The Temple AmeriCorps program is an example of how small interventions can produce successful results. In this instance, children in grades kindergarten through 5 in the Carroll County School District received tutoring and mentoring, with a focus on enhancing reading and math skills. Positive outcomes were noted when the students were tutored four to five days per week in half-hour or one-hour sessions before, during, or after school.

HOPE *worldwide*–Georgia

Child Development Program
400 Perimeter Center Terrace
Atlanta, GA 30346
Phone: (678) 320-9494
Web: www.ga.hopeww.org/index.htm

HOPE *worldwide*–Georgia's Child Development Program, a mentoring and tutoring program, was developed to meet the academic and social needs of Atlanta's most troubled inner-city youth. In operation since 1996, the Child Development Program has grown to become one of the leading mentoring and tutoring initiatives in the state of Georgia. Additionally, HOPE *worldwide*–Georgia trains and mobilizes its volunteers to successfully educate families concerning healthcare coverage.

Hawaii

Big Brothers Big Sisters of Honolulu, Inc.

418 Kuwili Street, Suite 106
Honolulu, HI 96817
Phone: (808) 521-3811
Fax: (808) 528-1599
Web: www.bigshonolulu.org

Big Brothers Big Sister of Honolulu, Inc. is affiliated with the national Big Brothers Big Sisters organization, providing one-on-one mentoring to children from single-parent homes or from other disadvantaged circumstances.

Idaho

After School Adventures and Youth Mentoring
Box 44095
Pocatello, ID 83205
Phone: (208) 233-9770
Fax: (208) 236–7316

This organization provides violence prevention through after-school sports/recreation activities and mentoring, targeting at-risk junior high school students and juvenile offenders. The After School Adventures program provides hands-on activities, an age appropriate curriculum, and homework tutoring via certified/qualified teachers at six licensed sites. Young people participating in the Youth Mentoring program engage in mentoring relationships with university students who volunteer nearly 20 hours per student per semester to work one-on-one or in small group activities at school. Services are based in schools in Pocatello and Chubbuck, Idaho. The program is funded by the U.S. Department of Agriculture, local government agencies, and universities. This project is operated by the University of Idaho, the Bannock County government, Idaho State University, School District 25, Southeast Idaho Community Action Agency, and Cre-Act School.

Idaho Youth Asset Builders, AmeriCorps
League of Idaho Cities
2214 Grace Street
Boise, ID 83703
Phone: (208) 333-7733
Fax (208) 344-8677
Web: http://www.serveidaho.com/AmeriCorps/IdahoYouthAsset
    Builders.html

The Idaho Youth Asset Builders assists Idaho communities in creating healthy environments for its youth by securing opportunities for youth involvement and by increasing youth developmental assets. Activities including mentoring youth, planning and developing Youth Action Councils, facilitating training on asset development, promoting youth-adult partnerships, and encouraging the inclusion of youth on community councils and boards of directors. This statewide program places AmeriCorps members with local organizations across the state.

Illinois

Good City
Free the Children
5049 W. Harrison
Chicago, IL 60644

Phone: (312) 322-3000
Fax: (312) 573-8881
Web: www.goodcitychicago.org

Good City is a faith-based organization that brings together businesses, churches, and civic leaders to provide needed services for the youth of Chicago. Good City's youth mentoring programs include the Lawndale Commnity Outreach, Chicago Communities in Schools, and the Free the Children Trust.

These programs focus on tutoring, mentoring, effective educational opportunities and/or creating opportunities for youth to serve and emphasize ongoing relationships with caring adults.

Jump Start Program
Literacy Volunteers of America—Illinois
30 E. Adams Street
Suite 1130
Chicago, IL 30303
Phone: (312) 857-1582
Fax: (312) 857-1586
Web: www.literacyvolunteers.org

Jump Start Mentoring and Tutoring Program began in 1995 and currently serves approximately 275 students. Children from preschool to third grade receive mentoring, tutoring, and literacy training. Low-literate delinquent teens, and low-literate parents of Head Start and grade school children are also eligible for assistance. The program actively recruits retired teachers to serve as mentors and tutors.

Northwestern University Settlement Association
Project YES
144 W. Augusta Boulevard
Chicago, IL 60622
Phone: (773) 278-7471
Fax: (773) 278-7536
Web: www.nush.org

AmeriCorps works with Project YES to provide community service, mentorship, arts and recreation activities for youth and adults. During the 2002–2003 school year, Project YES had 55 AmeriCorps members, 30 of them full-time, working in the Chicago area with youth. The three main components of Project YES are volunteerism, partnering with schools for creative instructional strategies, and before and after school programs for mentoring and tutoring.

Rend Lake College—Land of Lincoln

Land of Lincoln AmeriCorps
468 N. Ken Gray Parkway
Ina, IL 62846
Phone: (618) 437-5321
Fax: (618) 437-5403
Web: www.rcl.edu

The Land of Lincoln is the Governor's Initiative statewide program. A charter campus, it was established in 1993. The goals of the program are to bolster reading skills by providing literacy activities, and to improve academic performance, reduce student absenteeism, and enhance student self-esteem by providing tutoring and mentoring to at-risk middle school students and to elementary children as well. Participating students receive in-school mentoring and tutoring through small group and individual sessions and mentoring during structured school activities. Statewide, 600–700 youth are mentored and/or tutored through this organization.

The Tutor/Mentor Connection

800 W. Huron
P.O. Box 543401
Chicago, IL 60622
Phone: (312) 492-9614
Fax: (312) 492-9795
Web: www.tutormentorconnection.org

The Tutor/Mentor Connection (T/MC) seeks to support the development of comprehensive, long-term tutor/mentor programs in every poor neighborhood of Chicago. In early 1994, the T/MC began building a database of Chicago's nonschool tutor/mentor programs and now publishes the most comprehensive directory of Chicago tutor/mentor programs. While many efforts are aimed at mobilizing mentors, the T/MC and its Web site are aimed at building and sustaining a "village" of great tutor/mentor programs that function effectively. The T/MC demonstrates an innovative use of geographic information systems that allow

T/MC to produce maps of Chicago showing where programs are needed and where existing programs are located. T/MC actions are intended to help existing programs get volunteers, dollars, technology, and training while helping new programs. The Web site offers information useful to those interested in building or maintaining a mentoring program or network, as well as notices that invite program managers and other stakeholders (volunteers, educators, media, business, philanthropy, etc.) to come together for learning or volunteer recruitment, and/or fundraising events.

Indiana

Indiana University
Indiana Reading Corps
801 W. Michigan, BS 4080
Indianapolis, IN 46202-5152
Phone: (317) 278-2270
Fax: (317) 274–7860

AmeriCorps members act as mentors to young people transitioning out of juvenile correctional settings. Members work with the young offenders before they are released from three Central Indiana facilities, presenting a prerelease curriculum and creating a reentry plan with their youth matches. They also provide mentoring support to the young people upon their release from the facilities.

State Student Assistance Commission of Indiana
Twenty-first Century Scholars Program
150 W. Market Street, Suite 500
Indianapolis, IN 46204
Phone: (317) 233-2100
Fax: (317) 232-3260
Web: www.in.gov/ssaci

Fifteen hundred 8th- through 12th-grade students in the Twenty-first Century Scholars program across the state of Indiana receive tutoring, mentoring, and support as they strive to maintain their pledge to achieve academic excellence, drug abstinence, and responsible citizenship. Upon successful completion of their pledge, participating students receive a four-year scholarship at any Indiana state-funded college. The program operates 16 sites across the state. They provide direct service to youth and also support other mentoring efforts.

Iowa

Community Correction Improvement Association
NEIGHBORS in Action
951 29th Avenue, S.W.
Cedar Rapids, IA 52404
Phone: (319) 398-3675
Fax: (319) 398–3684

This program seeks to increase child and adolescent participation in community youth programs and decrease maladaptive youth behavior. Participating young people may receive mentoring, tutoring, and/or counseling, with a focus on academic and personal development. Efforts are also made to heighten youth interest in community service projects.

Fort Madison Family YMCA
A Safe Place to Grow and Learn
220 26th Street
Ft. Madison, IA 52627
Phone: (319) 372-2403
Fax: (319) 372-7488
E-mail: amerymca@interlinklc.net

Mentoring and tutoring youth constitute two of the many services offered by the YMCA after-school and summer programs.

Hospital Youth Mentoring Partnership
Johns Hopkins University
Iowa Healthy System
1440 Ingersoll Avenue, Suite 100
Des Moines, IA 50309-3114
Phone: (515) 241-3214
Fax: (515) 241-6969
Web: www.mentor.jhmi.edu/program/brief.html

Since June 1993, the Hospital Youth Mentoring Program, adminis-tered by the Johns Hopkins Hospital and funded by the Commonwealth

Fund (until 1999), has supported youth mentoring projects at 15 hospitals. The programs target at-risk youth from low-income families, matching them with mentors to help them to complete high school and make the transition to postsecondary education or work. By involving hospitals with youth from their communities, the program has encouraged the hospitals to take a more active role in addressing local community needs and in helping educate their future workforce.

Kansas

Books to Branches Program
Cowley County Community College
125 S. Second
Arkansas City, KS 67005
Phone: (800) 593-2222
Fax: (316) 441–5350

In the Books to Branches program, AmeriCorps members tutor and mentor at-risk youth in reading and school competency. The AmeriCorps members also supervise and train community volunteers in schools and coordinate service-learning activities for K–12 students.

Keys for Networking, Inc.
Topeka Cares for Topeka Kids
117 S.W. Sixth
Topeka, KS 66603
Phone: (785) 233-8732
Fax: (785) 235-6659
Web: www.keys.org

This AmeriCorps program serves youth in the Topeka area who have emotional and behavioral problems; assistance is also provided for their families. Students are guided through alternative programs and provided with adult-youth mentoring.

Kentucky

Kentucky Promise
227 Waterfield Hall
Morehead, KY 40351
Phone: (606) 783-2719

Fax: (606) 783-5080
Web: www.americaspromise.org

   In cooperation with community volunteers and organizations, volunteers serve in 11 Appalachian counties at 20 Family Resource Centers or Youth Service Centers. The volunteer adults provide tutoring, mentoring, and parental involvement activities to more than 1,000 at-risk students ranging from primary grades to high school in an effort to increase the educational success of the students served. The program has been in existence sine 1994.

Louisiana

City of West Monroe
Service Education Empowerment Corps (SEE Corps)
400 S. Fifth Street
West Monroe, LA 71292
Phone: (318) 387-4001
Fax: (318) 387–1443

   The Service Education Empowerment Corps, in existence since 1998, focuses on empowerment of youth through education. AmeriCorps members, volunteers, and cross age tutors provide a variety of services, including tutoring and mentoring for at-risk children and for youth in out-of-school-time programs.

East Baton Rouge School System
SERVE: Baton Rouge
555 St. Tammany Street, Suite B
Baton Rouge, LA 70806
Phone: (225) 924-9009
Fax: (225) 924–9082

   Students in grades K–5 receive tutoring and mentoring both in and out of school. Interventions focus on improving skills in reading and math, conflict resolution, and personal life enrichment. Participating students may also work on community-based service projects.

Maine

The Maine Mentoring Partnership
P.O. Box 406
Augusta, ME 04332

Phone: (207) 287-7669 or (888) 387-8755 in Maine
Fax: (207) 287-4375
Web: www.mainementoring.org

The mission of the Maine Mentoring Partnership is to insure that all children in Maine will have access to a mentor through high quality mentoring programs. The Maine Mentoring Partnership (MMP) promotes, supports, and fosters youth mentoring programs in Maine. Services include mentor recruitment, matching, technical assistance, public awareness campaigns, and financial resource development. The organization also maintains an inventory/catalog of training manuals, tools, policies, and procedures used in Maine and by national mentoring programs. The MMP also collects information to identify existing mentoring programs and the number of mentors statewide.

Maine's Care AmeriCorps
University of Southern Maine
Muskie School
400 Congress Street
Portland, ME 04112
Phone: (207) 780-5810
Fax: (207) 780–5817

AmeriCorps members serve in teams of two at 10 sites across the state to increase the life-skills competencies and protective factors of older juvenile offenders and youth in foster care. Members provide youth with weekly mentoring, along with an experimental life-skill program. The project aims to improve the leadership, communication, and team-building skills of participating youth. Volunteers also help the young people create a portfolio to catalogue their practical, personal, educational, and work-related achievements.

Maryland

Catholic Network of Volunteer Service
CNVS/AmeriCorps Education Awards Program
6930 Carroll Ave, Suite 506
Takoma Park, MD 20912
Phone: (301) 270-0900
Fax: (301) 270-0901
Web: www.cnvs.org

A recent move from the Washington, D.C., area has brought a new focus to this long established and nationally acknowledged volunteer agency. Catholic Network has worked with and coordinated the efforts of hundreds of human service agencies in the recent past, including scores of youth-based mentoring settings. Catholic Network has also traditionally partnered with AmeriCorps in delivering hands on services to youth and their families.

Civic Works, Inc.—Digital Discovery
Clifton Mansion
2701 St. Lo Drive
Baltimore, MD 21213
Phone: (410) 366-8533
Fax: (410) 366-1813
Web: www.civicworks.com
E-mail: civicworks@aol.com

AmeriCorps members and other volunteers tutor, mentor, and provide computer training and academic enrichment to students (ages 6 to 17) in after-school programs at nine Baltimore City Department of Parks and Recreation community centers. The program seeks to improve academic achievement, particularly in the area of technology literacy.

The Maryland Mentoring Partnership
517 N. Charles Street, Suite 200
Baltimore, MD 21201
Phone: (800) 741-2687 or (410) 685-8316
Fax: (410) 752-5016
Web: www.marylandmentors.org

This nonprofit organization serves the young people of Maryland by fostering mentoring relationships that promote growth and individual self-reliance, enhance academic and career choices, and develop self-esteem. It began as an organization in 1988 under the name Project RAISE and at inception, provided direct mentoring services for elementary school children. The Baltimore Mentoring Partnership engages in recruitment, fosters collaboration among agencies, facilitates mentor matching, and offers a range of technical assistance/training services. The Partnership also operates the Maryland State Mentoring Resource Center that contains manuals, videos, research documents, and directories related to mentoring. The Baltimore Mentoring Partnership implemented the Church Mentoring Initiative (1998) and the Workplace Mentoring Initiative (1990).

PAL Team/Goodnow PAL Center

Baltimore Police Athletic League
601 E. Fayette Street
Baltimore, MD 21202
Phone: (410) 396-2166
Fax: (410) 396–2545

Working out of Baltimore City Police Athletic League centers, police officers and AmeriCorps members tutor, mentor, and coach young people in academic and recreational activities after school. The project aims to improve attendance, retention, and academic skills and has been in existence for over 10 years.

Notre Dame Mission Volunteer Program, Inc.

403 Markland Avenue
Baltimore, MD 21212
Phone: (410) 532-6864
Fax: (410) 532-2418
Web: www.ndmva.org

The Notre Dame Mission Volunteers, Inc., is a nonprofit organization founded by the Sisters of Notre Dame, a religious institution that has served communities in need for more than 150 years. The Notre Dame Mission Volunteer Program is currently staffed with AmeriCorps members. Among other social issues that the organization addresses, the Notre Dame volunteers target the educational needs of disadvantaged youth and their families. The volunteers provide a vast array of services, including tutoring and mentoring for at-risk children of low educational achievement. Eight Baltimore City public elementary schools, alternative schools, and community-based organizations collaborate with this service. An after-school enrichment program is also offered.

Salisbury State University

Partnership for Adolescents on the Lower Shore (PALS)
1101 Camden Avenue
Salisbury, MD 21801

Phone: (410) 543-6137
Fax: (410) 543-6069
Web: www.salisbury.edu/community/AmeriCorps

At-risk adolescents on the Lower Eastern Shore of Maryland receive tutoring and mentoring from the Partnership for Adolescents, an Ameri-Corps program. The Partnership also offers conflict resolution training, health screenings, and health education events. Pregnant and parenting adolescents may participate in educational activities aimed at enhancing life and parenting skills.

Science Enrichment and Acceleration Academy

Johns Hopkins University School of Medicine
Office of Research Administration
720 Rutland Avenue, SOM 129
Baltimore, MD 21205
Phone: (410) 955-1567
Web: http://communityservices.jhmi.edu

The Science Enrichment and Acceleration Academy is an initiative designed to enhance the science curriculum and prepare underrepresented minorities for careers in health, biological sciences, and computer science. The academy serves students and teachers in The Dunbar/Hopkins Partnership. This collaborative effort between medical institutions and the Paul Lawrence Dunbar High School operates school-to-career transition initiatives. The program provides students with exposure to Johns Hopkins School of Medicine through tours, lectures, seminars, job shadowing, and paid work experiences.

UMBC/Shriver

The Choice Programs
971 Seagull Avenue
Baltimore, MD 21225
Phone: (410) 354-5511
Fax: (410) 354-4938
Web: www.choiceprogram.org

This program provides intensive case management and oversight of juveniles referred through the juvenile justice system, family services, or other social service agencies. Youth receive guidance and mentoring, and their families receive assistance in navigating the justice system, schools, and other public agencies. Established in the early 1990s, the program goals include decreased recidivism rates, increased attendance at school, and improved attitudes toward school.

U.S. Dream Academy
10400 Little Patuxent Parkway, Suite 300
Columbia, MD 21044
Phone: (800) USDREAM
Web: www.usdreamacademy.org

Founded in 1998, the U.S. Dream Academy offers a values-centered e-classroom designed to empower at-risk children to achieve their dreams. The academy emphasizes the needs of children of incarcerated adults and those at-risk for educational failure due to lack of financial, social, or academic support. Mentoring services are among the offerings of the academy, including one-to-one, group, and team mentoring formats.

Massachusetts

City Year Boston
285 Columbus Avenue
Boston, MA 02116
Phone: (617) 927-2500
Fax: (617) 927-2510
www.cityyear.com

AmeriCorps members tutor and mentor inner-city children in public elementary and middle schools throughout Boston. Established in 1998, City Year also sponsors in-class assistance, after-school and weekend programs, camps during school vacations, and the Young Heroes program. The goals of the program are to improve children's attitudes toward school and academic performance.

Franklin County DIAL/SELF
Greenfield AmeriCorps Program Youth Corps
196 Federal Street
Greenfield, MA 01301
Phone: (413) 774-7054
Fax: (413) 773–3335

Volunteers implement a variety of programs for children and youth, including individualized mentoring and support for at-risk youth. The organization has three service objectives: to provide consistent individual support to at-risk youth; to provide high-quality recreation, enrichment, and prevention programs for preschool and elementary school aged youth; and to provide high-quality after-school, recreation, and prevention programs for middle- and high-school aged youth.

Generations Incorporated
59 Temple Place, Suite 200
Boston, MA 02111
Phone: (617) 423-6633
Fax: (617) 422-0626
Web: www.generationsinc.org

Generations Incorporated provides tutoring and mentoring and promotes intergenerational activities, such as pairing students with elder partners in senior residences. The Leaps in Literacy and After School Reading Coaching programs offer one-on-one tutoring to second and third graders at elementary schools and in after-school programs.

The Greater Springfield Mentoring Partnership
Western New England College
1215 Wilbraham Road
Springfield, MA 01119
Phone: (413) 782-1265
Fax: (413) 796-2017
E-mail: mentoring@wnec.edu

Founded in 1999, the Springfield Mentoring Partnership (SMP) strives to increase mentoring services, to advocate for the expansion of mentoring, and to provide resources and technical assistance to mentoring programs. Initially focused on the city of Springfield, SMP expanded in 2001 to include the greater Springfield area and changed its name to The Greater Springfield Mentoring Partnership (GSMP). GSMP facilitates the work of mentoring organizations in greater Springfield, Massachusetts. These include the YWCA of Western Massachusetts, Springfield School Volunteers, Springfield College Partners Program, Dunbar Community Center, Partners for Youth with Disabilities, Girl Scouts of Pioneer Valley, Big Brothers Big Sisters of Hampden County, and Action Centered Tutoring Services.

Harvard Medical School

Project Success, Mentoring for Science and Saturday Science Academy Programs
164 Longwood Avenue, 2nd Floor
Boston, MA 02115
Phone: (617) 432-4697
Fax: (617) 432–3834

This program is one of several Harvard University Medical School K–12 programs that promote science literacy and interest in science careers for Boston middle and high school students. Three of the K–12 programs focus on mentoring. The Saturday Science Academy serves high school students and provides exposure to different fields of science through hands-on experiments and one-to-one mentoring. Mentoring for Science matches middle school students with Harvard Medical School faculty and students who encourage developing interests in math and science. Students go on field trips and receive an e-mail account to facilitate communication with mentors and other mentees. Students must commit to the program for at least one year. Project Success places minority high school students in paid summer research internships. Participating students receive hands-on laboratory learning experience, seminar and discussion series, and ongoing counseling and career support. The students also receive mentoring. Students are provided with laboratory mentors/advisors and medical/graduate student advisors to provide individual guidance regarding careers in the biomedical sciences.

The Mass Mentoring Partnership

150 Chauncy Street, 3rd Floor
Boston, MA 02111
Phone: (617) 695-1200 or (800) 397-1861
Fax: (617) 695-2435
Web: www.massmentoring.org

The mission of the Mass Mentoring Partnership (MMP) is to promote mentoring and economic self-sufficiency opportunities for youth. The partnership serves as the oversight agency for the Mentor Task Force Action Plan, tracking all new mentoring relationships formed in connection with the Massachusetts Promise. The Massachusetts Mentoring Partnership provides mentoring recruitment and matching, several different mentor training workshops and curricula, and several print resources. MMP programs include a faith-based mentoring network, the Institute for Youth Enterprise, a statewide mentor task force, a school-based mentoring initiative, Mentoring Day, the Pathways Initiative, and Massachusetts Mentor Programs networking opportunities.

Mentor Match Program
Partners for Youth with Disabilities
95 Berkeley Street Suit 407
Boston, MA 02116
Phone: (617) 556-4075
Fax: (617) 556-4074
Web: www.pyd.org

Partners for Youth with Disabilities, Inc. (PYD) strives to empower young people with disabilities to achieve their full potential. PYD is committed to providing one-to-one and group mentoring programs that match youth and adults with similar physical, sensory, or learning disabilities. Adult mentors function as positive role models and offer support, understanding, and guidance for youth as they strive to reach their personal, educational, and career goals.

PYD serves youth throughout New England and is expanding its presence throughout the country. Their mentoring model has been replicated for youth-serving organizations in Minnesota, Tennessee, and California.

Sharing Our Stories
Massachusetts College of Art
621 Huntington Avenue
Boston, MA 02115
Phone: (617) 879-7701
Web: www.massart.edu

Sharing Our Stories seeks to utilize the visual arts as a tool for building high quality mentoring relationships. In this after-school program, 40 second graders from the Young Achievers School come to MassArt to improve literacy skills through the visual arts. MassArt students fulfill the roles of both artists and mentors. Four program coordinators work with classroom teachers to select writing topics that allow the children to find their voices through both written and visual language.

Mentored children read their weekly writing to their mentors and then illustrate each "story" using a variety of art techniques. The outcome of the project is an individualized, bound biography. In a final capstone event, each child chooses a story and its corresponding illustration (to be made into slides) and presents their work to a live audience comprised of fellow students from Young Achievers, friends, family members, and guests from the community. An exhibition of all the Sharing our Stories books is then on view in the MassArt student gallery. More recently, Sharing Our Stories has expanded to include an older group of children from the Mission Safe program, who will be working on constructing artist books.

Springfield College AmeriCorps Program
263 Alden Street
Springfield, MA 01109
Phone: (413) 748-3610
Fax: (413) 748-3904
Web: www.msalliance.org/AmeriCorps.shtml

Under the Springfield College AmeriCorps Program, AmeriCorps members serve at an alternative high school where they tutor and mentor academically at-risk students and adjudicated youth. Some of the mentoring activities include anger management, conflict resolution, social skills, and social decision making. The program attempts to improve academic achievement and classroom behaviors.

Viva La Cultura! Club Mentoring Program
1530 Tremont Street
Roxbury, MA 02120
Phone: (617) 442-4299
Fax: (617) 442-4087
E-mail: soclatina@aol.com

Viva La Cultura! Club matches Latino adults with Latino youth ages 13 to 18 in a mentoring relationship. Group meetings are held once a month for two hours in which mentors and mentees read poetry, literature, and view films by and about Latinos. The program also involves fieldtrips to athletic events, music performances, bowling, photography, and art projects. Mentor and mentee commitment is four hours per month.

Michigan

B-H-K Child Development Board
Copper Country AmeriCorps
700 Park Avenue
Houghton, MI 49931
Phone: (906) 482-3663
Fax: (906) 482-7329
Web: www.bhkfirst.org

Incorporated in 1974, the B-H-K serves three rural counties in Northern Michigan. This program offers tutoring and mentoring for students in preschool through 12th grade schools in addition to an Even Start Program. AmeriCorps provides part of the staffing. Participating K–12 students were identified by teachers as individuals needing additional support to improve school success.

City Year Detroit
1 Ford Place 2A
Detroit, MI 48202
Phone: (313) 874-6825
Fax: (313) 874-6883
Web: www.cityyear.org

Established nationally in 1988 and in Detroit in 1999, City Year Detroit offers in-school and after-school tutoring and mentoring to inner-city youth in grades kindergarten through 9. Services exist in schools and community-based organizations. During the 2002–2003 school year, 95,600 hours of volunteer service were performed. Eighty percent of those service hours were mentoring and tutoring. The program seeks to enhance academic achievement and stimulate student involvement in community service activities.

Michigan Reading Readiness
Michigan State University
108 Agriculture Hall
East Lansing, MI 48824
Phone: (517) 432-7575
Fax: (517) 355–6473

The Michigan Reading Readiness project serves schools and community-based organizations in 15 counties, providing literacy tutoring and mentoring to kindergarten to 3rd-grade children and their families.

YouthFriends Michigan
521 S. Union Street
P.O. Box 694
Traverse City, MI 49684
Phone: (231) 947-3200 and toll-free (800) 344-9333
Fax : (231) 947-3201
Web: www.youthfriends.org

Founded in 1995, Youth Friends is a school-based mentoring program with three branches: Youth Friends Greater Kansas City, Youth Friends Kansas, and Youth Friends Michigan. Its mission is to motivate communities to help young people succeed by engaging adults in volunteerism with youth. Volunteers are matched with students, ages 5 to 18, with shared interests such as a special hobby, music, sports, reading, or computers. Mentor-mentee matches engage in a variety of activities, based on the needs of the individual child or adolescent. This program is flexible, with volunteer investment options that include working with one young person or a group and committing to as little as one hour a week for four weeks, a semester, a school year or more. Volunteers may select a preferred age group and school location.

Minnesota

Achieve Minneapolis
111 3rd Street S., Suite 120
Minneapolis, MN 55401
Tel (612) 3455-1530
Fax: (612) 455-1531
Web: www.achieveminneapolis.org

Achieve Minneapolis (AM) was created by a merger of Youth Trust, which started in 1989, with the Minneapolis Public Schools. Achieve Minneapolis seeks to promote the development of local youth by promoting the attitudes, knowledge, and skills needed to succeed at school and in the world of work. The key goal of this organization is to help students develop marketable skills and transition effectively from school to work. The focus of AM's work is on collaboration, and the agency serves as an intermediary that fosters partnerships between employers and schools. Students are connected to business professionals through three programs—School Partners, New Workforce, and High-School Partners.

AmeriCorps Southern Minnesota
South Minnesota Initiative Foundation
525 Florence Street
P.O. Box 695
Owatonna, MN 55060
Phone: (507) 455-3215
Fax: (507) 455-2098
Web: www.smifoundation.org
E-mail: semif@semif.org

In this project, AmeriCorps members work in a statewide program tutoring youth during and after school, coordinating service-learning activities for students, mentoring young people, and facilitating mentoring programs.

Amherst H. Wilder Foundation—Future Force
911 Lafond Avenue
St. Paul, MN 55104
Phone: (651) 642-2090
Fax: (651) 659–6027

This project makes mentoring and tutoring services available to inner-city students in low-achieving classrooms, with a focus on improving academic skills and test scores. After-school and summer programs are also provided for children ages 6 to 16.

Higher Education Service Office/Get Ready
1450 Energy Park Drive, Suite 350
St. Paul, MN 55108-5227
Phone: (651) 642-0533
Fax: (651) 657–3866

This program helps low-income students and their parents in Minneapolis and St. Paul. The goal is to advance these young people educationally and economically. Interventions include education regarding academic and career options, and tutoring and mentoring for children in grades 4 through 8. Volunteers also work with parents to enhance their understanding of how their children can succeed in higher education.

Kinship of Greater Minneapolis

3210 Oliver Avenue N.
Minneapolis, MN 55412
Phone: (612) 588-4655
Fax: (612) 488-4680
Web: www.kinship.org

Established in the 1950s and incorporated 30 years later, this Christian mentoring program serves children ages 5 to 15 from single-parent homes in Minneapolis and the surrounding area. Matches are made with individuals, couples, and families. There were almost 300 matches made during the 2002–2003 school year, with the average match lasting two and a half years.

The Mentoring Partnership of Minnesota

81 S. Ninth Street, Suite 200
Minneapolis, MN 55402
Phone: (612) 370-9180
Fax: (612) 370-9195
Web: www.mentoringworks.org

This partnership, which began in 1994, advocates for mentoring and providing young people with experiences that will increase their chance of gaining economic self-sufficiency. The program collaborates with more than 400 mentor programs in the Twin Cities area, providing resources such as recruitment, technical assistance, and training support. The partnership offers a training institute, the Minnesota Mentoring Conference, Metro Mentor Network, a Minnesota Business Partnership Connections tool kit, a mentor evaluation tool kit, and two resource directories. Information about these offerings is available on the Web site.

Mississippi

Big Brother Big Sisters of Mississippi

175 E. Capitol Street, #222

Jackson, MS 39201
Phone: (601) 961-9286
Fax: (601) 961-9288
Web: www.bbbsms.org

Big Brother Big Sisters of Mississippi is the local Jackson, Mississippi branch of the national Big Brother Big Sisters program, providing one-on-one mentoring to children from single-parent homes. Other branches of BBBS are located in Mississippi as well.

Missouri

Seneca R-7 School District

Seneca AmeriCorps Project
1110 Neosho Street
Seneca, MO 64865
Phone: (417) 776-3690
Fax: (417) 776–1509

AmeriCorps members tutor students in grades 1 through 6 in the Seneca School District who are reading below grade level. The program also provides mentoring for students in the middle school grades. There is an after school program for grades 1 through 8. The program seeks to improve students' behavior and academic performance.

United Way of the Ozarks

Community Partnership
1330 N. Jefferson
Springfield, MO 65804
Phone: (417) 888-2020
Fax: (417) 888–2322

This project offers one-to-one tutoring and mentoring to teacher-identified low-achieving K–5 students, as well as mentoring to middle school youth.

YouthFriends

1000 Broadway, Suite 302
Kansas City, MO 64105
Phone: (877) 842-7082 or (816) 842-7082
Fax: (816) 842-7907

Web: www.youthfriends.org
E-mail: youthfriends@youthfriends.org

This program links adults and school children in an effort to promote the positive development of youth and build stronger communities. The project began in 1995 as a pilot effort in six metropolitan Kansas City school districts and currently serves 77 school districts in the greater Kansas City area. Working one hour a week, volunteers choose the age group they want to work with and the activities that most appeal to them. For example, YouthFriends might read to elementary school students, help middle school students on a special project, eat lunch with a young person who needs a friend, or offer career guidance to a high school senior. Volunteers may choose to work one-to-one with a single young person, interact with a small group of students, or sponsor an entire class. YouthFriends engages in recruitment and provides technical assistance to participating school districts. One hundred thousand children have been mentored through this program.

Montana

Child Advancement Project (CAP)
Prevent Child Abuse, Inc.
400 E. Babcock Street
Bozeman, MT 59715
Phone: (406) 587-3840
Fax: (406) 586–9376

Established in 1992, this school-based project pairs K-12th grade students with adults who meet with them one hour per week in an effort to enhance academic and social functioning. During the 2002–2003 school year, 430 students were matched with a mentor. Most of the mentoring relationships are one-on-one.

Gemini Program
P.O. Box 5244
Kalispell, MT 59903
Phone: (406) 257–4624

Developed to provide 9th grade girls with crucial support, this program matches young girls with an adult volunteer. The pairs meet outside of the school setting. The program emphasizes goals such as increasing self-esteem, increasing motivation and involvement, career exploration, and improved academic and social competencies.

Montana 4-H
Montana State University
210 Taylor Hall
Bozeman, MT 59717
Phone: (406) 994-3501
Web: www.montana.edu/www4h

This 4-H program is open to youth ages 6 to 19 years. These young people are matched with adults, and the pairs engage in a variety of activities aimed at promoting mental, physical, moral, and social development. Montana 4-H sponsors innovative mentoring programs such as Bridging the Gap of Isolation, a program that serves the Northern Cheyenne Reservation and Powder River County youth.

Nebraska

All Our Kids, Inc.
The Midlands Mentoring Partnership
1004 Farnam Street
Omaha, NE 68102
Phone: (402) 930-3000
Fax: (402) 930-3006
Web: www.am1st.com

The mission of All Our Kids, started in the 1940s and later merged into the Midlands Mentoring Partnership, is to expand opportunities for at-risk youth in the greater Omaha metropolitan area. Their method is to engage at-risk students in positive relationships with caring adults. The partnership recruits prospective adult volunteers, engages in public awareness campaigns, and operates a mentor training institute and resource center that assist community partners. The All Our Kids mentoring program strives to promote academic achievement.

Lincoln Public Schools Foundation
Comprehensive School Health Initiative
1845 S. 11th Street
Lincoln, NE 68502

Phone: (402) 436-1035
Fax: (402) 436–1037

Lincoln public school students receive in-school tutoring and mentoring, as well as after-school Kids Clubs programs.

Teammates Mentoring Program
6801 O Street
Lincoln, NE 68510
Phone: (402) 323-6250
Fax: (402) 323-6255
Web: www.teammates.org

This school-based mentoring program serves children vulnerable to school difficulties. There are many community Teammates organizations throughout Nebraska, modeled after the original program begun by Tom and Nancy Osborne in 1991. Adult volunteers are matched with middle school students, serving as positive role models for students needing extra adult attention. Pairs meet at least one hour a week during school hours, sharing in a variety of activities.

Nevada

Mentor Center of Western Nevada
Western Nevada Community College
Cedar Building, Room 209
P.O. Box 2740
Carson City, NV 89700
Phone: (775) 445-3346
Fax: (775) 887–3160

This community-supported program, founded in 2000, matches youth with adults and/or older adolescents. The center is housed at Western Nevada Community College.

Southern Nevada Mentoring Coalition
1660 E. Flamingo Road
Las Vegas, NV 89119
Phone: (702) 892-2323
Web: www.uwaysn.org

Founded in 1998, the coalition unites mentoring efforts in southern Nevada.

New Hampshire

Granite State Youth Mentors
15 Constitution Drive, Suite 105
Bedford, NH 03110-6041
Phone: (603) 589-8003
Fax: (603) 589-8004
Web: www.nhmentors.org

Granite State Youth Mentors (GSYM), established in October 2000, is a statewide umbrella organization formed and funded by the New Hampshire Department of Justice, the New Hampshire Charitable Foundation, and New Futures. Its mission is to sustain mentoring programs statewide in an effort to enhance the quality of life for youth in New Hampshire. GSYM operates a toll-free, statewide mentor hotline. The New Hampshire Department of Justice provides grant funding to expand mentoring programs, especially programs serving first-time juvenile offenders. GSYM also plans to initiate extensive public awareness campaigns promoting mentoring as an effective youth development strategy.

New Jersey

A+ for Kids Teacher, AmeriCorps.
Mercer County Reads Literacy and After-School Program
P. O. Box 5975
Trenton, NJ 08638
Phone: (609) 278-8248
Fax: (609) 656–8570

This program involves literacy tutoring, after-school homework assistance, a summer reading lab, and mentoring services for children in Trenton's most troubled schools.

BBBS of Metro Newark
35 James Street
Newark, NJ 07102
Phone: (973) 242-1142

Fax: (973) 242-0945
Web: www.bbbs.org

This program assists young people by pairing them with adult volunteers who offer support, guidance, companionship, and challenge. The goal of the relationship is to decrease drug use and foster a work ethic within youth. Eight hundred youth were mentored through this program in the 2002–2003 school year.

Department of Law and Public Safety

Juvenile Justice Commission AmeriCorps Junior Mentor Program
275 Hobart Street
Perth Amboye, NJ 08861
Phone: (732) 293-5026
Fax: (732) 293-5027
Web: www.ntlAmeriCorpsone.org

In this unique and successful program established in 1997, Junior Mentors, young people who have successfully graduated from the juvenile justice system mentor youth still in the juvenile justice system. These successful graduates also provide community service to victims and the community. Junior Mentors are supervised by adults in the Juvenile Justice system. There are an average of 200 youth being mentored throughout the state at any given time.

New Jersey Reads

Cumberland County College and Kean University
100 Riverview Plaza
Trenton, NJ 08625-0500
Phone: (609) 633-0793
Fax: (609) 633–2939

Part of a statewide initiative, this program provides tutoring, mentoring, and family literacy assistance to K–3 students in an effort to bring the reading abilities of students up to or above grade level.

New Mexico

New Mexico MESA

2808 Central Avenue, S.E.
Suite 122

Albuquerque, NM 87106
Phone: (800) 544-2617
Fax: (505) 262-1119
Web: http://nmmesa.nmt.edu

Established in 1983, New Mexico MESA (Mathematics Engineering Science Achievement) prepares students in grades 6 through 12 for college majors and careers in mathematics, engineering, science, and related technological fields. While open to all eligible students, the project targets Native Americans, African Americans, and Hispanics. Strategies include field trips, tutoring, competitions, leadership workshops, and summer enrichment classes. The project serves young people in five distinct areas of New Mexico: Central, North Central, Northern, Southern and Western.

New Mexico Young Fathers Project
3214 Purdue Place, N.E.
Albuquerque, NM 87106
Phone: (505) 265-5976
Fax: (505) 266-1017
Web: www.youngfathers.org
E-mail: contact@youngfathers.org

This project serves the needs of young male parents, with the goal of reducing repeat pregnancies and developing support networks. There are currently eight sites. Interventions seek to improve parenting skills, educational levels, employment capabilities, and social stability. Adults work with youth at-risk for teen pregnancy, serving as mentors, coaches, and community educators.

San Juan Service Corps
4601 College Boulevard
Farmington, NM 87401
Phone: (505) 566-3585
Fax: (505) 599-0385
Web: www.sjc.cc.nm.us/AmeriCorps/

AmeriCorps members serve at-risk youth from disadvantaged communities in rural northwestern New Mexico. Activities include science-based tutoring, English, and family literacy instruction, civic responsibility affirmation, mentoring, and out-of-school enrichment.

The program seeks to promote academic improvement, increased positive behaviors, and decreased negative behaviors.

New York

AmeriCorps Kids First Initiative
The Institute for Human Services
6666 County Road 11
Bath, NY 14810-7722
Phone: (607) 776-1104
Fax: (607) 776-9482
Web: www.ihsnet.org
E-mail: ackf@ihsnet.org

This initiative assists 20 mentoring programs in rural Steuben County and the Southern Tier/Finger Lakes region of New York state. Operating since 1997, currently AmeriCorps participants provide area youth with positive role models and alternative activities through tutoring, mentoring, and planned activities. Specific member services include providing safe places such as youth centers and after-school programs, pregnancy/early childhood/parenting counseling, Head Start and other early childhood programs, literacy training, and alternative education programs. One thousand youth are served each year in the Kids First Initiative.

Big Brother Big Sister of New York City
223 E. 30th Street
New York, NY 10016
Phone: (212) 686-2042
Web: www.bigsnyc.org

The Big Brother Big Sister (BBBS) of New York City organization offers both school site and community-based mentoring opportunities for adult volunteers and their mentees. As with other Big Brother Big Sister branches, the New York City branch provides at-risk youth with an intensive one-on-one mentoring relationship with a fully screened adult volunteer. The pair meets regularly for a period of at least one year. BBBS also offers a 32 hour certificate program in mentoring supervision in partnership with Fordham University Graduate School of Social Service. The certificate program is designed to help an organization develop, start, expand, or improve a mentoring program for youth.

ESCORT
State University College of NY at Oneonta
308 Bugbee Hall
Oneonta, NY 13820
Phone: (888) 922-4673
Fax: (607) 432-7102
Web: www.escort.org

ESCORT is a national resource center dedicated to improving the educational opportunities for migrant children. ESCORT staff maintains the National Migrant Education Hotline and conducts workshops with local school districts and community resources to enable them to better serve migrant children as well as English language learners. ESCORT volunteers, including AmeriCorps members, provide mentoring, tutoring, and positive activities for migrant students, conducting home visits, encouraging parental involvement, and providing appropriate referrals.

Families First in Essex County
P.O. Box 565
Elizabethtown, NY 12932
Phone: (518) 873-9544
Fax: (518) 873-9570
Web: www.behaviorhealthnet.org/template1.htm#overview

Families First is a not-for-profit community organization in Sussex County, New York, designed by parents to offer support to families who are overwhelmed by the needs of an emotionally disturbed or behavior disordered child. Built on the premise of wraparound, or coordinated, services, Families First provides these families with a number of programs designed to keep their children either at home or in the most family-like environment possible. Working with Families First, Essex County AmeriCorps members and other volunteers provide the identified youth with positive adult mentors and role models. The mentoring may take the form of tutoring, educating, role modeling, supporting, or leading recreational activities with the identified child or adolescent.

The Mentoring Partnership of Long Island
150 Motor Parkway, Suite 90
Hauppauge, NY 11788

Phone: (631) 761-7800
Fax: (631) 761-7803
Web: www.mentorkids.com

The Mentoring Partnership of Long Island serves at-risk youth by promoting and supporting mentoring and economic empowerment across the Long Island community. Available services include mentor recruitment and training, technical assistance for programs, public awareness campaigns, resource development, and data collection. A mentoring connection links volunteers and local programs. A mentoring academy provides classes for volunteers and staff. Mentoring efforts include Teens on the Job/Groundhog Job Shadow Day, Mentoring Futures, Golf-Mentoring Teams, and faith-based mentoring. The partnership Web site connects interested individuals with a variety of resources.

The Mentoring Partnership of New York
122 E. 42nd Street, Suite 1520
New York, NY 10168
Phone: (212) 953-0945
Fax: (212) 953-1057
Web: www.mentoring.org/newyork

Established in 1991, the Mentoring Partnership of New York provides an umbrella of support for youth mentoring efforts in the five boroughs of New York City. Although the partnership does not provide direct mentoring services, it expands the city's capacity for mentoring opportunities by providing training, technical support, referrals, and resources for the local mentoring programs. In addition, the partnership promotes mentor recruitment and public awareness, citywide, and provides celebratory activities for mentors and mentees. The partnership also sponsors educational workshops, a speaker series, the New York City Youth Council, the Business Partners Roundtable, a yearly mentoring symposium, and provides an opportunity for member organizations to gather and share ideas. Two major programs of the Mentoring Partnership of New York are the school-based Youth Mentoring Youth Program and the Faith-Based Mentoring Program. The partnership offers several print resources as well.

Mentoring USA
113 E. 13th Street
New York, NY 10003
Phone: (212) 253-1194

Fax: (212) 253-1267
Web: www.mentoringusa.org

Mentoring USA was founded by Matilda Raffa Cuomo in 1995 as an early intervention mentoring program to prevent school dropout. It is currently the largest one-on-one mentoring program in New York City. The program has specialized areas of mentoring, including youth where English is a second language, youth in foster care or who have been homeless, and other high risk youth populations, along with early intervention mentoring for children who are struggling with school and/or social problems. The programmatic design of Mentoring USA calls for trained adult mentors to meet at least four hours a month with their mentees. The one-on-one mentoring takes place at a supervised site in the child's community. Multiple mentors and mentees meet simultaneously at the site under the supervision of a teacher or trained child-care professional. Mentoring USA currently operates in more than 60 locations. It is affiliated with HELP USA, the nation's largest provider of transitional housing and on-site services for homeless families.

Research Foundation of SUNY–New Paltz

SUNY New Paltz—AmeriCorps EAP
75 S. Manheim Road
HAB 705
New Paltz, NY 12561-2443
Phone: (845) 257-3236
Fax: (845) 257-3674
Web: www.newpaltz.edu

AmeriCorps members tutor and mentor at-risk youth two to five days per week, with a focus on improving academic achievement and self-esteem. The AmeriCorps program is a partnership with the State University of New York at New Paltz.

RF/CUNY on behalf of New York City Technical College

CUNY TechCorps
300 Jay Street N-422
Brooklyn, NY 11201
Phone: (718) 260-5117
Fax: (718) 260–5198

With a focus on literacy and school success, AmeriCorps members tutor and mentor students in after-school programs at sites in the Ft. Green area of Brooklyn.

State University of New York at Stony Brook
Community Outreach Program Effort (COPE)
SUNY @ Stony Brook Career Center
Melville Library, Lower Level W-0550
Stony Brook, NY 11794-3363
Phone: (631) 632-6814
Fax: (631) 632-9146
Web: www.sunysb.edu/career/

This program assists at-risk elementary and secondary school students and their families. Youth receive tutoring, coaching, and mentoring, as well as organized after-school activities four days per week for a total of three hours per visit. The program aims to positively impact academic achievement and decrease truancy.

North Carolina

Children First of Buncombe County
Project POWER, AmeriCorps Mentoring Program
50 Doctors Drive, Suite 202
Ashville, NC 28801
Phone: (828) 259-9717
Fax: (828) 281-3308
Web: www.childrenfirsbc.org

This project assists children in grades kindergarten through 12th grade in order to promote academic achievement. Students receive mentoring, tutoring, and conflict-resolution and anger-management skills training. In the past, high school students volunteered as mentor/tutors for the after-school program, but the current service providers are largely adults.

East Carolina School of Education
Project HEART
Joyner East 122
East Carolina University

Greenville, NC 27858
Phone: (252) 328-4357
Fax: (252) 328–4219

Project HEART, an East Carolina School of Education mentoring program, serves students in grades 4 through 8 both in the public schools and in the juvenile justice alternative sentencing programs and settings. Participating youth receive tutoring and mentoring services.

North Carolina's Promise
Governor's Mentoring Initiative
Office of the Governor
116 W. Jones Street
Raleigh, NC 27601
Phone: (919) 715-3470
Fax: (919) 733-2120
Web: www.governor.state.nc.us

North Carolina's Promise aims to increase the quality and quantity of mentors so that every child in North Carolina who needs a mentor is matched with a caring adult. North Carolina's Promise recruits prospective mentors. Training is provided through statewide institutes, which are open to all mentoring agencies for a nominal fee. In collaboration with various nonprofit organizations, other training services are open to all mentoring groups. Training materials and resources are also available through the North Carolina's Promise office. The partnership engages in public awareness campaigns, resource development, public policy development, and tracking/data collection.

North Dakota

Big Brothers Big Sisters of the Village Family Center
1201 25th Street S.
Fargo, ND 58106
Phone: (701) 451-4900
Fax: (701) 451-5058
Web: www.thevillagefamily.org

The Village Family Center is the local branch of national Big Brother Big Sister program, providing one-on-one mentoring to children from single-parent homes.

Kinship Program
1900 N. 4th Street
Wahpeton, ND 58704
Phone: (701) 642–2811

The Kinship Program matches children ages 6–16 years who have special needs with caring adults willing to volunteer an hour a week for one year as a positive role model.

Ohio

Mentoring Center of Central Ohio
195 N. Grant Avenue
Columbus, OH 43215
Phone: (614) 233-6368
Fax: (614) 224-6866
Web: www.firstlink.org/public/mentoring/mentoring.php
E-mail: mentor@firstlink.org

The Mentoring Center represents a partnership between Big Brothers Big Sisters of Greater Columbus, Inc., FIRSTLINK, Inc., and more than 35 youth mentoring organizations. It is also an element of Ohio Reads, Governor Bob Taft's initiative to increase literacy among elementary school students, and helps to recruit for Mayor Coleman's Cap City Kids after school programs, and trains mentors for the Ohio Department of Aging's STARS program (Seniors Teaching and Reaching Students) and the Chamber's Career Academies.

Working to make quality mentoring more accessible, the center functions as a source of mentoring resources and services. It offers recruitment, screening, training, placement, and technical assistance.

Reaching Our Youth (ROY)
2 E. Main Street
Norwalk, OH 44857
Phone: (419) 663-2525
Web: http://homepages.accnorwalk.com/hcjpc/reach%
    20our%20youth.htm
E-mail address: roy@accnorwalk.com

Reach Our Youth (ROY) is a one-to-one mentoring program that was started in 1978 by Huron County Juvenile Court. Volunteers are matched with children (ages 6 to 18 years old) in a mentoring relationship. The program is open to any child living in Huron County who could use a special friend.

The Volunteer Action Center of Greater Lorain County
Project STRIVE
1905 N. Ridge Road, E.
Lorain, OH 44055
Phone: (440) 240-1990
Fax: (440) 240–1992

AmeriCorps members provide tutoring/mentoring in reading in 19 schools and in 10 after-school programs and recruit community volunteers to improve reading scores of educationally and economically challenged students.

Oklahoma

Ponca City United Way
Partners Building a Stronger Tomorrow
205 N. 2nd
Ponca City, OK 74601
Phone: (580) 765-2476
Fax: (580) 765–8369

AmeriCorps members tutor and mentor disadvantaged and underserved children in Ponca City and rural Ponca County. In addition, volunteers provide structured after-school recreational and educational events in low-income neighborhoods.

Seminole County Youth Promise Foundation
401 N. Main Street
Seminole, OK 74868
Phone: (405) 382-7688
Fax: (405) 382-7688
E-mail: YouthPromise@aol.com

The foundation provides before and after-school tutoring and reading programs, drug, gang and violence prevention. The project also offers a mentoring program through drop-out prevention and career and educational counseling for children and youth.

Youth Services for Stephens County
Yes 2 Kids!
16 S. 7th Street
Duncan, OK 73533
Phone: (580) 255-8800
Fax: (580) 255–8842

This program aids low-achieving and at-risk youth in rural Southern Oklahoma, with offerings such as during and after-school mentoring and tutoring.

Oregon

CyberSisters
P.O. Box 1518
2300 Leo Harris Parkway
Eugene, OR 97440
Phone: (541) 682-7884
Fax: (541) 484-9027
Web: www.cyber-sisters.org
E-mail: cybersisters@sciencefactory.org

In operation since 1997, CyberSisters unites teachers and college mentors in an effort to promote interest in math, science, and technology among middle school girls. College mentors serve as one-on-one mentors and role models in these fields, using both e-mail and face-to-face interactions. The larger CyberSisters organization works to create a supportive community for gender equity in Oregon K–12 education, and to advance the science, math, and school-to-work goals of Oregon's Education Act for the Twenty-first Century. The organization offers workshops, conferences, and training for parents and educators.

Forest Grove School District
Partnerships for Student Achievement
1728 Main Street
Forest Grove, OR 97116
Phone: 503-359-8110 ext. 254
Fax: (503) 359-2520
Web: www.fgsd.k12.or.us/AmeriCorps

This program serves selected K–12 Washington County schools with the goal of improving academic achievement through tutoring, mentoring, extended-school-day activities, parental involvement programs, and volunteer generation.

Friends of the Children
44 N.E. Morris Avenue
Portland, OR 97212-3015
Phone: (877) 493-2707
Fax: (503) 281-6819
Web: www.friendsofthechildren.com
E-mail: national@friendstochildren.org

Founded in 1993, this program uses highly trained, professional full-time mentors hired on a salary basis, as opposed to volunteers. Each mentor (known as a Friend in the program) works intensely with eight kids, four hours a week with each child. Friends follow children for 12 years, starting in first grade.

Oregon Mentors
221 N.W. Second Avenue
Portland, OR 97209
Phone: (503) 450-0890
Fax: (503) 228-5126
Web: www.ormentor.org
E-mail: info@ormentors.org

Oregon Mentoring Initiative (OMI) is a community-driven nonprofit organization advocating for the expansion of quality mentoring in Oregon. OMI offers assistance with volunteer recruitment and referral and matching of prospective volunteers to mentoring programs. Affiliated with the Portland Business Alliance, the initiative also provides information on program start-up, strategies to increase program capacity, and technical assistance.

Summer Experience in Science and Engineering for Youth (SESEY)
Oregon State University
Department of Chemical Engineering
103 Gleeson Hall, OSU
Corvallis, OR 97331-2702
Phone: (541) 737-2408
Web: www.che.orst.edu/SESEY

SESEY is one of several Oregon State University bioengineering out-reach activities. This program gives high school students a chance to work with faculty and student mentors in bioengineering and chemical engineering laboratories. SESEY targets high school girls and minorities who are traditionally underrepresented in science and engineering, although others may apply. To qualify, students must be sophomores, juniors or seniors in high school at the time of their participation. Partic-ipating high school students collaborate with mentors on weeklong research projects. Founded in 1997, SESEY is coordinated by the Departments of Chemical Engineering and Bioengineering and funded through grants from the Camille and Henry Dreyfus Foundation, the Oregon State University Pre-College Programs, the National Science Foundation, and the Bridges Family Foundation.

The SMILE Program
Oregon State University
18 Gladys Valley Center
Corvallis, OR 97331-3510
Phone: (541) 737-2388
Fax: (541) 737-3554
Web: www.orst.edu/precollege/TheSMILE

Founded in 1988, the Science and Math Investigative Learning Experi-ences (SMILE) program is a partnership between Oregon State University and 10 Oregon school districts, mostly rural, to provide science and math enrichment for educationally disadvantaged students in grades 4 through 12. SMILE seeks to promote retention and college attendance for educa-tionally disadvantaged students. In particular, SMILE works to encourage qualified students to pursue careers related to science, math, health, engi-neering, and teaching. SMILE offers year-round activities designed to pro-vide hands-on science experience, strengthen students' knowledge, and raise students' academic and career aspirations. The project involves a col-laborative effort between students, teachers, Oregon State University resource faculty and SMILE professional staff. Participating schools and their students receive instruction, access to equipment, mentoring, com-puter networking, teacher training, and administrative support.

Pennsylvania

Achievers Program YMCA of Philadelphia
2000 Market Street

Philadelphia, PA 19102
Phone: (215) 963–3726

The Achievers Program matches successful minority professionals with adolescents, using a group mentoring format. The program goal is to help youth achieve high academic and career goals.

Across Ages
Temple University
Center for Intergenerational Learning
1601 N. Broad Street
Room 206 (083-40)
Philadelphia, PA 19122
Phone: (215) 204-6160
Web: www.temple.edu/cil

This program links older adults (55 years and over) with young people 5 to 14 years of age. These one-to-one, community-based matches emphasize increasing youth involvement in community service, providing drug prevention education, and teaching life skills.

The Colours Organization
Mentor/Mentee Project
1201 Chestnut Street, 15th Floor
Philadelphia, PA 19107
Phone: (215) 496-0330
Web: www.coloursinc.org

The Colours Mentor/Mentee project provides one-to-one mentoring relationships, matching youth ages 15 to 21 with adult mentors.

Communities in Schools of Philadelphia
734 Schuylkill Avenue
JFK Building, Room 450
Philadelphia, PA 19146
Phone: (215) 875-3171
Web: www.cisphila.org/cisp

Communities in Schools of Philadelphia, Inc. (CISP) is the third-largest affiliate of 193 independently incorporated affiliates of Communities in Schools, Inc., the country's largest stay-in-school network. Incorporated in 1986, CISP partners with the School District of Philadelphia to mobilize community resources on behalf of students and their families. CISP goals include helping young people successfully learn, stay in school, and prepare for life. CISP programs are targeted to disadvantaged, low income, underserved students. Among the agency's "Five CIS Basics" is a belief that every child needs and deserves a personal, one-on-one relationship with a caring adult.

Lock Haven University
Office of Community Service
Lock Haven, PA 17745
Phone: (570) 893-2498
Web: www.lhup.edu

This office provides many services, among them the Youth Leadership and Development Team (YLDT). YLDT is affiliated with AmeriCorps and offers tutoring and mentoring to students in grades K through 12.

National School and Community Corps—Philadelphia
Stevens Administration Building
13th and Spring Garden, Room 105
Philadelphia, PA 19123
Phone: (215) 351-7654
Fax: (215) 351-7258
Web: www.educationworks-online.org

The National School and Community Corps enhances the capacity of urban schools to serve students, their families, and the community; creates safe, educationally rich environments for children during nonschool hours and the summer; and collaborates with organizations to support communities. Among the services provided by AmeriCorps members are mentoring, homework help, club activities, youth leadership, and conflict resolution.

One to One: The Greater Philadelphia Mentoring Partnership
7 Benjamin Franklin Parkway
Philadelphia, PA 19103

Phone: (215) 665-2606
Fax: (215) 665-2531

Serving at-risk youth, One to One combines mentoring and economic empowerment. The Partnership includes the United Way of Southeastern Pennsylvania, as well as local businesspeople, educators and social activists. One to One is also a signature partner of the National Mentoring Partnership. One to One goals include heightening attention to mentoring as a valuable intervention, mobilizing individuals to volunteer as mentors, cultivating the development of novel mentoring initiatives, and expanding the financial resources that support mentoring programs. The partnership also supports a variety of school-to-work programs (such as a job shadowing day) while striving to incorporate entrepreneurial activities in mentoring programs in order to increase at-risk young people's exposure to the economic mainstream. One to One supports a Coordinators and Providers Network that encourages resource sharing among the 130 member programs in Philadelphia. The partnership provides the Coordinators and Providers Network with technical assistance, recruitment support, recognition, training, a newsletter, and a ticket clearinghouse. Another service provided by this partnership is the Church Mentoring Network, which promotes and supports religious-based mentoring programs. The Network provides 250 mentors from 66 churches, serving more than 500 young people.

One to One: The Mentoring Partnership of Southwestern Pennsylvania
2934 Smallman Street, 2nd Floor
Pittsburgh, PA 15201
Phone: (412) 281-2535
Fax: (412) 281-6683
Web: www.mentoringpittsburgh.org
E-mail: info@mentoringpittsburgh.org

The Mentoring Partnership of Southwestern Pennsylvania is a network of community leaders and organizations that provides support and resources to enhance quality mentoring and encourage economic self-sufficiency opportunities for youth. This program is an affiliate of the National Mentoring Partnership and offers connections to training via a mentor training database, as well as regular general mentor training sessions conducted by the partnership. Other services include program development, referrals, and an annual mentoring symposium. The Greater Pittsburgh Mentoring Association is a network of organizations that sponsor mentoring programs in Greater Pittsburgh and the surrounding area. Representatives of the various organizations hold monthly meetings to network and share ideas. The partnership is also associated with Kujichagulia, an African American–based model for mentoring, which incorporates components of values, life skills, academics, culture, and parental involvement.

Teens-N-Technology Mentoring
Southwest Enrichment Center
1341 S. 46th Street
Philadelphia, PA 19143
Phone: (215) 386–8250

This program matches adolescents ages 15 to 18 years in one-to-one mentoring relationships aimed at preparing mentees for postsecondary education and careers.

Puerto Rico

Centros Sor Isolina Ferre, Inc.
Museum and Communities Working Together
30213
Ponce, PR 00734-0213
Phone: (787) 844-4646
Fax: (787) 284-2537
E-mail: censoris@coqui.net

Communities Working Together involves a collaboration between the art museum and colleges in an effort to serve the needs of children in rural and urban communities. A wide variety of services are offered, including mentoring, tutoring, family outreach, and establishing AmeriCorps Jr. and AmeriKids programs.

Rhode Island

Child and Family Services of Newport City
Volunteer Program
19 Valley Road

Middletown, RI 02842
Phone: (401) 848–4210

This program matches residentially placed young people between 5 and 18 years of age in one-to-one mentoring matches.

City Year Rhode Island
77 Eddy Street, 2nd Floor
Providence, RI 02903
Phone: (401) 553-2500
Fax: (401) 553-2510

AmeriCorps members tutor and mentor elementary school children, implement an after-school program, and present special issues workshops. In middle schools, volunteers teach a six-week Creating Community curriculum and operate Young Heroes, which is a junior service and service-learning program.

Public Education Fund
Parents Making a Difference
797 Westminster Street
Providence, RI 02903
Phone: (401) 453-8614
Fax: (401) 861-5768

This school-reform project entails the operation of family centers in 14 Providence public elementary, middle, and high schools. Youth services include before and after-school tutoring, mentoring, and homework helper sessions. The program includes a Learn and Serve initiative, Story Tellin', which engages students in grades K–6, adults, and senior citizens in literacy activities for children in grades K–2.

South Carolina

Communities in Schools
1300 Pickens Street, Suite 202
Columbia, SC 29201
Phone: (803) 254-5520
Fax: (803) 254-5377
E-mail: LPNCISSC@AOL.COM

This project focuses on improving academic achievement and provides tutoring, mentoring, and life-skills training for K–12 students.

School District of Pickens County
Project TEAM
200 W. D Street—Simpson Academy
Easley, SC 29640
Phone: (864) 855-8190
Fax: (864) 850–8116

This academically focused program offers tutoring and mentoring to children in elementary and middle school. Sessions take place during the school day, after school, during intersessions, and in the summer. Outreach efforts encourage parents to become involved in their child's education.

Winthrop University
Winthrop AmeriCorps: Empowerment Through Literacy
218 Dinkins Student Center
Rock Hill, SC 29733
Phone: (803) 323-2520
Fax: (803)323-4369
Web: www.winthrop.edu

AmeriCorps members tutor and mentor students in grades 1–6 and grades 8–12 at three sites in Rock Hill.

South Dakota

JUMP program
Department of Corrections
Mentor Coordinator
3200 E. Highway 34, c/o 500 E. Capitol Avenue
Pierre, SD 57501-5070
Phone: (605) 773-3478 or (800) 298-1677
Fax: (605) 773-3194
E-mail: MentorCoordinator@state.sd.us

This community program, part of the Department of Corrections mentoring initiative, pairs adults and adjudicated juveniles. The program is part of an aftercare plan for youth involved in the court system and is designed to support the philosophies and objectives of the department's juvenile institutions as the young person is transitioned from an institutional environment. Adult mentors provide support, supervision and involvement over a six-month period.

Tennessee

Best I Can Be Mentoring Program
309 Queen Avenue
Nashville, TN 37207
Phone: (615) 227–1595

This faith-based mentoring program provides one-to-one, group, and team mentoring with a Christian emphasis. Positive male mentors work with boys and young men with the goal of helping them reach their potential. Mentors provide support, guidance, friendship, and spiritual teaching.

Upper Cumberland Community Services
School Achievement Partnership Project
417 E. Broad Street
Cookesville, TN 38501
Phone: (931) 520-0200
Fax: (931) 520–3438

This project serves low-achieving students in five counties of the Upper Cumberland region of Middle Tennessee. These students are provided with tutoring, and truant students receive mentoring. Goals include improving academic performance and attendance.

Texas

Central Texas Armed Services YMCA
KISSS (Kids Involved Safely and Successfully in Service)
415 N. Eighth Street
Killeen, TX 76541
Phone: (254) 634-5445
Fax: (254) 634-4202
E-mail: bigcforddaddy@yahoo.com

The Kids Involved Safely and Successfully in Service program offers tutoring and mentoring to disadvantaged youth across the greater Killeen area of central Texas. The program seeks to increase school success and promote positive attitudes regarding education.

Communities in Schools of Hidalgo/Willacy Counties
Y2 Kids
3700 N. Tenth Street, Suite 290
McAllen, TX 78501
Phone: (956) 630-0016
Fax: (956) 630-0019
E-mail: cishidalgo@aol.com

This project assists two economically disadvantaged counties in the southern Rio Grande valley. During and after school hours, youth are offered tutoring and mentoring, with the goal of boosting school success and retention.

Hispanas Unidas
2507 N.W. 36th Street
San Antonio, TX 78228
Phone: (210) 434–2550

Hispanas Unidas offers early intervention, culturally based leadership, and mentoring programs. Latina youth between 5 and 14 years of age are provided one-to-one or group mentoring, with the goal of building on strengths and empowering young women in academic, cultural, personal, and social areas.

Governor's Mentor Initiative
Texas Commission on Volunteerism and Community Service
P.O. Box 13385
Austin, TX 78711
Phone: (512) 936-3587
Fax: (512) 463-1861
Web: www.txserve.org

The Governor's Mentoring Initiative (GMI) of the Texas Commission on Volunteerism and Community Service serves as the central coordinator of information to promote, support, and develop high-quality mentoring programs in Texas. The GMI provides statewide services, including a training and technical assistance program, along with a speaker's bureau. GMI has developed mentoring program quality assurance standards, and collaborates with the Office of the Governor and state legislators to create legislation that promotes mentoring and volunteering in Texas. The Governor's Volunteer Leadership Conference has long offered training and technical assistance to Texas volunteer leaders and administrators.

San Antonio: Making Mentoring a Partnership
The Greater San Antonio Chamber of Commerce
P.O. Box 1628
San Antonio, TX 78296
Phone: (210) 229-2190
Web: www.utsa.edu

The Making Mentoring a Partnership initiative provides a vehicle for the Greater San Antonio Chamber of Commerce to function as a liaison, uniting the business community, mentor programs, and local schools in an effort to serve young people. The MMAP recruits new mentors and links them with established mentoring programs.

San Marcos Youth Service Bureau
YAHOO! San Marcos
518 S. Guadalupe Street
San Marcos, TX 78666
Phone: (512) 396-5437
Fax: (512) 396–5374

This program seeks to promote the academic skills and emotional well-being of young people. Local students in need receive one-on-one support such as mentoring and tutoring.

St. Edward's University Community Mentor Program
3001 S. Congress Avenue
Austin, TX 78704-6489
Phone: (512) 448-8594
Fax: (512) 448–8549

The St. Edward's University Community Mentor Program mentors and tutors elementary school children, as well as youth being held in detention at the juvenile justice center.

University of Texas at El Paso—Department of Political Science
Paso Del Norte Assets for Youth
El Paso, TX 79968
Phone: (915) 747-6582
Fax: (915) 747–5400

This program seeks to prevent high-risk behaviors and foster healthy development among disadvantaged youth in El Paso. Interventions include structured tutoring, mentoring, and enrichment activities.

Utah

Salt Lake County Reads and Promotes Service
YOUTH FORCE
2001 S. State Street, S-2100
Salt Lake City, UT 84190
Phone: (801) 468-3604
Fax: (801) 468-3671
Web: www.slcoedcr.org/html/AmeriCorps.html

This Salt Lake City area program provides tutoring and mentoring to students in grades kindergarten through 6, with the goal of increasing academic achievement and attendance.

Utah Mentor Partnership
120 North 200 West, #419
Salt Lake City, UT 84103
Phone: (801) 538-9811
Fax: (801) 261-2753
Web: www.utahmentors.org

The Utah Mentor Partnership (UMP) advocates for collaboration between mentoring programs with the goal of promoting the development of quality mentoring programs. The Utah Mentor Partnership works to recruit new mentors statewide and provides technical assistance and training to mentoring organizations. The UMP sponsors a Mentor Day, as well as a Mentor of the Year award. Resources provided by the network include brochures, training videos, a computer-aided presentation, and a Web site.

Youth and Families with Promise—Washington County
197 E. Tabernacle
St. George, UT 84770
Phone: (435) 652–5814

This early-intervention agency serves at-risk children and families. They offer one-to-one mentoring between a young person and young adult mentor, or mentoring between a child and senior-age couples. The goals include improving academic performance, enhancing interpersonal competencies, and improving family bonds.

Youth Volunteer Corps of Washington County
46 W. St. George Boulevard, Suite C
St. George, UT 84770
Phone: (435) 674-5757
Fax: (435) 674-9105
E-mail: vcofwc@infowest.com

Youth Volunteer Corps of America (YVCA) is a national program dedicated to promoting volunteer opportunities that enrich America's youth, address community needs, and encourage a lifetime commitment to service. In this affiliated program, AmeriCorps members act as service learning coordinators, recruiting and training school-age youth to recognize and address community problems, and provide tutoring, mentoring, and reading support.

Vermont

Everybody Wins! Vermont
Verizon Building
119 Gates Street
White River Junction, VT 05001
Phone: (802) 296-READ (7323)
Fax: (802) 296-7300
Web: www.everybodywinsvermont.org

Everybody Wins! is a not-for-profit children's literacy and mentoring organization dedicated to encouraging positive attitudes about reading in elementary school children. The program was launched in Washington, D.C., by the U.S. Senate, headed by Senator James Jeffords (I-VT), in 1995. Everybody Wins! Vermont (EW! VT), is the first statewide EW!

program in a rural location. Launched in October of 2000, today over 640 adults and students participate in seven EW! VT locations each week. EW! VT consists of six main programs designed to increase literacy skills and to cultivate a lifelong love of reading and learning: Power Lunch, parent programs, gift books, book clubs, readers as leaders, and summer pen pals.

Lyndon State College
Northeast Kingdom Initiative AmeriCorps Program
1001 College Road
Lyndonville, VT 05851
Phone: (802) 626-6357
Fax: (802) 626–4803

AmeriCorps members serve Vermont's Northeast Kingdom, providing after-school enrichment, mentoring, and recreational activities. Members also provide youth with tutoring, job shadowing, technology training, and conflict resolution training.

Middlebury College Community Friends
Center for Campus Activities and Leadership
McCullough Student Center
Middlebury, VT 05753
Phone: (802) 443-3010
Web: www.middlebury.edu

Community Friends community-based mentoring began in 1960. Middlebury student volunteers are matched with children or adults for mentoring. Mentor-mentee pairs spend approximately two hours per week in activities, on or off campus.

Virginia

Child Aide Program
800 Preston Avenue
Charlottesville, VA 22903
Phone: (434) 970-2160
Fax: (434) 970–2104

Child Aide is a therapeutic mentoring program providing three to eight hours of direct contact per week. Young people between the ages of 4 and 18 from the Charlottesville/Albemarle area receive one-on-one mentoring that may entail a social/recreational and/or academic focus. Young participants are referred by schools, courts, Region 10, and the Department of Social Services. Mentors are paid for their work.

The Fairfax Mentoring Partnership
10530 Page Avenue
Fairfax, VA 22030
Phone: (703) 246-3895
Fax: (703) 246-4662
Web: www. volunteerfairfax.org

Formed in an effort to promote access to quality mentoring programs, the Fairfax Mentoring Partnership engages in recruitment, volunteer training, technical assistance, and public relations efforts. Mentorworks, a school-based mentoring program, represents a collaborative effort partnership formed with the Fairfax County Public Schools and Fairfax County Council of PTAs.

Family Counseling and Mentoring
Family Preservation Services
609 High Street E.
Charlottesville, VA 22902
Phone: (434) 293-4262
Fax: (434) 293–3077

Family Preservation Services provides intensive services tailored to meet the unique needs of its clients, with a focus on solutions-based strategies and challenges. Adolescents ages 12 to 18 may be referred for services by the Department of Social Services, the Health Department, or schools, or they may be self-referred. Paid mentors commit 5 to 10 hours per week to mentoring and engage in therapeutic recreation, outdoor activities, and tutoring with their mentees. Mentoring may occur in one-on-one or group format. Considerable parental involvement is expected.

Madison House Big Sibling Program
The Student Volunteer Center
University of Virginia
170 Rugby Road

Charlottesville, VA 22903
Phone: (434) 977-7051
Web: www.student.virginia.edu/~madison/

Madison House is a student volunteer center at the University of Virginia. Through Madison House, 3,000 University of Virginia students engage in various forms of community service. Among the many programs sponsored by Madison House is the Big Siblings program. This program fosters a long-term one-to-one relationship of friendship and trust between the volunteer and the child. The volunteer commits to spending a fall and spring semester as a mentor for a 5- to 12-year-old child from Charlottesville or Albemarle County. Big Sibling pairs meet weekly for two to three hours.

Monticello Avenue
Web: http:Monticello.avenue.org/mentorville

This is not a community agency in the traditional sense. Rather, Monticello Avenue is an innovative attempt to promote civic use of the World Wide Web using a community information server located in Charlottesville, Virginia. Among the valuable resources offered by this server is Mentorville, an online guide to Charlottsville-area youth mentoring programs. From this link, interested individuals can take steps to become a mentor or to find a mentor.

Teens GIVE Service Mentors
Community Attention Adolescent Home and Family Group Homes
907 E. Jefferson Street
Charlottesville, VA 22902
Phone: (434) 970-3334
Fax: (434) 970–3577

Teens GIVE Service Mentors develop relationships with at-risk youth by performing community service projects together with them. The program emphasizes skill-building and academic growth. Volunteer mentors perform supervised community service work with the youth in the program and also do some one-on-one tutoring and counseling. The program services youth ages 9 to 18 in the Charlottesville/Albermarle area who may be referred by the courts, the Department of Social Services, area schools, or parents, including residents of the Community Attention Adolescent Home and Family Group Homes.

Virginia Commonwealth University
VCU AmeriCorps
1103 W. Marshall Street
P.O. Box 843034
Richmond, VA 23284-3034
Phone: (804) 828-8850
Fax: (804) 828–1418

AmeriCorps members provide intensive, one-on-one reading support and mentoring to students in grades 1 and 2 in the Richmond metro area. The project also entails adult literacy and parental involvement programs through school-based parent resource centers.

Virginia's Future: The Attorney General's Mentoring Initiative
Office of the Attorney General
900 E. Main Street
Richmond, VA 23219
Phone: (804) 786-2071 or (804) 371-8946 TDD or (804) 786-1991
Web: www.oag.state.va.us/Special%20Projects/Mentoring/
E-mail: mentoring@oag.state.va.us

This initiative provides a forum for collaborative efforts among law enforcement, community leaders, educators, parents, and other concerned members of the public, with the goal of supporting Virginia youth. The Web site provides information regarding mentoring opportunities throughout Virginia.

Virginia One to One: The Mentoring Partnership
327 W. Main Street, #280
P.O. Box 843066
Richmond, VA 23284
Phone: (804) 828-1536
Fax: (804) 828-1418
Web: www.vcu.edu/vamentor

Virginia One to One nurtures a collaborative partnership among Virginia's mentoring community, while increasing the number of mentors serving Virginia youth. The partnership offers a centralized mentor training program. It also engages in public awareness, public policy, and resource development activities.

Washington

Central Puget Sound Council of Camp Fire
YVC of Muskegon County
8511 15th Avenue N.E.
Seattle, WA 98115
Phone: (206) 461-8550
Fax: (206) 525-3351
Web: www.campfire-usa.org

Youth Volunteer Corps of America (YVCA) creates and increases volunteer opportunities to enrich America's youth, address community needs, and develop a lifetime commitment to service. In this YVCA branch, AmeriCorps members function as service-learning coordinators and provide tutoring, mentoring, and reading support. Members also recruit, lead, and supervise volunteers in youth-generated service projects.

Community for Youth
2802 E. Madison, Suite 186
Seattle, WA 98112
Phone: (206) 325–8480

Community for Youth has developed and implemented mentoring and self-development programs for teens in the Seattle area for more than 10 years. The Steps Ahead and Steps Beyond programs teach high school students the personal values and social skills necessary for academic and future life success. Community for Youth offers one-on-one mentoring with carefully trained adults, tutoring, monthly personal growth workshops, enrichment activities, leadership training, career preparation, and community service projects. The program develops a strong supportive community among mentors, students, and staff.

The Daughters-Sisters Project
P.O. Box 4492
Rolling Bay, WA 98061
Phone: (206) 842-3000
Web: www.daughters-sisters.org
E-mail: daughtersi@aol.com

The theme of interconnection unites the goals of this Washington state based nonprofit organization. A primary goal of the Daughters-Sisters Project is to empower young women and to cultivate mentoring relationships between girls and women. The group also strives to promote understanding between genders, generations, and cultures. Programs supported by the project include weekly girls' focus groups, as well as various workshops and conferences. The Daughters-Sisters Project also publishes *InContext* magazine.

Sound Youth AmeriCorps
Notre Dame AmeriCorps—Seattle Sound Youth
4759 15th Avenue N.E.
Seattle, WA 98105-4404
Phone: (206) 525-1213 ext. 3202
Fax: (206) 525-1218
Web: www.21mainstreet.com/soundyouth/

Notre Dame Mission Volunteers, Inc., is a nonprofit organization founded by the Sisters of Notre Dame, a religious institution that has been serving communities in need for more than 150 years. The Notre Dame volunteers address many issues, including the educational needs of the disadvantaged youth and their families. Sound Youth Ameri-Corps participants collaborate with faith-based community-school partnerships to provide tutoring, mentoring, and after-school enrichment programs to help children and youth develop to their full potential.

Washington State Mentoring Partnership
Department of Social and Health Services
Division of Alcohol and Substance Abuse
612 Woodland Square Loop S.E., Building "C"
P.O. Box 45330
Olympia, WA 98504-5330
Phone: (360) 438-8494
Fax: (360) 438–8053

Formed in 1999, the Washington State Mentoring Partnership advocates for the expansion of mentoring services to at-risk youth. The partnership provides technical assistance and training related to mentoring, as well as a variety of resources and materials.

Yakima Valley Community College
P.O. Box 22520
Yakima, WA 98907-2520
Phone: (509) 574-4754
Fax: (509) 574–4737

The Career Connection Center (CCC) at Yakima Valley Community College is designed to serve nontraditional students as they transition into workforce training arenas. Staff is equipped to serve Displaced Homemakers, Worker Retraining, and WorkFirst students. Individual advising and referral services are available through the CCC.

West Virginia

Big Brothers Big Sisters of Northern Panhandle, Inc.
1310 Jacob Street
Wheeling, WV 26003
Phone: (304) 232-0520
Fax: (304) 232-3851
Web: www.bbsnp.org
E-mail: bbbs@stratuswave.com

This is the local branch of BBBS, providing one-on-one mentoring to children from single-parent homes.

Wisconsin

Outagamie County Mentoring Program
Outagamie County Division of Youth & Family Services
500 W. 5th Street
Appleton, WI 54911
Phone: (920) 832–2460

This program links youth ages 10–17 involved with the juvenile justice system with mature adults in their community to help foster the youth's development of character, competence, self-confidence, and self-esteem on a one-to-one basis through weekly contact.

Outagamie County PALS Program
401 S. Elm Street
Appleton, WI 54911
Phone: (920) 832–5161

The PALS Program matches children in the child protection system between the ages of 5–17 with positive adult mentors for at least one year. The mentor spends time with the child, usually one to two hours a week, doing recreational activities and teaching life skills.

Wyoming

Northern Arapaho Tribal Housing
AmeriCorps Program
774 White Hawk Drive
Ethete, WY 82520
Phone: (307) 332-4126
Fax: (307) 332–4107

AmeriCorps participants offer cultural, mentoring, and homework assistance activities after school and during the summer. This project serves young people living in five low-income housing areas on a central Wyoming reservation.

6

Selected Print and Nonprint Resources

"I've been waiting a long time. When am I going to get a mentor?"

Michael, 11 years old

A vast array of print and nonprint resources exist that relate to the field of mentoring, and the following chapter details both types of resources. Print resources include books, periodicals, state and national government documents, curriculum kits, manuals, and substantive brochures/pamphlets. Nonprint resources consist of Web sites.

The presentation of mentoring print resources is divided into three sections:

I. Books
II. Youth Mentoring Curricula, Instructional Materials, and Reference Works
III. Federal Government Documents and Reports

The presentation of nonprint mentoring resources is dedicated to resources available on the World Wide Web.

PRINT RESOURCES

While the majority of mentoring publications focus on professional mentoring—for example, the mentoring of first-year teachers or the mentoring of corporate professionals—there are many useful publications related specifically to youth mentoring and youth mentoring programs. The following list of print resources focuses on publications directly related to the mentoring of children and youth. A limited number of adult-focused mentoring volumes are included. In these instances, as is specified in the annotations, the publications provide information that is equally relevant to youth mentoring, or the materials contain ideas that may be readily adapted to a younger population. Print resources may be obtained through a variety of sources, including bookstores, university or public libraries, Internet Web sites, online bookstores, or by direct contact with the publisher or agency that developed the book or resource.

I. Books

The following selection of books is divided into five main areas:

- General Mentoring-Related Books
- Resource Books Related to Supporting Girls and Young Women
- Resource Books Related to Supporting Boys and Young Men
- Resource Books for Mentors and Protégés/Mentees
- Print Materials Offering Programmatic Information

General Mentoring-Related Books

Becker, J. M. (1994). *Mentoring high-risk kids.* Minneapolis, MN: Johnson Institute. ISBN 1562460927 (51 pages, paperback).

This book examines the challenges evident in the mentoring of young people experiencing difficult family or personal situations. The author discusses mentoring joys and pitfalls from the vantage point of both the mentor and the mentee. Although currently out of print, this text is readily available in libraries or via online book sources such as Amazon (www.amazon.com) or Powell's Bookstore (www.powells.com).

Beiswinger, G. L. (1985). *One to one: The story of the Big Brothers/Big Sisters movement in America.* Philadelphia: Big Brothers/Big Sisters of America. ASIN 0961382007 (290 pages).

This work offers an overview of the Big Brothers/Big Sisters of America organization, from its beginnings at the turn of the century to the mid-1980s. The book includes appendixes listing agencies affiliated, as well as agencies that are unaffiliated, with Big Brothers/Big Sisters. The organization is significant to the mentoring movement because of its longevity, its proven record of successful outcomes with youth, and its well-documented organizational and procedural structure. Although currently out of print, this useful book may be obtained through online used book sources such as Amazon (www.amazon.com) or Powell's Bookstore (www.powells.com).

Brooks, V. & Sikes, P. (1997). *The good mentor guide: Initial teacher education in secondary schools.* Buckingham, UK: Open University Press. ISBN 0335197590 (188 pages, hardcover) and 0335197582 (paperback).

This book explores various models of mentoring and examines in depth the roles and responsibilities of a mentor. The book includes an overview of how to work with students, as well as strategies for functioning as an effective mentor. Originating from Great Britain, it is one of a number of excellent reference works written for traditional "new teacher" mentoring. The material is fully adaptable and useful for programs that feature the mentoring of children and youth.

Daloz, L. A. (1999). *Mentor: Guiding the journey of adult learners* (2nd ed.). San Francisco: Jossey-Bass. ISBN 0787940720 (304 pages, paperback).

This book is targeted to postsecondary educators and is written by educational mentoring expert Laurent A. Daloz. In this work, Daloz adopts the metaphor of the mythic journey as a framework from which to consider life changes. Although focused on issues related to adult learners, including nontraditional students, the book touches on numerous issues relevant to the field of mentoring in general, including the qualities of both good teachers and good mentors.

Dortch, T. W., Jr., & Joyner, T. (2000). *The miracles of mentoring: The joy of investing in our future.* New York: Doubleday. ISBN 0385499914 (224 pages, hardcover).

In this book, the highly acclaimed 100 Black Men of America organization shares the successful blueprint of its Miracles of Mentoring program, from which more than 100,000 children of all ethnicities have benefited. Both a how-to and an inspirational guide, this work outlines the mechanics of establishing a mentoring partnership in one's community or workplace, including the 10 essential elements of mentoring, how a person can determine if mentoring is for him or her, and the five stages of a mentoring relationship. Also included are stories from adult mentors (all members of the 100 Black Men organization who mentor primarily, but not exclusively, in African American communities) and stories from the young people whose lives have been enriched and strengthened by their relationships with their adult mentors.

Dortch, T.W., Jr., & The 100 Black Men of America, Inc. (2001). *The miracles of mentoring: How to encourage and lead future generations.* New York: Broadway Books. ISBN 0767905741 (224 pages, paperback).

This is a revised but essentially similar version of the preceding book, *The Miracles of Mentoring: The Joy of Investing in our Future* (ISBN 0385499914).

Drury, K.W. (Ed.). (1998). *Successful youth mentoring: Twenty-four practical sessions to impact kids' lives.* Loveland, CO: Group Publishing. ISBN 0764421042 (128 pages, paperback).

This publication offers a step-by-step program for adult mentors seeking to develop leadership characteristics in young people. Twenty-four sessions are outlined. These sessions include active and interactive experiences. The book is available through www.grouppublishing.com.

Ellis, J., Small-McGinley, J., & De Fabrizio, L. (2001). *Caring for kids in communities: Using mentorship, peer support, and student leadership programs in schools.* New York: Peter Lang. ISBN 082041834X (296 pages, paperback).

Caring for Kids in Communities provides research and case studies that highlight the potential of interventions such as mentorship, peer support, and student leadership programs. The book offers practical material for implementing such programs in the schools.

Evans, T.W. (1992). *Mentors: Making a difference in our public schools.* Princeton, NJ: Peterson's Guides. ISBN 1560791527 (247 pages, paperback).

This work profiles successful mentors and mentor programs across the country, describing different styles of mentoring and a variety of management approaches. Not a how-to volume, the book is, nonetheless, a starting place for the development of a breadth of knowledge regarding successful educational mentoring of children and youth. Funding information and organizational resources are located in the appendixes.

Freedman, M. (1988). *Partners in growth: Elder mentors and at-risk youth.* Philadelphia: Public/Private Ventures. ISBN N/A (73 pages).

This volume presents the findings from a study of several successful intergenerational mentoring programs. It outlines in depth the linkage of elders to children and youth in a mentoring relationship. In the work, the author discusses research findings related to the nature of intergenerational relationships, the benefits of elder-youth mentoring, and elements of an effective relationship.

Freedman, M. (1993). *The kindness of strangers: Adult mentors, urban youth, and the new voluntarism* (1st ed.). San Francisco: Jossey-Bass. ISBN 1555425577 (182 pages, hardcover).

A well-received book in both the professional and the lay community, *The Kindness of Strangers* presents a comprehensive overview of the role that caring adults play in the development of young people. It also provides a historical review of the mentoring movement, as well as addressing the benefits and challenges of mentoring programs. The author combines experience and research in presenting the big picture of America's mentoring movement. The book is often used as a recruitment tool for organizations seeking to increase their pool of adult mentors.

Freedman, M. (1999). *The kindness of strangers: Adult mentors, urban youth, and the new voluntarism* (Reprint ed.). New York: Cambridge University Press. ISBN 0521652871 (162 pages, paperback).

See annotation above. This edition contains an updated introduction.

Goodlad, S. (Ed.). (1995). *Students as tutors and mentors.* Philadelphia: Kogan Page. ISBN 07494917927 (334 pages, paperback).

This volume addresses cross-age mentoring, a mentoring configuration in which older students are paired with younger students, or in some cases with same-age peers. The book contains an introduction to the concept of using older students as tutors and mentors to younger students, as well as a section on how students effectively fill these roles. Additionally, the book contains chapters on the benefits to participants

in a mentoring relationship and the process of initiating and institution-
alizing a cross-age mentoring program. Currently out of print, the book
highlights mentoring case histories from New Zealand, Australia, South
Africa, and the United Kingdom.

Goodlad, S. (Ed.). (1998). *Mentoring and tutoring by students.* Sterling,
VA: Kogan Page. ISBN 0749425598 (352 pages, paperback).

This book seeks to promote the use of students as tutors and mentors
among teachers in tertiary and secondary education, outlining how this
educational technique can bolster academic success. Goodlad continues
in the easy-to-read, inspirational mode of his 1995 work, and provides
information that is applicable to youth mentoring.

Gray, W.W., & Albrecht, B. (1999). *Mentoring youth for success.* Madison, WI: Wisconsin Dept. of Public Instruction. ISBN 1573370592
(26 pages).

While this workbook and guide for parents, employers, and mentor
trainers focuses on work-based mentoring, several of the sections,
including those on mentoring young learners and mentoring activities,
could be readily adapted to fit local needs. This book can be ordered
through the Wisconsin Department of Public Instruction Web site
(http://www.dpi.state.wi.us/) or by contacting publication sales at (800)
243-8782 (U.S. only) or (608) 266-2188.

Greif, R.S. (1997). *Big impact: Big Brothers making a difference.* New
York: New Hat. ISBN 0965813002 (208 pages, paperback).

The enduring success and influence of adult mentors on the lives of
youth and children is highlighted in this work. According to the author,
an estimated 15 million children in the United States are currently considered at risk. Big Impact stresses the ways that mentoring positively
influences the lives of America's at-risk youth. *Big Impact* cites stories
specifically about the mentoring of boys and adolescents involved in the
Big Brothers Big Sisters program. Based on 200 interviews with current
and former Big and Little Brothers, the text anecdotally walks the reader
through the components of this unique mentoring program, which
include (a) matching mentors and mentees, (b) the development of
mentoring relationships, (c) the qualities of a successful mentor, (d)
activities that enrich the mentoring bond, and (e) the positive impact on
everyone affected, including the Big Brothers, Little Brothers, their
friends and family, and the greater community in general.

Grossman, J. B. (Ed.). (1999). *Contemporary issues in mentoring.* Philadelphia: Public/Private Ventures. ISBN N/A (100 pages).

This book examines operational questions that must be addressed in order for mentoring programs to reach their full potential. The volume covers current mentoring issues and topics, including the elements of an effective mentoring program, measuring program outcomes and results, financial aspects of mentoring efforts, and the recruitment of volunteers. This publication can be either ordered or downloaded at www.ppv.org.

Mecca, A. H. (2001). *The mentoring revolution: Growing America one child at a time* (Part I). Tiburon, CA: California Mentor Foundation. ISBN: 0971368007 (77 pages).

With a foreword by George Lucas, this publication discusses mentoring as a national strategy, while also providing general mentoring-related information. An overview of the HOSTS program is provided, as well as information on key figures in the mentoring movement. The appendixes offer resources, with a focus on California coalitions and mentor programs.

Peddy, S. (2001). *The art of mentoring: Lead, follow, and get out of the way* (Rev. and exp. ed.). Corpus Christi, TX: Bullion Books. ISBN 096513766X (264 pages, paperback).

Using the style of storytelling to convey her message, the author introduces Rachel, the workplace mentor of the story, who finds that her own son needs mentoring support also. Although written for the business world, the book has much to offer to anyone whose goal is to make a positive difference in the lives of others. The book presents three key concepts: (1) "lead," where knowledge and skills are passed down; (2) "follow," where advice and counsel become the mentor-mentee link; and (3) "get out of the way," where the mentee has reached the set goals of the relationship and it is time to either terminate amicably or to set new mentoring goals.

Pitman, M. A., & Zorn, D. (Eds.). (2000). *Caring as tenacity: Stories of urban school survival.* Crosskill, NJ: Hampton Press. ISBN 1572732113 (141 pages, paperback).

This book details Project Hope, an urban mentoring program for youth that emphasizes a network of relationships built on the qualities of caring, respect, and values. The book grew out of a research project that focused on a mentoring support program in a large urban school district.

Having universal appeal to both professionals and the general public, this is a book of stories about survival and caring. Beyond stories and vignettes, a concept introduced as "tenacious caring" details the next steps to take in establishing and/or maintaining a network of adults reaching out in care and connection to children and adolescents.

Reilly, J. M. (1992). *Mentorship: The essential guide for schools and business.* Scottsdale, AZ: Gifted Psychology Press. ISBN 0910707189 (278 pages, paperback).

This book offers a well-articulated and comprehensive overview of mentoring in general, along with practical details on issues such as locating mentors, forming relationships, and collaborating with school personnel, parents, and community members. The author offers both breadth and an in-depth look at a specific mentoring program as a model for program development. The principles are relevant to mentorships in organizations ranging from high schools to businesses. The text offers numerous activities and concepts that can be instantly replicated or implemented, especially at the high school level. Checklists are included in the book, making implementation user-friendly.

Rhodes, J. E. (2002). *Stand by me: The risks and rewards of mentoring today's youth.* Cambridge, MA: Harvard University Press. ISBN 0674007379 (176 pages).

Mentoring expert Jean Rhodes provides a synthesis of research on the topic of youth mentoring in an attempt to bring some caution and complexity to the dialogue about this popular topic. Within this context, Rhodes discusses some of the factors that have fueled the recent interest in mentoring and evaluates evidence for program effectiveness. Research and case examples are provided to highlight both the benefits of enduring relationships and the potentially harmful effects of relationships that fail to deliver consistent support. The findings highlight the need for sufficient program resources to ensure reasonable levels of mentor screening, training, and postmatch support. The book also describes the underlying processes by which volunteers are thought to bring about change and draws on research from psychotherapy and personal relations to address some of the training issues that arise in mentoring. Finally, the book describes research and policy priorities with particular attention to how programs might better respond to the developmental needs of youth.

Schwiebert, V. L. (2000). *Mentoring: Creating connected, empowered relationships.* Alexandria, VA: American Counseling Association. ISBN 1556202237 (182 pages, paperback).

This book provides an overview of the history of mentoring and common mentoring models, along with strategies for implementing successful mentoring relationships. The content emphasizes the relationship between mentoring and counseling. The work considers the issues related to creating mentoring relationships between people of diverse ages, genders, and cultural backgrounds. The power of mentoring as a learning relationship is emphasized. The rewards for both members of the mentoring partnership are underscored.

Shulman, J. H., & Colbert, J. A. (Eds.) (1987). *The mentor teacher casebook.* San Francisco: Far West Laboratory for Educational Research and Development. ISBN 0865520941 (104 pages, paperback).

Developed in partnership with the Los Angeles Unified School District and the Far West Laboratory, this handbook reviews the extensive research conducted by Public/Private Ventures over a decade. The findings are organized according to five key areas: (1) tangible benefits of mentoring, (2) effective practices, (3) programmatic structure and support, (4) integration of mentoring programs with large-scale youth-serving institutions, and (5) viability of volunteers. The report includes the executive summaries of 11 Public/Private Ventures studies on mentoring.

Sinetar, M. (1998). *The mentor's spirit: Life lessons on leadership and the art of encouragement* (1st ed.). New York: St. Martin's Press. ISBN 0312186304 (176 pages, hardcover).

Calling true mentors "artists of encouragement" who help others discover their true selves and who empower their mentees to pursue their dreams, Sinetar's work is a departure from the traditional books on mentoring. Seeing the world and everything in it as a potential mentor, Sinetar calls for individuals to be open to the mentoring that abounds, unrealized, in the form of literature, children, nature, and the like. This work can serve as a resource to adult mentors who themselves feel the need for mentoring and encouraging to sustain them in their mentoring and support work with children and youth.

Sipe, C. L. (1996). *Mentoring: A synthesis of Public/Private Ventures' research: 1988–1995.* Philadelphia: Public/Private Ventures. ISBN 1556202237 (76 pages).

This publication details Public/Private Ventures' extensive research program related to youth mentoring. It includes findings related to the investigation of the efficacy of forming adult-youth mentoring relationships, as well as findings regarding elements of effective practice. This publication may be ordered or downloaded at www.ppv.org.

Steele, R. (1998). *Mentoring and the rites of passage for youth.* Baton Rouge, LA: RAVLON Books. ISBN 1570874085 (106 pages, paperback).

This book is a guide for both mentors and mentees. It would be extremely useful for anyone who desires to become a mentor. Referred to as a daily mentoring reference, the book will help schools, communities, and churches develop youth via mentoring relationships. The book has been recommended for use as a college supplemental textbook on contemporary youth issues and interventions.

Taylor, A. S., & Bressler, J. (2000). *Mentoring across generations: Partnerships for positive youth development.* New York: Kluwer Academic/Plenum. ISBN 0306464136 (115 pages, paperback).

This book features Across Ages, a multigenerational and multifaceted mentoring intervention that matches older adult volunteers with children and youth. Designed as a school-based model, Across Ages can be easily adapted to fit other agency- and community-based organizations. Each major component of the mentoring program (mentoring, community service, life skills instruction, and family support) is described in precise detail. Across Ages is deemed cost effective and easily implemented, even with limited resources. The program is applicable to children and youth felt to be highly at risk, as well as to youth needing less intense support and guidance.

Tierney, J., Grossman, J. B., & Resch, N. L. (2000). *Making a difference: An impact study of Big Brothers/Big Sisters* (Reissued). Philadelphia: Public/Private Ventures. ISBN N/A (58 pages).

This recently reissued publication presents findings from a 1995 study of Big Brothers Big Sisters mentoring relationships. The original study demonstrated that mentoring according to the Big Brothers Big Sisters model is associated with a number of significant beneficial effects. This publication may be ordered or downloaded at www.ppv.org.

Wickman, F., & Sjodin, T. (1997). *Mentoring: The most obvious yet over-looked key to achieving more in life than you ever dreamed.* New York: McGraw-Hill Professional Publishing. ISBN 0786311355 (250 pages, hardcover).

This book thoroughly covers the strategies and methods for finding mentors to help with every aspect of life. Written for the adult professional mentor-mentee audience, this book is an excellent resource for mentoring program administrators and trainers, as well as for the adult considering becoming involved as a mentor. The volume focuses on the benefits and the "magic" of mentoring and offers "16 laws of mentoring" as a chapter topic.

Wicks, R. J. (2000). *Sharing wisdom: The practical art of giving and receiving mentoring.* New York: Crossroad. ISBN 0824518381 (160 pages, paperback).

Developed in the format of 40 small chapters (one to three pages each), this book offers practical wisdom and insight into the complexities of human relationships, be they formal youth mentoring matches, students involved in peer helping programs, parents guiding their offspring, or corporate executives mentoring "rising stars." The resources can be used to inspire the individual mentor or as short discussion starters between mentors and mentees.

Resource Books Related to Supporting Girls and Young Women

Bolden, T. (Ed.). (1998). *33 things every girl should know: Stories, songs, poems, and smart talk by 33 extraordinary women.* New York: Crown. ISBN 0517709368 (159 pages, paperback).

Billed as a "call to self-esteem," this book directs girls to focus on developing a bright future for themselves. Easily readable, with text ranging from comic strip graphics about unpleasant girls who are mean to others to moving essays about living with physical challenges, the work highlights 33 essential elements to growing up healthily with a purpose for life. The book would be an excellent mentoring resource when working with older children and adolescent girls, either individually or in a group.

Echevarria, P. (1998). *For all our daughters: Five essentials to help young women and girls master the art of growing up.* Worcester, MA: Chandler House Press. ISBN 186628413X (228 pages, paperback).

Originally published under the title *For all our daughters: How mentoring helps young women and girls master the art of growing up,* this book provides a rationale for the importance of mentoring in the development of young women. Targeted to parents as well as women interested in mentoring, this book offers strategies for helping young women in the transition through adolescence. The book covers mentoring techniques as well as the key areas of development that mentors may address. The "five essentials" include a focus on physical development, intellectual development, emotional development, spiritual development, and financial accountability. The book also provides tips to parents interested in finding mentors for their daughters. The book includes a variety of mentoring stories as well as a brief list of resources such as books, organizations, and Web sites related to female development and interests.

Glennon, W. (1999). *200 ways to raise a girl's self-esteem: An indispensable guide for parents, teachers and other concerned caregivers.* Berkeley, CA: Conari Press. ISBN 1573241547 (220 pages, paperback).

The author addresses the decline in self-esteem among adolescent girls and provides practical suggestions for assisting young women in this area. Parents, teachers, and others who interact with young women gain information on how to impart a strong sense of self-worth to girls in their daily lives.

Harper, S., & Cascardi, A. (Eds.). (2001). *Hands on: 33 more things every girl should know: Skills for living your life from 33 extraordinary women.* New York: Crown. ISBN 0517800985 (160 pages, paperback).

A companion to Bolden's *33 Things Every Girl Should Know: Stories, Songs, Poems, and Smart Talk by 33 Extraordinary Women,* this book is a powerful collection of advice from 33 women, ranging from serious (such as Eileen Collins's essay on being prepared) to humorously stress-releasing (such as Tina Howe's recipe for the appropriate revenge cake in honor of the boyfriend who dumps you). The list of contributors is impressive, and the book signals to the reader that women have many choices in life, both professionally and personally. Fun and thought provoking, the content is ideal to be read out loud in a mentoring setting and then discussed in terms of applicability to the mentee's present and future life.

Hughes, K. W., & Wolf, L. (1997). *Daughters of the moon, sisters of the sun: Young women and mentors on the transition to womanhood.* Stony Creek, CT: New Society. ISBN 0865713774 (240 pages, paperback).

This book presents personal accounts of almost fifty young women, ages 13 to 23, from a variety of backgrounds. It also includes interviews with several prominent women. The narratives are an outgrowth of the Girls Focus Group, a project that unfolded between 1994 and 1997. Sections include "The Emerging Self," "Taking It to the Edge," "Growing Up Fast and Speaking Out," "Find Our Power," and "Gendertalks." This work serves as a resource book for individuals and groups who are interested in conducting comparable focus groups, as well as for teenagers interested in hearing from peers going through similar transitions.

Pipher, M. (1995). *Reviving Ophelia: Saving the selves of adolescent girls* (Reissue ed.). New York: Ballantine. ISBN 0345392825 (304 pages, paperback).

This book, written by a clinical psychologist, examines current societal pressures faced by adolescents and the difficulty girls have in sustaining healthy development. Punctuated with vignettes, research, and examples from the author's own work with young women, the book offers concrete suggestions of ways in which young girls and adolescents can develop and sustain a strong sense of self. The book is an excellent tool for mentor-mentee discussion. It is also useful as a text or teaching tool for mentors who want to understand the current effects of culture on young girls and adolescents.

Shandler, S. (1999). *Ophelia speaks: Adolescent girls write about their search for self.* New York: Harper Perennial. ISBN 0060952970 (285 pages, paperback).

Stories from teenage girls who are struggling with their passage into adulthood are highlighted in this book. Through stories in their own words, the young women reflect on issues ranging from parental expectations, eating disorders, racial relations, and drug abuse to faith and pride in being a female. The book would be helpful to adult mentors who want to understand some of the issues and pressures faced by their mentees or by their mentees' peer groups. It would also be a helpful discussion tool for use by administrators in mentor training or for the mentors and mentees themselves as a mutual discussion tool.

Shehyn, A. (2000). *Picture the girl: Young women speak their minds.* New York: Hyperion. ISBN 078688567X (128 pages, paperback).

This book is a collection of 35 profiles of young women, ages 14 to 19, who speak out about their lives, their expectations, and their beliefs. The book helps the reader—adult or adolescent—to get into the mindset of developing young females and can be a powerful discussion tool for a mentor-mentee discussion. Reader alert: The language used is brash and at times colorful and is not appropriate for young children.

Singer, M. (Ed.). (1999). *Stay true: Short stories for strong girls* (Reprint ed.). New York: Scholastic Paperbacks. ISBN 0590360337 (208 pages, paperback).

Stories of young women finding their own inner strength are highlighted in this collection of 11 short stories. Outlining what it takes to develop a strong and unique personality, the wildly differing situations and challenges presented in these stories contain a common theme of young girls finding their own voice. The book is recommended as a discussion tool, with adolescent mentees and adult mentors engaging in a thoughtful conversation about the struggles of discovering and exposing one's true self.

Wiltshire, S. F. (1998). *Athena's disguises: Mentors in everyday life.* Louisville, KY: Westminster John Knox Press. ISBN 0664221017 (176 pages, hardcover).

Although targeted to adult women, this book would also be of interest to adolescent girls and young women. The author discusses how females develop and flourish, considering the unique role of mentors in this process. She considers the important role of natural mentors as well as spontaneous connections with special people who will significantly impact development. The author illustrates key points with examples from her own experience.

Resource Books Related to Supporting Boys and Young Men

Davis, H. (1998). *Leader's guide for talks my father never had with me: Helping the young black male make it to adulthood* (2nd ed.). Champagne, IL: KJAC. ISBN 0963855328 (256 pages, paperback).

The purpose of this faith-based text is to provide mentors of African American young men with instructions for establishing mentoring programs in churches and other organizations. The text includes sample forms and conversation stimulators based on questions and passages from Scripture. The guide also includes the complete student text, which aims to provide young men with the perspective that aided their forefathers in overcoming great obstacles. The advice given in the student text is based on the Bible, common sense, and the rich African American heritage.

Glennon, W., Elium, J., & Elium, D. (2000). *200 ways to raise a boy's emotional intelligence: An indispensable guide for parents, teachers, and other concerned caregivers.* Berkeley, CA: Conari Press. ISBN 1573240206 (272 pages, paperback).

This book is a practical resource for helping young boys and adolescent males develop into emotionally and mentally healthy men. Each of the chapters contains activities that may be used by mentors at school in a mentoring capacity or by parents at home with their children. Focusing on ways to avoid the typically evolved stoicism of young men in our society, the book offers the reader realistic approaches to cultivate positive, healthy attitudes and responses in the developing adolescent. This is an excellent resource for mentors desiring to model appropriate communication skills and emotionality to their male mentees.

Gurian, M. (1997). *The wonder of boys: What parents, mentors, and educators can do to shape boys into exceptional men.* New York: Tarcher/Putnam. ISBN 0874778875 (294 pages, paperback).

Taking a practical approach to the developmental support boys need to grow into healthy men, Gurian offers guidelines for channeling boys' natural tendencies for competition and aggression into positive areas for growth. Maintaining that boys are at high risk for gang involvement, sexual misconduct, and crime if they are not provided appropriate role models and support, the author proposes that what boys need most of all is a primary and an extended family, including mentors. This work is a useful tool for both mentors and mentees, as well as for the families and teachers of boys and young men.

Gurian, M. (1999). *A fine young man: What parents, mentors, and educators can do to shape adolescent boys into exceptional men.* New York: Tarcher/Putnam. ISBN 0874779693 (297 pages, paperback).

This work examines the needs of adolescent boys as a key at-risk group, focusing on the problems and positive attributes of boys ages 10 to 20 and considering the impact of both nature and nurture. The book also addresses ways adults can help this group.

Kindlon, D. J., & Thompson, M. (2000). *Raising Cain: Protecting the emotional life of boys.* New York: Ballantine. ISBN 0345434854 (298 pages, paperback).

This book focuses on the authors' views of the way masculinity is understood in our current society, which defines "being male" in a narrow and emotionally illiterate manner. Citing the current thrust for boys to be "tough" and our current "culture of cruelty," the authors call for a better understanding of what boys need in order to grow and develop mentally, physically, and spiritually. A seven-point list of "What Boys Need" clearly outlines the steps to understanding boys and young men and to the development of emotional literacy among male youth. Identifying the social and emotional challenges that boys encounter in school can show parents, teachers, and mentors how to help boys develop the empathy and emotional awareness needed to plot a course through the social pressures related to growing up. The book is seen as an excellent resource tool for mentoring programs.

Pollack, W. S. (1999). *Real boys: Rescuing our sons from the myths of boyhood.* New York: Owl Books. ISBN 0805061835 (480 pages, paperback).

This book draws on 20 years of research on young men in our society, including research on the ways boys manifest their "social and emotional disconnectedness" through violence and anger. Core focus is placed on an unspoken "boy code" that influences how boys act (and are allowed to act) and demands that boys cover up their emotions. In addition to outlining the problems that boys and male adolescents face, as well as the background behind those problems, the author offers solid advice on supporting boys as they transition from child to adolescent to adult. The information and advice in the text may be used by parents, teachers, and mentors in their work with and support for youths. The book highlights ways to effectively help boys first interpret their own moods and emotions and then learn to respond appropriately.

Pollack, W. S., & Shuster, T. (2001). *Real boys' voices.* New York: Penguin Books USA. ISBN 0141002948 (392 pages, paperback).

This book is a follow-up to the author's *Real Boys: Rescuing Our Sons from the Myths of Boyhood.* In this volume the voices of boys are heard through their compelling, candid recollections of what it is like to "grow up male" in America. Citing the pressures and problems of modern male adolescence, the book contains practical advice on how to respond to challenges such as bullying, depression, friends, peer pressure, and communication. The book is recommended both for adolescent males and for the adults in their lives. It is especially suited for those working with young males and boys in a support situation, be it parenting, mentoring, coaching, or ministerial support.

Silverstein, O., & Rashbaum, B. (1995). *The courage to raise good men: You don't have to sever the bond with your son to help him become a man* (Reprint ed.). New York: Penguin USA. ISBN: 0140175679 (244 pages, paperback).

Written specifically for parents of sons, this book is also a helpful resource for mentors of boys and youth. Questioning the traditional manner in which boys are raised and the societal expectations for boys and youth, the author calls for a holistic or "wholeness" approach to the development of the child, including the development of healthy emotional expression.

Thompson, M., & Barker, T. (2000). *Speaking of boys: Answers to the most-asked questions about raising sons.* New York: Ballantine. ISBN 0345441486 (288 pages, paperback).

Written specifically for the parents of boys, this text is an excellent resource for mentors and mentoring programs as it addresses a myriad of situations that arise for young boys, including many of the challenges arising in school or during other peer-interactive times. Chapters focus on one general topic area developed from a question, such as "Feelings and Communication: Is Our Sensitive Boy a Sitting Duck for Bullies?" that offer insight into the background of the featured topic, along with methods of prevention and strategies for intervention when needed. Mentors, especially those working with the parents of the mentee, will find this a valuable resource.

Resource Books for Mentors and Protégés/Mentees

The Abell Foundation. (1991). *The two of us: A handbook for mentors.* Baltimore, MD: Author. ISBN N/A (214 pages).

This handbook is designed to guide individual mentors in getting the most out of their mentoring relationships—whatever the focus of the relationship, from developing a friendship, to role modeling, to achieving academic goals. The activities in the handbook were developed for one-on-one mentoring between an adult and a young person ages 8 to 18 but can be adapted for group mentoring, peer mentoring, and other models. The handbook contains specific activities and ideas organized around seven themes, including health, fitness, and general well-being; improving academic skills and performance; exploring and improving self-esteem; and combining fun and learning with opportunities to get to know one another.

Benson, P. L., Galbraith, J., & Espeland, P. (1998). *What kids need to succeed: Proven, practical ways to raise good kids* (Rev., exp., and upd. ed.). Minneapolis, MN: Free Spirit. ISBN 1575420309 (256 pages, paperback).

Revised and updated, this award-winning book covers 40 developmental assets critical to fostering positive youth development and preventing at-risk behavior. The book also covers contemporary information on asset building, while offering concrete suggestions for promoting the 40 developmental assets in a variety of contexts, including home, school, community, and congregation. A Spanish language version of this book is also available.

Clinton, H. R. (1996). *It takes a village: And other lessons children teach us.* New York: Simon & Schuster. ISBN 0684825457 (336 pages, paperback).

Addressing the changed landscape of family life, the author challenges society to search the past for resurrectable structures to support children as they grow and develop. The book is based on the belief that how a child develops and what a child needs to succeed is intensely linked with the society in which the child lives and how well that society sustains and supports children, families, and individuals. How to make our society into the kind of "village" that enables all children to grow into competent, resilient, caring adults is the thrust of this work. An excellent resource for mentoring organizations seeking community and corporate support, the book substantiates the purpose and meaning behind the mentoring of youth and children. Mentors, in effect, become an important part of that village of support.

Cuomo, M. R. (Ed.). (1999). *The person who changed my life: Prominent Americans recall their mentors.* Secaucus, NJ: Carol Publishing Group. ISBN 1559725087 (256 pages, hardcover).

Seventy-five contributors tell stories of the caring adult mentors who made profound differences in their lives in this collection of essays written by individuals who have distinguished themselves in professional fields. Contributors include Walter Cronkite, Marian Wright Edelman, Gloria Estefan, and Larry King, among others. Beginning with the introduction, in which the author describes mentoring and details how to develop a mentoring program in a local community and how to become a mentor, the book is an essential mentoring resource. Informative and heartfelt, the chapters will inspire adults to get involved by becoming positive role models to children in need of extra support.

Edelman, M. W. (2000). *Lanterns: A memoir of mentors.* New York: HarperCollins. ISBN 0060958596 (180 pages, paperback).

In this book, child advocate Marian Wright Edelman offers a tribute to the mentors who guided her life's journey. In addition to the famous names (such as Martin Luther King Jr., Robert F. Kennedy, Fannie Lou Hamer, and William Sloane Coffin) are ordinary citizens who provided love, guidance, inspiration, and support during her youth.

Gaetano, R. J., Grout, J., & Klassen-Landis, M. (1994). *Please talk with me: A guide to teen-adult dialogue.* Dubuque, IA: Kendall/Hunt. ISBN 0840364881 (96 pages, spiral-bound).

This book focuses on opening and sustaining conversation and communication between teens and adults, be the adult a parent, teacher, mentor, or family friend. It dispels the myth that adolescents do not want to communicate with adults and offers practical solutions to initiating and sustaining communication across the ages.

Galbraith, J. (1998). *The gifted kids' survival guide for ages 10 and under* (Rev. and upd. ed.). Minneapolis, MN: Free Spirit. ISBN 1575420538 (88 pages, paperback).

This revised, updated version of a classic book provides valuable information on intelligence and "giftedness" for young people. The information provided is based on contemporary surveys of gifted children and offers various how-to tips for gifted young people, covering areas such as coping with high expectations and making friends.

Galbraith, J., & Delisle, J. (1996). *The gifted kids' survival guide: A teen handbook* (Rev., exp., and upd. ed.). Minneapolis, MN: Free Spirit. ISBN 1575420031 (304 pages, paperback).

Targeted to youth ages 11 to 18, but also useful for the adults in their lives, this book came about with the assistance of hundreds of gifted teenagers. In addition to providing information on concepts such as intelligence and giftedness, the book also includes topics related to promoting healthy functioning, including positive relationship building. The current version of this publication reflects a recent revision and update to the popular 1987 edition.

Gershen, K., Raphael, L., & Espeland, L. (1999). *Stick up for yourself! Every kid's guide to personal power and positive self-esteem* (Rev. and upd. ed.). Minneapolis, MN: Free Spirit. ISBN 1575420686 (128 pages, paperback).

An excellent resource for both mentees and mentors (as well as a tool for mutual discussion), this book presents an in-depth view of many problems faced by young people as they make choices, learn about themselves and discover who they are, accept and appreciate themselves, and solve problems in life. It is seen as a self-help guide to positive thinking and responsible personal power and behavior, and it supports commonly held goals in mentoring relationships.

Greene, R. (2000). *The teenagers' guide to school outside the box* (1st ed.). Minneapolis, MN: Free Spirit. ISBN 1575420872 (272 pages, paperback).

This innovative guide to alternative learning is useful for teens as well as school guidance and career personnel. The book covers topics such as internships, apprenticeships, networking, job shadowing, and service learning, and includes specific suggestions for finding opportunities, selecting alternative learning approaches, and accessing these opportunities.

Hendricks, W. (1998). *Intensive caring: Practical ways to mentor youth.* Loveland, CO: Group Publishing. ISBN 0764420682 (112 pages, paperback).

This book is a practical guide to implementing a youth mentoring program. The book includes practical mentoring suggestions and descriptions of actual church-based programs.

Kanfer, F. H., Englund, S., Lennhoff, C., & Rhodes, J. (1995). *A mentor manual: For adults who work with pregnant and parenting teens.* Washington, DC: Child Welfare League of America. ISBN 0878685804 (136 pages, hardcover).

This concrete and user-friendly manual provides an overview of the changes and challenges facing pregnant adolescents and offers mentors tips on helping the pregnant/parenting teen through this transition. Discussed are ways to help the mentored teen build self-confidence and self-reliance. This work outlines key lessons regarding the development and maintenance of the mentor-mentee relationship and highlights skills for effective mentoring. Included are fact sheets with useful information related to pregnancy and parenting.

Kouri, M. K. (1990). *Volunteerism and older adults.* Santa Barbara, CA: ABC-Clio. ISBN 0874365627 (197 pages).

Part of Choices and Challenges: An Older Adult Reference Series, this book offers an overview of volunteerism, with a focus on providing older adults interested in volunteering with direction in locating volunteer placements that best meet their needs. This publication includes an overview of the types of volunteer activities available, information on finding volunteer opportunities that are suitable to the volunteer's needs and interests, and suggestions for volunteer directors, as well as an extensive resource guide that includes a directory of organizations, associations, and agencies, and print and nonprint resources. Although currently out of print, this useful book may be obtained through online used book sources such as Amazon (www.amazon.com) or Powell's Bookstore (www.powells.com).

Larson, S., & Brendtro, L. K. (2000). *Reclaiming our prodigal sons and daughters: A practical approach for connecting with youth in conflict.* Bloomington, IN: National Education Service. ISBN 1879639696 (250 pages, paperback).

A faith-based resource that focuses on connecting caring, healthy adults with children and youth in need of support, this book offers practical information based on 60 years of research and experience working with at-risk youth. The text's compelling plan for reconnecting with troubled youth convinced the National Education Service to publish this work, its first faith-based publication ever. Real-life stories are blended with practical solutions based on the experiences and wisdom of historical figures from both the youth development field and from the Bible. In addition to mentors, the book will be especially helpful to teachers, coaches, and foster care providers.

Nelson, F. W. (2000). *TalkPoints: Conversation starters for youth and adults in mentoring relationships.* Woodbury, MN: TalkTrips. ISBN N/A (48 pages).

This workbook, developed in collaboration with the Mentoring Partnership of Minnesota, contains 10 "talksheets" designed to encourage conversation between adult and youth in mentor/mentee partnerships. The reproducible activity sheets come in pairs, one for the mentor and one for the mentee.

Norwalk Mentor Program (1995). *Mirror, Mirror on the Wall, Who is the Greatest One of All?* Norwalk, CT: Author. ISBN N/A (48 pages).

This is a workbook for mentors and mentees and students in grades kindergarten through 6. Self-esteem building activities and exercises focus on such topics as the school scene, favorite things, high hopes, friends, wishes, and steps to success. Mentors can follow in some of the areas along with the mentees.

Parks, S. D. (2000). *Big questions, worthy dreams: Mentoring young adults in their search for meaning, purpose, and faith.* San Francisco: Jossey-Bass. ISBN 0787941719 (288 pages, hardcover).

Targeted toward help professionals, educators, community leaders, and parents, this book examines the unique challenges of young adulthood and how, through mentoring, concerned adults can help the next generation in this transition. The author integrates her own research, along with wisdom from developmental psychology, religion, theology, leadership, and ethics. She also stresses the key role of mentoring in promoting positive aspirations in young adults, as well as in creating citizenship and leadership essential to the twenty-first century.

Phillips-Jones, L. (2001). *The new mentors and protégés: How to succeed with the new mentoring partnerships.* Grass Valley, CA: Coalition of Counseling Centers. ISBN 1890608009 (250 pages, paperback).

This update of the 1982 publication *Mentors and Protégés* emphasizes mentoring from a career development perspective. The author elaborates on how mentoring may be useful for the career advancement of the mentee, as well as providing benefits to the mentor. The book outlines the role mentors play and identifies important factors in finding the right mentor, while examining key elements of and potential problems in the mentor-protégé relationship. Although this book appears targeted to adults, it provides information that may be useful to adolescents seeking mentors. The Coalition of Counseling Centers publishes Phillips-Jones's other mentoring works, which are also geared toward the adult professional mentoring relationship: *The Mentee's Guide: How to Have a Successful Relationship with a Mentor; The Mentor's Guide: How to Be the Kind of Mentor You Once Had or Wish You'd Had; The Mentoring Program Coordinator's Guide: How to Plan and Conduct a Successful Mentoring Program.*

Shore, B. (2001). *The cathedral within: Transforming your life by giving something back.* New York: Random House. ISBN 0375758291 (320 pages, paperback).

Through the metaphor of architecture, the author examines the way individuals allocate their resources to improve public life. The founder of Share Our Strength, a national nonprofit devoted to raising funds for antihunger and antipoverty organizations worldwide, the author showcases through stories some of the social entrepreneurs he has come across in the course of his work.

Smith, R., & Grayer, J. (1999). *How to be a great mentor.* New York: Newsweek (special issue). Order by calling 1-800-272-8306 or 703-803-8171, order #210; $5.95 plus shipping, bulk discount available. Ordering information may also be found at www.mentoring.org (the National Mentoring Partnership Web site).

A practical guide to making mentoring work, this *Newsweek* special edition is a combined effort of *Newsweek* magazine, Kaplan Educational Centers, and the National Mentoring Partnership. The guide is replete with stories of successful mentoring relationships, including those of notables such as author John Updike and sports hero Grant Hill. It is an interestingly written, practical guide outlining the how, the why, and the where of getting started as a mentor. Topics covered include mentor training, tips on effective mentor behavior, methods for connecting with appropriate mentoring programs, and inspirational stories.

Sommer, R. B. (Ed.). (1998). *Inspiring others to win.* Torrance, CA: Griffin. ISBN 1882180941 (192 pages, paperback).

This book is a compilation of inspiring stories by people who have overcome challenges and have succeeded in their dreams. It also includes the stories of those mentors who inspired them. The stories of contributors, who include athletes, business leaders, media personalities, educators, and other high achievers, offer inspiration as well as useful strategies for leading and motivating people to accomplish their aspirations. This book is appropriate for mentors, teachers, managers, and parents.

Spoden, J. (Ed.). (1999). *To honor a teacher: Students pay tribute to their most influential mentors.* Kansas City, MO: Andrews McMeel. ISBN 0740700510 (256 pages, hardcover).

This work is a collection of narratives focused on the teacher as mentor. The stories highlight the mentoring role teachers may play. Stories in this book are organized according to the concepts of the teacher as healer, thinker, sage, maestro, dancer (inspiration), believer, guide, and torchbearer.

Stanley, P. D., & Clinton, R. J. (1992). *Connecting: The mentoring relationships you need to succeed in life.* Colorado Springs, CO: Navpress. ISBN: 0891096388 (252 pages, paperback).

For those interested in faith-based Christian-oriented mentoring, this book explores ways to connect with others for healthy development and fulfillment.

Weinberger, S. G. (1992). *The Mentor Handbook* (2nd ed.). Norwalk, CT: Educational Resources Network. ISBN 096231614 (32 pages).

This guide is for adult volunteers, sponsoring companies and organizations, and schools involved in a one-to-one mentor/student support program. The ideas in this guide are based on the mentor program in Norwalk, Connecticut, which began in 1986 as a partnership between an elementary school and a local company, and expanded throughout the Norwalk area in subsequent years. The handbook is filled with practical information, including how to start, implement, and evaluate a mentor program; tips for working with elementary school–aged children; and mentor roles and responsibilities. Nine sample forms are also provided. This publication can be ordered from Educational Resources Network, Inc., 18 Marshall Street, Norwalk, CT 06854.

Wynn, M. (1994). *Building dreams: Teacher, parent, mentor workbook.* Marietta, GA: Rising Sun. ISBN 1880463423 (125 pages).

This work offers an extensive array of mentoring-related exercises organized around the ideas of developing a dream, setting goals, formulating an action plan, and taking self-directed steps toward achieving one's vision. Exercises are tailored to either the needs of the mentor or those of the protégé/student. This workbook is part of the Building Dreams: Helping Students Discover Their Potential program, which includes a companion book, audiotape set, and poster series. The materials may be purchased at www.rspublishing.com.

Zachary, L. (2000). *The mentor's guide: Facilitating effective learning relationships.* San Francisco: Jossey-Bass. ISBN 0787947423 (224 pages, paperback).

The author clearly details the journey of the mentoring process, illustrating concepts using examples and metaphors. She offers insights on relationship building and demarcates classical models of mentoring from more contemporary views of mentoring as a partnership. The book combines discussion and workbook-like elements to support those who are in the process of facilitating learning in mentoring relationships. Building strategies, examples, and exercises into the text, the author emphasizes "facilitating effective learning relationships." Easy to read and with compelling vignettes, the book is inspiring as well as educational.

Print Materials Offering Programmatic Information

Avani, N. (1998). *Mentoring works! Peer helping program for middle and high school students.* Plainview, NY: The Bureau for At-Risk Youth. ISBN 1566884403 (94 pages, paperback).

This book presents a comprehensive peer helping program for middle and high school students using the programmatic structure of cross-age peer helping and mentoring. This curriculum entails a four-part program designed to assist peer mentors and their mentees in achieving greater self-awareness, self-confidence, trust, and decision-making skills. The program addresses the following skills: values identification, goal setting, critical thinking, and problem solving and communication skills. Supporting materials (available separately) are a facilitator's guide, a student workbook, Mentoring and You handouts, and Mentoring Works! posters.

Balcazar, F. E., & Fawcett, S. B. (1992). *Recruiting mentors and potential helpers.* Lawrence, KS: University of Kansas Press.

This is a workbook-style manual that comes in two volumes. Volume I challenges the reader to select personal goals and provides strategies for identifying possible helpers and mentors. Volume II provides information on building relationships with potential mentors. The manual includes information regarding specific skills, as well as exercises and study guides. Although targeted at individuals with disabilities, the exercises and information may be useful for mentoring programs focusing on other populations.

Creative Mentoring. (2000). *Creating an effective youth mentoring program: A technical assistance manual.* Wilmington, DE: Author. ISBN N/A (70 pages).

This technical assistance manual addresses the all-important issue of program infrastructure. The manual's purpose is to walk the program designer (the principal in an in-school program) and the day-to-day program coordinator (usually a counselor in a school setting) through virtually every aspect of program design and implementation via a series of thought-provoking questions and checklists to assure that all bases have been covered. Multiple examples of forms that various mentoring programs use are also included. This workbook/manual comes in a half-inch three-ring binder and can be ordered from the organization's Web site (www.creativementoring.org).

Creative Mentoring. (2001). *Elements of effective mentoring: A mentor training manual.* Wilmington, DE: Author. ISBN N/A (214 pages).

This mentor training manual includes not only important lessons for the mentor, but also many suggested activities in a variety of areas for different grade levels. A 1998 Athena Award winner for Best Complete Set of Mentor Training Materials Produced by a Non-Profit, *Elements of Effective Mentoring* stresses the Creative Mentoring process: how to build higher purpose into all mentoring activities, the foundations of unconditional love/acceptance, mentoring in the present moment, appropriate and inappropriate roles for mentors, and teaching universal values. Other topics include building the relationship; listening and communication skills; self-esteem building; tips on providing academic support; tutoring guides for reading, language arts, and math; special activities for K–3 students; and a journal for mentors. This publication comes in a one-inch three-ring binder. The Creative Mentoring Web site (www. creativementoring.org) contains ordering information. Volume discounts are available.

Dare Mighty Things. (2000). *A MentorActive approach to reclaiming youth at risk.* Bloomington, IN: National Educational Service. ISBN 1879639742 (28 pages).

These packs of 10 mentor's guides complement A MentorActive Approach to Reclaiming Youth at Risk training sessions. The group authoring this publication works with organizations seeking to start self-sustaining initiatives aimed at helping high-risk youth and adults. These materials may be purchased at www.nesonline.com.

Ellis, S. J. (1996). *The volunteer recruitment and membership development book* (2nd ed.). Philadelphia: Energize Books. ISBN 094057618X (152 pages).

This publication offers practical solutions to the problem of recruiting volunteers and includes a discussion of how organizational image can impact the recruitment process. The book contains a vast array of suggestions and recommendations on the subject of the recruitment and retention of volunteer workers.

Garringer, M., Fulop, M., & Rennick, V. (2003). *Foundations of successful youth mentoring: A Guidebook for program development.* Portland, OR: Northwest Regional Educational Library. ISBN: N/A (110 pages).

Foundations of Successful Youth Mentoring: A Guidebook for Program Development is aimed at helping both new and established mentoring programs, whether they be community-based, school-based, or faith-based. The book synthesizes information gleaned from a comprehensive literature review related to youth mentoring, as well as results of the national evaluation of Juvenile Mentoring Program (JUMP) grantees and the National Mentoring Center's own experience as a technical assistance provider. The guidebook outlines the essential components for successful and sustainable mentoring programs. In addition to an overview of each program component, the guidebook includes self-assessment questions designed to help foster thorough consideration of issues related to program design and implementation, and recommended resources that can assist in the planning and growth of the program. Print copies can be ordered from the NWREL Marketing Office at 1-800-547-6339 x-519 or through the NWREL online catalog.

Graff, L. L. (1997). *By definition: Policies for volunteer programs: A manual for executive directors, board members, and managers of volunteers* (2nd ed.). Philadelphia: Energize Books. ISBN 0968476007 (91 pages, spiral-bound).

This publication, geared toward agency-based volunteer programs, examines the importance of making policies regarding volunteers, and shares general and specific policies for volunteer programs. It also includes seven steps to help program leaders design their own policies. This book is applicable to any agency-based volunteer program.

Graff, L. L. (1999). *Beyond police checks: The definitive volunteer and employee screening guidebook.* Philadelphia: Energize Books. ISBN 0968476015 (150 pages, paperback).

This comprehensive guidebook offers explicit tips for enhancing screening effectiveness and program safety. The book includes practical suggestions as well as reproducible checklists and assessment tools. Oriented toward volunteer programs in general, the book also discusses how to match screening methods to the requirements of the program and particular position.

Henderson, N., Benard, B., & Sharp-Light, N. (Eds.). (2000). *Mentoring for resiliency: Setting up programs for moving youth from "stressed to success."* San Diego, CA: Resiliency in Action. ISBN 0966939417 (88 pages, paperback).

This collection contains articles previously published in the journal *Resiliency in Action* and is an excellent resource for anyone looking for inspiration about meeting the needs of at-risk youth or seeking an overview of youth mentoring approaches in general. Chapters by Bonnie Benard and Marc Freedman are highlighted, along with other notable figures in the youth mentoring movement. The power of the relationship between youth and their mentors is emphasized. Practical strategies for setting up youth support mentoring connections are featured. The book may be ordered at www.resiliency.com.

Herrera, C. (1999). *School-based mentoring: A first look into its potential.* Philadelphia: Public/Private Ventures. ISBN N/A (20 pages).

This report examines the strengths, challenges, and possible benefits of school-based mentoring. It includes an overview of two model programs. The report may be ordered or downloaded at www.ppv.org.

Herrera, C., Sipe, C. L., McClanahan, W. S., Arbreton, A. J. A., & Pepper, S. K. (2000). *Mentoring school-age children: Relationship development in community-based and school-based programs.* Philadelphia: Public/Private Ventures. ISBN N/A (48 pages).

This report draws on interviews of more than 600 mentors, examining their experiences as mentors. It includes discussion of the mentors' views of the process of developing a relationship with a mentee, as well as an overview of factors related to successful relationships. The report may be ordered or downloaded at www.ppv.org.

Jucovy, L. (2000). *The ABCs of school-based mentoring* (Technical Assistance Packet #1). Portland, OR: Northwest Regional Educational Laboratory. ISBN N/A (54 pages).

The first of several joint ventures between Public/Private Ventures, Big Brothers Big Sisters of America, and the Office of Juvenile Justice and Delinquency Prevention, this technical assistance packet covers school-based mentoring. The packet includes valuable information on partnering with a school. The packet also includes strategies for mentor recruiting, screening, orientation, and training. Various resources are provided, including a wide array of sample forms and mentoring program worksheets.

Jucovy, L. (2000). *Mentoring sexual minority youth* (Technical Assistance Packet #2). Portland, OR: Northwest Regional Educational Laboratory. ISBN N/A (46 pages).

This National Mentoring Center technical assistance packet was completed in a joint venture between Public/Private Ventures, Big Brothers Big Sisters of America, the National Youth Advocacy Coalition, and the Office of Juvenile Justice and Delinquency Prevention. It provides practical advice for mentoring sexual minority youth. The packet reviews issues confronting sexual minority youth and strategies for making organizations safe for this population. Training issues are covered and valuable resources provided. As with other National Mentoring Center technical assistance packets, this publication can be downloaded from the Public/Private Ventures Web site (www.ppv.org).

Jucovy, L. (2001). *Building relationships: A guide for new mentors* (Technical Assistance Packet #4). Portland, OR: Northwest Regional Educational Laboratory. ISBN N/A (43 pages).

This National Mentoring Center technical assistance packet was completed in a joint venture between Public/Private Ventures, Big Brothers

Big Sisters of America, and the Office of Juvenile Justice and Delinquency Prevention. This research-based publication offers an overview of essential relationship-building skills and issues, as well as useful questions for mentors to consider. As with other National Mentoring Center technical assistance packets, this publication can be downloaded from the Public/Private Ventures Web site (www.ppv.org).

Jucovy, L. (2001). *Recruiting mentors: A guide to finding volunteers to work with youth* (Technical Assistance Packet #3). Portland, OR: Northwest Regional Educational Laboratory. ISBN N/A (50 pages).

This National Mentoring Center technical assistance packet was completed in a joint venture between Public/Private Ventures, Big Brothers Big Sisters of America, and the Office of Juvenile Justice and Delinquency Prevention. It provides practical advice for developing a recruitment plan and information on recruiting particular populations. The publication provides resources and sample forms. As with other National Mentoring Center technical assistance packets, this publication can be downloaded from the Public/Private Ventures Web site (www.ppv.org).

Jucovy, L. (2001). *Supporting mentors* (Technical Assistance Packet #6). Portland, OR: Northwest Regional Educational Laboratory. ISBN N/A (30 pages).

Completed in a joint venture between Public/Private Ventures, Big Brothers Big Sisters of America, and the Office of Juvenile Justice and Delinquency Prevention, this technical assistance packet covers issues related to supporting mentors. Topics covered include monitoring the mentoring relationship, training, and support. The publication also contains additional resources and useful checklists. As with other National Mentoring Center technical assistance packets, this publication can be downloaded from the Public/Private Ventures Web site (www.ppv.org).

Jucovy, L. (2001). *Training new mentors* (Technical Assistance Packet #5). Portland, OR: Northwest Regional Educational Laboratory. ISBN N/A (56 pages).

Another joint venture between Public/Private Ventures, Big Brothers Big Sisters of America, and the Office of Juvenile Justice and Delinquency Prevention, this technical assistance packet covers issues related to mentor training. The publication contains concrete tips for trainers, as well as useful training activities. As with other National Mentoring Center technical assistance packets, this publication can be downloaded from the Public/Private Ventures Web site (www.ppv.org).

Keim, N., & Tolliver, C. (1993). *Tutoring and mentoring: Starting a peer helping program in your elementary school.* San Jose, CA: Resource Publications. ISBN 0893902594 (152 pages, paperback).

Guiding the reader through the mechanics of developing and implementing a peer tutoring and/or mentoring program in an elementary school, this book begins with an overview of the concept of peer helping and its differentiation from mentoring. The book contains stories of success and an elaboration on what makes peer helping successful. Planning and customizing the school's program and establishing an effective system of in-school communication are the main focuses of the text. More than 20 reproducible forms are located in the appendixes, including parent permission forms, peer helper application forms, agendas for training sessions, and the like.

Lacey, K. (2000). *Making mentoring happen: A simple and effective guide to implementing a successful mentoring program.* Warriewood, N.S.W, Australia: Business and Professional Publishing. ISBN 1875680683 (123 pages, paperback).

This guide is aimed primarily at the business community but incorporates many strategies and practical ideas applicable to all mentoring programs, as well as a straightforward explanation of mentoring and why it has become so important to many successful organizations. The characteristics of an effective program are analyzed, with the aim of helping programs meet the specific needs of an organization. The book includes easy-to-follow training activities, advice on building mentoring relationships, and potential pitfalls.

Malderez, A., & Bodóczky, C. (1999). *Mentor courses: A resource book for trainer-trainers.* New York: Cambridge University Press. ISBN 0521566908 (232 pages, paperback).

This resource book provides an array of activities for use in mentor-based teacher training. Although targeted toward the mentoring of student teachers, individuals working in mentoring programs for youth will find the collection of activities interesting and useful in their work with youth and children. Many of the resource book activities can be adapted for mentoring work with a younger population. This book is suitable for all individuals involved in the training of mentors.

McCurley, S. H., & Vineyard, S. (1998). *Handling problem volunteers.* Downer's Grove, IL: Heritage Arts. ISBN 0911029478 (60 pages, paperback).

This publication addresses the concern of managing problematic volunteers. Targeted to a wide variety of volunteer-based programs, the authors provide information on discerning true problems and their possible causes. The book includes advice regarding managing differences, resolving impasses, redirecting good intentions, dealing with disruptions, and firing volunteers, as well as managing conflict and legal actions. Suggestions on how to work with the mildly problematic volunteer (such as the merely annoying person) as well as with the most severely dysfunctional volunteer are provided.

National Association of Partners in Education (1992). *Organizing effective school-based mentoring programs.* Alexandria, VA: Author. ISBN N/A (140 pages).

This manual, produced by the National Association of Partners in Education, helps schools and their community partners set up mentoring programs to connect adults with students identified by their schools as likely to benefit from mentoring relationships. Based on the experiences of school districts that have successfully launched and maintained mentoring programs, the manual includes steps for planning and implementing programs and a comprehensive index with numerous handouts and examples from existing programs. This publication can be ordered through the organization's Web site (www.napehq.org).

National Black Child Development Institute (1996). *The spirit of excellence: A manual for mentoring and tutoring African-American children and youth.* Washington, DC: Author. ISBN N/A (14 pages).

This manual, a cooperative effort of the National Black Child Development Institute and One to One, is designed to aid volunteers who work with African American children and youth. The guide provides information on child development, discipline, encouragement, and building self-esteem, as well as practical skills for tutoring. A suggested reading list for children of various age groups is included.

National Mentoring Partnership. *Team Mentoring Guide.* Washington, DC: Author. ISBN N/A.

School-based team mentoring matches a group of three adults—a teacher or administrator from the school, a college student, and a community or business volunteer—with a group of 10 to 12 middle school students. Throughout the school year, youths and adults participate in leadership training, field trips, volunteer community service, and ongoing team and one-on-one mentoring. Team mentoring is the brainchild of two high school students who saw the value in mentoring but felt that kids relate better in groups. It was launched in the 1992–93 academic year at Horace Mann Middle School in South Central Los Angeles and currently serves 900 students in six Los Angeles middle schools. This manual gives schools and businesses everything they need to start a team mentoring program.

Police/Youth Mentoring Program. (1996). *Police and youth "looking to the future": Executive summary of the final report of the Pilot Project Police/Youth Mentoring Program.* ASIN 0662214617 (18 pages).

A replicable youth mentoring program is highlighted in this work that captures the spirit of a pilot project developed by a Canadian police department that matched police officer mentors with high school students. The small study set as its goals to develop tolerance, mutual respect, cooperation, and appreciation between police and youth and to increase the awareness of career opportunities in police service. Currently out of print, the summary of the results of the Police/Youth Mentoring Project in Kingston, Ontario, may be secured by contacting the Policing Division, 340 Laurier Avenue, Ottawa LIA OP8, Canada.

Portner, H. (2001). *Training mentors is not enough: Everything else schools and districts need to do.* Thousand Oaks, CA: Corwin Press. ISBN 0761977384 (120 pages, paperback).

This book was written for the educational leader interested in developing or improving an exemplary mentoring program for his or her school site. Intended as a how-to guide for mentoring program implementers, a reference guide for administrators, and a supplemental text for advanced training or graduate education purposes in the area of mentoring, this work commits itself to the "validation, support, and celebration" of all facets of the mentor-mentee relationship. Focused on the mentoring of new teachers, the volume is replicable in the development of a similar program for children and youth. Each of the book's nine chapters highlights an essential element of an exemplary mentoring program: commitment to mentoring, development of an implementation committee, systems and climates, roles and responsibilities, policies and procedures, professional development, evaluation, related programs, and the planning and management guide.

Reglin, G. (1998). *Mentoring students at-risk: An underutilized alternative education strategy for K–12 teachers.* Springfield, IL: Charles C. Thomas. ISBN 039806833X (93 pages, paperback).

The book addresses issues of school restructuring, with an emphasis on alternative education programs. Offering an in-depth description of key components of alternative education, the author addresses how two programs, the Truancy Court Conference Program and the Mentoring and Tutoring Help Program, increase student investment in school. Significant components of the Mentoring and Tutoring Help Program are reviewed, including concrete tips for implementing such a program. The volume is well documented, with more than 50 research projects. It also includes an extensive bibliography for teachers and administrators working in at-risk student support programs.

Reilly, J. M. (1992). *Mentorship: The essential guide for schools and business.* Scottsdale, AZ: Gifted Psychology Press. ISBN 0910707189 (278 pages, paperback).

This book describes how to establish a highly successful mentoring program. It presents an in-depth analysis of the efforts of mentoring interventions (called mentorship) on high school students, high school staff, and the schools themselves, as well as on the mentors and their respective businesses. Honored as an exemplary school-to-work model, the mentorship model illustrated how many students work best in a career mentoring situation, either as an addition to the traditional school schedule or as an alternative school experience. The book includes criteria and replicable sample forms for developing a career-focused mentoring program.

Sipe, C. L., & Roder, A. E. (1999). *Mentoring school-age children: A classification of programs.* Philadelphia: Public/Private Ventures. ISBN N/A (50 pages).

This report examines mentor programs serving school-aged youth, looking at characteristics such as goals and activities as well as various types of relationships.

Smink, J. (1999). *A training guide for mentors.* Clemson, SC: National Dropout Prevention Center. ISBN N/A (70 pages).

This publication of the National Dropout Prevention Center provides program planners and coordinators useful information on conducting a comprehensive training program for adults and young people volunteering to be mentors. Copies can be ordered from the Web site at www.dropoutprevention.org.

Stromei, L. K., & Phillips, J. J. (Eds.). (2001). *In action: Creating mentoring and coaching programs.* Alexandria, VA: American Society for Training and Development. ISBN 1562862847 (195 pages, paperback).

Designed for a primarily adult audience, this work includes 12 case studies of mentoring and coaching relationships in both educational and organizational settings around the world. The book would be helpful in planning new mentoring programs or in augmenting a current program. Youth and educational organizations will find the material replicable to a nonemployment setting. The application of the case studies to career-based youth mentoring programs is especially pertinent.

Sullivan, C. G. (1992). *How to mentor in the midst of change.* Alexandria, VA: Association for Supervision and Curriculum Development. ISBN 0871201917 (39 pages, paperback).

This small, easy-to-read book reviews a variety of approaches to mentoring, ranging from the formal approach of many state-mandated programs to informal efforts similar to the "old-boy network" of industry. The work highlights the particular need for mentors working with women and minorities. Relationships between mentors and mentees are stressed in this work, with special emphasis given to building rapport, trust, and respect; determining goals; sharing information and resources; coaching for development; and developing mentees as future mentors.

United Way of Southeastern Pennsylvania. (1994). *Church-based mentoring: A program manual for mentoring ministries.* Washington, DC: Points of Light Foundation. ISBN N/A (44 pages).

This publication is a workbook designed to concretely address forming mentoring ministries based out of religious institutions. Although written for the church audience, many of the strategies and resources presented are highly adaptable to traditional mentoring programs. The workbook also addresses the wide range of social problems that are often at the root of a young person's personal and educational sense of failure. The publication takes a how-to approach for beginning and structuring ministries based out of religious institutions. It explores ways to increase self-image and develop a sense of usefulness and purpose. The workbook was written by staff of the United Way of Southeastern Pennsylvania Volunteer Center.

Vineyard, S., & McCurley, S. (1988). *101 tips for volunteer recruitment.* Washington, DC: Points of Light Foundation. ASIN 0911029133 (72 pages).

This resource provides a helpful array of lists and explanations aimed at optimizing volunteer recruitment, including how to engage specific populations (youth, low-income people, board members, males, etc.). It would be a useful resource to administrators of mentoring programs.

Walters, J. L., Furnas, M. E., & Renstrom, D. (1990). *Volunteer mentor training program: To promote independent living skills in young adults preparing to leave foster care.* Tulsa, OK: National Resource Center for Youth Services. ISBN 1878848046 (200 pages).

This guide assists foster care providers in becoming mentors to the youth in their care. The training program is designed to encourage young adults to identify their strengths and skills in preparation for independent living. This coordinator's handbook comes in a three-ring looseleaf binder. A 96-page participant's manual is also available.

White, L. T., Patterson, J., & Herman, M. L. (1998). *More than a matter of trust: Managing the risks of mentoring.* Washington, DC: Nonprofit Risk Management Center. ISBN 0963712098 (59 pages, paperback).

This book outlines the exposure to harm that might be associated with mentoring programs, while providing an overview of risk management fundamentals. Harm to children and youth are the highest concern. This book reviews the legal liability issues relevant to mentoring programs and offers suggestions for ways to implement and monitor risk management techniques in their operations. The publication is available from www.nonprofitrisk.org.

Youth Trust. (2000). *E-mentoring: A model and guide for a new concept in mentoring.* Minneapolis, MN: Author. ISBN N/A (47 pages).

This manual guides the reader through the process of planning and structuring an e-mentoring program.

II. Youth Mentoring Curricula, Instructional Materials, and Reference Works

Avani, N. (2001). *YouthLinks: Developing effective mentoring programs.* Plainview, NY: Bureau for At-Risk Youth.

A three-part curriculum, this material is a flexible guide to developing a mentoring program that will be unique to a specific population or locale. Topics include the efficacy of mentoring; program planning; recruitment, screening, and training of mentors; relationship building between mentors and mentees; program evaluation; and developing outside support. The curriculum kit includes a facilitator's guide with a comprehensive overview of how to set up a mentoring program, a youth workbook containing activities for keeping youth involved, and advertising material. All may be purchased separately by calling (800) 99-YOUTH or from the organization's Web site (www.at-risk.com).

Bellm, D., Whitebook, M., & Hnatiuk, P. (1997). *The early childhood mentoring curriculum: A handbook for mentors.* Beltsville, MD: Gryphon House. ISBN 1889956007 (144 pages, paperback).

This program includes both a handbook for mentors and a trainer's guide. The handbook details the goals and principles of mentoring programs in general and strategies for developing child-adult mentoring skills and relationships, as well as diversity issues. The authors describe this program as appropriate for child-care classes, workshops, formal mentoring programs, and related college courses. The trainer's guide presents a sample five-day mentoring course outline, as well as training activities, teaching tips, handouts, and supplemental readings.

Borba, M. (1989). *Esteem builders: A K–8 self-esteem curriculum for improving student achievement, behavior, and school climate.* Rolling Hills Estates, CA: Jalmar Press. ISBN 0915190532 (444 pages, paperback).

This volume is a comprehensive, developmentally appropriate curriculum for use with students and mentees ages 5 to 14. Developed as classroom resource material, the lessons and activities are easily adaptable for use in small groups or with students in a one-on-one mentoring relationship.

Enterprise Foundation and the United Way of America. (1990). *Partnerships for success: A mentoring program manual.* Alexandria, VA: Author. ISBN N/A.

This publication offers guidelines for developing structured mentoring programs in any organization. The work provides information relevant to assessing the needs of participants, program management and administration, screening volunteers, matching participants, and maintaining the mentoring program.

Erickson, J. B. (1998). *The directory of American youth organizations: A resource guide to 500 clubs, troops, teams, societies, lodges, and more for young people* (7th ed.). Minneapolis, MN: Free Spirit Press. ISBN 1575420341 (200 pages, paperback).

This resource provides a comprehensive listing of organizations that serve children and youth in the United States. Organized alphabetically and by subject matter, the volume is a comprehensive guide to the descriptions and contact locations of the major youth-service entities. Mentor organizations have long used this resource to network and problem solve with other organizations serving similar populations.

Jucovy, L. (1999). *Training Mentors: Part Two of Strengthening Mentor Programs.* Portland, OR: National Mentoring Center. ISBN N/A.

This curriculum is a product of a joint venture between the Northwest Regional Educational Laboratory, Public/Private Ventures, the Office of Juvenile Justice and Delinquency Prevention, and Big Brothers Big Sisters of America. It provides activities for training mentors in areas such as communication skills and diversity issues.

National Assembly of Health and Human Services Organizations. (1997). *The new community collaboration manual* (Rev. ed.). Philadelphia: Energize Books. (76 pages, paperback).

This curriculum presents a systematic approach to building effective community collaboration. While this curriculum manual was developed to help build youth collaborations, the principles are readily adaptable to building any type of community collaboration. Material addresses starting and building collaboratives, maintaining momentum, working effectively with youth, and involving business and the media. Appendixes include model bylaws, characteristics of good chairpersons, setting objectives, and program evaluation.

National Mentoring Partnership. (1990). *Mentoring: The elements of effective practice.* Alexandria, VA: Author.

This brochure outlines program elements and policies that have proven effective in a wide range of existing mentoring settings. It was developed by the National Mentoring Working Group, a representative group of national and community-based nonprofit organizations with significant experience in running mentoring programs. The brochure is available free of charge to any individual or organization wanting to develop, operate, volunteer in, or fund a mentoring program. It is also downloadable from the National Mentoring Partnership Web site (www.mentoring.org).

National Mentoring Partnership. (1995). *ABC's of mentoring kit.* Washington, DC: Points of Light Foundation.

The *ABCs of Mentoring* kit is a resource to help organizations create and maintain a mentoring program. The kit includes a sample business plan; templates for a recruitment brochure, recruitment advertisement, and newsletter; a manual with a step-by-step action plan for structuring a program, establishing an image for the program, and clarifying responsibilities of organizations and mentors; and recommendations for evaluating programs. There is also a video that features interviews with business leaders, mentors, and students.

National Mentoring Partnership (1999). *How to become a mentor.* Alexandria, VA: Author. ISBN N/A (49 pages).

This brochure may be reproduced for distribution or adapted to meet the needs of an individual organization. More than 75,000 adults have received this brochure, which educates them on mentors' roles, how they would like to work with young people, where to begin the process of volunteering as mentors, and tips for successfully connecting with appropriate volunteering opportunities. This brochure can be requested by contacting the National Mentoring Partnership; it is also downloadable from the organization's Web site (www.mentoring.org).

Norwalk Mentoring Program (1995). *CONNECTIONS from school to career.* Norwalk, CT: Author. ISBN N/A (56 pages).

This is a curriculum workbook for mentors and students in grades 6 through 12. Career strategies include interviewing skills, filling out job applications, completing a career interest inventory, opening a bank account, setting goals, and following dress codes on the job.

United Way of America/One to One, Inc. (1999). *Mentor training curriculum.* Washington, DC: National Mentoring Network. ISBN N/A (109 pages).

This manual contains a comprehensive curriculum for training mentors. The curriculum includes a "train the trainer" component, information regarding workshop preparation, training outlines, handouts, timelines, and objectives. Training/workshop topics include mentor value clarification, goal setting, communication skills, trust building, problem solving, initiating and maintaining a relationship with participants, and dealing with diversity. The manual also explores three categories of youth participants and provides training and orientation guidelines for each grouping. It is available at www.mentoring.org.

FEDERAL GOVERNMENT DOCUMENTS AND REPORTS
ERIC Digests

There are thousands of youth-related publications available through the Educational Resources Information Center (ERIC), easily accessible through public and university libraries. Most articles are also available online via the Department of Education or through the ERIC homepage. Included in the vast resources are excellent articles on the mentoring of children and youth. A small sampling follows in this section.

The Mentoring of Disadvantaged Youth. ERIC/CUE Digest No. 47.

ERIC Identifier: ED306326

Publication Date: 1988

Author: Ascher, Carol

Source: ERIC Clearinghouse on Urban Education, Teachers College, Box 40, Columbia University, New York, NY 10027

School-College Alliances: Benefits for Low-Income Minorities. ERIC/CUE Digest No. 53.

ERIC Identifier: ED308277

Publication Date: 1989

Author: Ascher, Carol; Schwartz, Wendy

Source: ERIC Clearinghouse on Urban Education, Teachers College, Box 40, Columbia University, New York, NY 10027

Mentor Relationships and Gifted Learners. ERIC Digest No. E486.

ERIC Identifier: ED321491

Publication Date: 1990

Author: Berger, Sandra L.

Source: ERIC Clearinghouse on Handicapped and Gifted Children, Reston, VA

Community Involvement in K–12 Career Education. ERIC Digest No. 177.

ERIC Identifier: ED402473

Publication Date: 1996

Author: Brown, Bettina Lankard

Source: ERIC Clearinghouse on Adult Career and Vocational Education, Columbus, OH

Cultivating Resilience: An Overview for Rural Educators and Parents. ERIC Digest.

ERIC Identifier: ED372904

Publication Date: 1994

Author: Finley, Mary

Source: ERIC Clearinghouse on Rural Education and Small Schools (CRESS), P.O. Box 1348, Charleston, WV 25325-1348

Youth Mentoring: Programs and Practices. Urban Diversity Series No. 97.

ERIC Identifier: ED308257

Publication Date: 1988

Author: Flaxman, Erwin; Ascher, Carol; Harrington, Charles

Source: ERIC Clearinghouse on Urban Education, Teachers College, Box 40, Columbia University, New York, NY 10027

Migrant Students Attending College: Facilitating Their Success. ERIC Digest.

ERIC Identifier: ED423097

Publication Date: 1998

Author: Morse, Susan; Hammer, Patricia Cahape

Source: ERIC Clearinghouse on Rural Education and Small Schools (CRESS), P.O. Box 1348, Charleston, WV 25325-1348

Helping Minority Students Graduate from College: A Comprehensive Approach. ERIC Digest.

ERIC Identifier: ED308795

Publication Date: 1988

Author: Richardson, Richard C., Jr.; de los Santos, Alfredo G., Jr.

Source: ERIC Clearinghouse on Higher Education, The George Washington University, One Dupont Circle, Suite 630, Washington, DC 20036

Additional Documents and Reports

Many federal agencies provide print materials, documents, and reports related to the mentoring of children and youth. Two of the most prolific providers are the United States Department of Education (www.ed.gov) and the United States Department of Justice, Office of Juvenile Justice and Delinquency Prevention (www.ojjdp.ncjrs.org). Documents and reports are available online from these sources.

NONPRINT RESOURCES

World Wide Web Sites

The following are examples of Internet sites providing key resources for mentoring:

All Our Kids
  www.allourkids.org/

Based in Nebraska, All Our Kids is dedicated to helping at-risk youth in the community. The organization supports the belief that these students can benefit from an ongoing, one-to-one relationship with a mentor. All Our Kids has joined with the National Mentoring Partnership to develop community initiatives and recruit more mentors. All Our Kids operates a comprehensive mentoring program and works with other organizations to help them develop their own effective mentoring programs. All Our Kids has also established a scholarship program to provide opportunities to young people who have graduated from high school and participate in a mentoring relationship. The organization's Web site includes links to safe Web sites for kids, answers to questions about what defines mentoring and who mentors are, and scholarship information.

America's Promise
www.americaspromise.org
America's Promise was founded at the Presidents' Summit for America's Future and is chaired by General Colin Powell. The mission is to provide every at-risk child in America with access to the fundamental resources needed in order for him or her to lead a happy and healthy life.

Bad Dog Rediscovers America
www.baddogkids.org

Bad Dog Rediscovers America is a nonprofit organization whose mission is to teach and mentor kids interested in art and technology. It is a creativity-based program that mentors disadvantaged at-risk children and youth ages 5 to 18. This Web site includes news events, sponsors, and additional links.

Big Brothers Big Sisters of America
www.bbbsa.org

This Web site includes: history, news, agency locations to volunteer, links, stories, and profiles.

California Mentor Resource Center
www.mentors.ca/mentorprograms.html

This Web site includes mentoring definitions, contact information, and a peer resources network. General details and more specific contact information (such as the name, address, telephone, fax, and e-mail address of a certain mentoring program coordinator or the organization itself) are only available to members of this peer resources network. Membership is fee-based and includes subscriptions to print and Internet mentor publications, toll-free mentor program consultation, and discounts on training workshops and publications. Also, access to additional documents is only available in the password-protected area of this Web site.

Create Now!
www.createnow.org/

The mission of Create Now! is to educate institutionalized at-risk children and youth through the creative arts in an effort to bring stability and direction into their lives. The program serves youth ages 5 to 21 living in court-ordered residential care facilities in the Los Angeles and Orlando areas. Founded in 1996, this program provides an array of mentoring programs involving various types of intervention strategies such as writing, painting, music, dance, and video production, with an emphasis on the crafts of the film and TV industry. This Web site includes success stories, mentoring news and updates, specific projects, feedback from kids, tips for working with at-risk youth, and information about cyber-mentoring.

Daughters-Sisters Project
www.daughters-sisters.org

The theme of interconnection unites the goals of this Washington state–based nonprofit organization. A primary goal of the Daughters-Sisters Project is to empower young women and to cultivate mentoring relationships between girls and women. The group also strives to promote understanding between genders, generations, and cultures. The project, part of the Northwest Girls Coalition, inspired the publication *Daughters of the Moon, Sisters of the Sun* (Hughes & Wolf, 1997; see print resources for more information). The Daughter-Sisters Project Web site includes an overview of the organization, a listing of current workshops and programs, and interviews with inspiring individuals.

Educating Jane
www.EducatingJane.com

EducatingJane.com seeks to provide information that optimizes the educational experiences of girls and helps them succeed. The site provides specific informational materials for girls, parents, and educators. The "Mentors" link offers girls information on mentoring, including tips on how to find a mentor and links to organizations that support mentoring.

Electronic Emissary Project
http://emissary.ots.utexas.edu/emissary/index.html

Online since 1993, this national telementoring program housed at the University of Texas at Austin helps teachers establish and maintain curriculum-based electronic exchanges between students and professionals in a variety of disciplines. Individuals interested in serving as volunteer experts can complete an online application. This application collects information regarding the volunteer's areas of expertise. Educators can search for experts in relevant areas. The Web site contains a sample of project descriptions, which highlight a variety of interesting telementoring activities. The Electronic Emissary Project has also conducted research on online educational experiences, and the Web site features a bibliography of research papers.

Filipino Integrated Learning Through Mentoring
www.veranda.com.ph/fsi/filmentor.html

FIL-MENTORING, INC. (Filipino Integrated Learning Through Mentoring, Inc.) was conceptualized and established to motivate and encourage Filipino children to pursue higher education. It is a formally organized nonprofit and voluntary organization involved in expanding mentoring opportunities and in developing supplemental learning, particularly for Filipino children. This Web site includes benefits of mentoring, program objectives, and international links and support.

Friends for Youth Mentoring Institute
www.mentoringinstitute.org

The Friends for Youth Mentoring Institute promotes the utilization and effective application of mentoring as an intervention to help individuals succeed. The institute's Web site provides general information regarding mentoring, including a checklist for effective mentoring organizations and an overview of 12 elements of success for mentoring programs. The site also describes recent research measuring the effectiveness of the Friends for Youth mentoring program. An overview of the institute's technical assistance training is provided to assist new or existing mentoring projects.

INSITE Mentoring Program
www.mentoringnetwork.org

INSITE is a Michigan Web-based mentoring network that uses its Web site and database to facilitate the matching of middle and high school students with prescreened adults according to shared interests and career goals. This program's primary goal is the large-scale matching of teens with caring, responsible adults. The Web site includes the following resources: databases (Career Exploration and Life Experiences databases searchable by category or key words); career categories; job shadowing information; descriptions of typical days at work for various careers; adult feedback; online career mentors who answer e-mail inquiries; a list of mentors who are available to meet face-to-face for academic help, job shadowing, or other activities; background information on the effectiveness of mentoring; and a listing of mentoring programs.

International Telementor Center
    www.telementor.org/

This resource is an outgrowth of the Hewlett-Packard Telementor Program. The International Telementor Program facilitates electronic mentoring relationships between professionals and students worldwide. The program seeks to create project-based online mentoring support in math, science, engineering, communication, and career/education planning for students and teachers. Sponsors include Hewlett-Packard, Agilent Technologies, Thomson Financial, Merck Institute for Science Education, Cinergy, Sun Microsystems, Berks Business Education Coalition, eDave, Inc., Pitney Bowes, George Lucas Education Foundation, and MasterCard International.

The Mentor Directory/Peer Resources—Navigation Tools for the Heart, Mind and Soul®
    www.peer.ca/mentor.html

This Web site emphasizes mentoring as a community of wisdom; a gift of flight for the soul; and the balancing of heart, mind, and spirit. On this Web site one can obtain tips from the experts, take a brief mentor test, and receive feedback about one's mentor quotient. Notices of seminars, workshops, and conferences on mentoring are available. This site tracks and regularly updates the best mentor sites on the Internet. It also has many great books and videos that focus on mentoring and has links to purchase them. Also available is a virtual mentor, as well as summaries of research, professional, and popular articles published on mentoring. The Web site offers a demonstration of how different organizations have designed their mentor programs and defines the differences between a coach, mentor, and therapist.

Mentors, Inc.
www.mentorsinc.org/

The mission of Mentors, Inc., is to promote the academic, career, and personal development of public high school students through one-on-one mentoring relationships and enrichment activities. This comprehensive Web site includes the following resources: a compilation of online resources; definitions of mentoring; partnership lists; links to the National Mentoring Partnership, Save the Children: "Do Good. Mentor a Child" Campaign, U.S. Department of Justice, Juvenile Mentoring Program (JUMP),Tutor/Mentor Connection, and America's Promise—Alliance for Youth.

National Mentoring Center
www.nwrel.org/mentoring/

The Northwest Regional Educational Laboratory's National Mentoring Center provides training and technical assistance for mentoring programs through a variety of services and conferences. Created and funded by the Office of Juvenile Justice and Delinquency Prevention (OJJDP), the National Mentoring Center seeks to create connections between children and caring adults in the community. The National Mentoring Center contends that because mentoring makes a tangible difference in the lives of young people, the organization's hope is to provide the skills and tools necessary for successful mentoring relationships. This Web site includes news updates, a resource collection, publications, training session and conference listings, a database search capability, detailed information on OJJDP, and a list of collaborative partners.

The National Mentoring Partnership
www.mentoring.org/

The National Mentoring Partnership is an advocate for the expansion of mentoring and is a resource for mentors and mentoring initiatives nationwide. The site is dedicated to the expansion of quality mentoring. This Web site includes how to run a mentoring program, finding a local mentor, resource listings by state, and news updates, as well as information on how to become a member. The Web site also houses the National E-Mentoring Clearinghouse, which offers a wealth of information and resources related to online mentoring.

Points of Light
www.pointsoflight.org

The mission of the Points of Light foundation is to help people get involved by connecting with others through volunteer service. This Web site includes information about volunteer/mentoring opportunities, listings of mentoring volunteer centers, and online discussion groups. There is also information on how Points of Light helps businesses, nonprofit organizations, and youth organizations to create and improve volunteer programs.

Rotary Reader
www.rotaryreader.org/

This is a K–5 mentoring program sponsored by the Rotary Club. The mentor's mission is to serve as a "loyal friend," "a reader," an "advisor," and "a mentor." This Web site includes information on why mentors are important and positive feedback from guidance counselors, parents, readers, and students.

Save the Children
http://savethechildren.org/mentors/index.html

Save the Children's campaign mission is to help meet the urgent need for mentors in the lives of children in the United States. The organization is founded on the belief that one of the most effective ways to help young people overcome challenges and achieve their potential is through mentoring. This Web site includes information on what mentors do, how to become a mentor, fact sheets about mentoring, and how to register online for Save the Children's national mentoring database, which connects to numerous resources and links.

Tutor/Mentor Connection
www.tutormentorconnection.org

The Tutor/Mentor Connection is the Chicago partner of the National Mentoring Partnership. The belief is that after-school tutoring/mentoring programs, in which children work with adult role models in one-on-one and group activities, can be a means of giving children hope, support, and learning tools that will build the self-esteem and confidence necessary for students to succeed in school. The organization has piloted programs in Chicago that have helped more than 250 tutor/mentor programs grow and expand, and it works to develop new programs where voids exist. This Web site includes news, lessons learned, information on how to add partners to the organization's efforts, special events, and other links.

United Way of America
   www.unitedway.org

The mission of the United Way of America is to support and serve local United Way chapters in order to help increase the organized capacity of people to care for one another. This Web site includes ways to get involved, what community building means, news, and partnerships.

Virtual Volunteering Project
   www.serviceleader.org/vv/

Based at the University of Texas at Austin, this internationally recognized site offers the most detailed information available on using the Internet to recruit and involve volunteers. The Web site also features comprehensive information regarding online mentoring programs and resources, particularly programs that are youth-focused. Online mentoring resources include guidelines for online safety, suggestions for mentoring activities, a grid of administrative responsibilities involved in launching and maintaining a program, and profiles of more than 35 programs around the United States. The project is part of ServiceLeader. Org, which offers comprehensive information about volunteerism and volunteer management in general.

Watoto World On-Line Mentor Program (MELANET—Our Children, and Education)
   www.melanet.com/watoto/mentor.html

A K–12 African American–based mentoring program, this project was created to explore the possibilities of matching technologically savvy Internet users with K–12 students and working jointly toward bridging the gap between the technology "haves" and "have-nots." The primary objectives of this program are to introduce students to the Internet and online technologies. This Web site includes electronic resources for homework assistance, project research, and technological encouragement to assist educators in using the Internet for classroom activities. It also addresses why online mentoring is of value to students, teachers, and mentors.

A World Fit for Kids!
   www.worldfitforkids.org/

A World Fit for Kids! is a program based out of Los Angeles. The mission of the program is to train teens to become role models or heroes to the kids in their own neighborhoods by using the vehicles of school, fitness, and sports. The program has received considerable recognition as a successful gang, drug, and dropout prevention program because it prepares teens to become mentors and coaches themselves. With the help of college coordinators, the teens run the programs, which engage elementary through high school students in healthy activities that build self-esteem, teach conflict resolution, and foster leadership skills. A World Fit for Kids! unites parents, teachers, local businesses, police, city and public health officials, churches, youth service organizations, universities, and national sponsors. This Web site includes articles, a list of partnerships, information on how to create a chapter, and public service announcements.

Your Time—Their Future
   www.health.org/yourtime/

This is the home page for the Your Time—Their Future Positive Activities Campaign, a national public education campaign developed by the U.S. Department of Health and Human Services. The campaign urges adults to become involved in volunteering, mentoring, and other efforts that help young people ages 7 to 14 participate in positive activities that build skills, self-discipline, and competence. The campaign mission is to prevent new use and reduce existing use of alcohol, tobacco, and illicit drugs among youth. This Web site includes information and materials on how to keep kids drug free, how to become a mentor or volunteer, user feedback, and links to additional resources.

Youth Starts with YOU
   www.youthstartswithyou.org/

The mission of this organization, which is based out of Ohio, is to teach adult volunteers how to work effectively with young people. Youth Starts with YOU has a training program for adult volunteers, which is delivered in a variety of ways. This Web site includes a description of the program delivery model, partnerships, key word searches, additional Web links, and announcements.

The Web sites listed are intended for use as resources, and inclusion is not intended as endorsement by the authors. All Web addresses were accurate and all sites listed were open at the time of publication. The core address (i.e., the address before the first backslash) may work if problems are encountered in accessing the Web site address as listed.

7

Chronology

I know his whole family. I'm going to be in his life for a long, long time.

                    Chris, adult mentor

As noted in chapter 1, mentoring is an old concept. While the term "mentor" can be traced to Homer's *Odyssey*, the practice of mentoring has most likely existed since the earliest human relationships. Across the ages, the idea of a wise, trusted, nonfamilial adult contributing in a special way to the education and development of a young person has been a part of many societies. The specific form and nature of mentoring relationships has varied and evolved across time and culture. Throughout much of its history, mentoring occurred as a natural process wherein members of the community offered guidance and support to young people. In the past several decades, mentoring has become increasingly formalized. This formal mentoring process involves a third party, such as an agency, uniting young people and prospective mentors. Such programs operate on the assumption that two people, initially strangers, can cultivate a meaningful relationship that confers the benefits attributed to naturally occurring adult-youth relationships.

The following chronology highlights some of the important events in the mentoring movement.

1200   Odysseus appoints Mentor as a surrogate father to his son.
B.C.

Late   Volunteer "Friendly Visiting" emerges as a popular strategy to
1800s assist the poor. According to this model, Friendly Visitors offer
           counsel and personal support as a means of influencing the
           character and aspirations of the poor. This personal contact is
           viewed as a substitute for providing welfare funds. Although,
           like mentoring, this approach ostensibly focuses on friendship,
           role modeling, and the formation of a personal relationship,
           such intervention also possesses a patronizing element and is
           soon replaced by the social work movement.

1903   On July 4, Irvin Westheimer befriends a young, fatherless boy,
           later leading to the formation of a Big Brothers group in Cincin-
           nati.

1904   On December 3, Ernest K. Coulter addresses the Men's Club of
           the Central Presbyterian Church of New York. His speech
           decries the severe reformatory approach inflicted on juvenile
           offenders and argues that the best hope for reforming these
           young people is for responsible adult men to volunteer as caring,
           connected "big brothers." Forty of those present enlisted as the
           first "big brothers."

1905   In New York, the Ladies of Charity changes its name to Catholic
           Big Sisters. Mrs. John O'Keefe is credited as being the first Big
           Sister.

1908   Mrs. Willard Parker establishes a Big Sister program for Protes-
           tant girls in New York City.

1909   Coulter and many of the original "Big Brothers" formally incor-
           porate the nation's first Big Brothers Big Sisters agency, Big
           Brothers of New York, Inc.

           A Big Sisters agency forms in Milwaukee.

1910   Irvin Westheimer founds the Big Brother Association in Cincin-
           nati.

1916   In April, a rally for the Big Brothers Big Sisters movement takes
           place at the Casino Theatre in New York. This inspirational,
           nondenominational rally includes addresses from clergymen of

diverse faiths. Two thousand men and women of diverse ethnic backgrounds are present.

1921 The first Big Brothers Big Sisters Federation is created. This federation establishes guidelines and standards for BBBS programs.

1954 National Kinship Affiliate Network, an interdenominational Christian youth mentoring program, is established.

1958 The United States Congress officially charters Big Brothers of America.

1963 A national alliance of leading African American men of business, industry, public affairs, and government emerges. This alliance, 100 Black Men of America, seeks to improve the quality of life for African Americans and other minorities through interventions such as mentoring.

1970 The United States Congress officially charters Big Sisters International.

1971 In Vancouver, Washington, teacher Bill Gibbons starts the HOSTS program, the nation's first and largest structured academic mentoring program. The initiative began in a "reading lab" with volunteer mentors and a single reading instructor.

1977 Big Brothers and Big Sisters organizations merge to form Big Brothers Big Sisters of America, with national headquarters in Philadelphia.

The HOSTS program, which has grown significantly since its founding in 1971, becomes an independent organization.

1978 The *Harvard Business Review* publishes an article entitled "Everyone Who Makes It Has a Mentor." This article is one of many articles over the next several decades to argue that mentoring plays a key role in an individual's success in the corporate world.

1979 The Center for Intergenerational Learning at Temple University is established. The CIL is a national resource for programs seeking to improve the lives of individuals and families by creating opportunities for youth and elders to contribute to their communities and by promoting partnerships among organizations serving young people, families, and older adults.

1981   Eugene M. Lang originates the "I Have a Dream" project at New York's P.S. 121. Fifty years before, Mr. Lang had attended elementary school at P.S. 121 in East Harlem. A prominent New York businessman and multimillionaire, Mr. Lang returned to his elementary school to give a speech on the importance of hard work for success in life and subsequently made a spontaneous promise to provide partial college scholarships to the children present if they graduated from high school.

1986   The national "I Have a Dream" Foundation is created. In the coming years, the foundation supports a nationwide network of projects that encourage children to stay in school, graduate, and go to college or obtain meaningful employment.

State chapters of 100 Black Men unite to form a national organization, 100 Black Men of America, Inc. Local chapters of this organization have existed for decades, dedicated to empowering young people and nurturing academic achievement, social responsibility, and creativity. Mentoring is a primary vehicle through which this mission is met.

1987   Matilda Raffa Cuomo establishes Mentoring USA, which will become the largest one-on-one mentoring program in New York City. The program provides community-based mentoring to at-risk children, such as the homeless and those in foster care.

100 Black Men of America, Inc., holds its first national conference.

1988   Public/Private Ventures launches a research initiative to assess the viability and impact of mentoring. The initial 1988 study examines five projects that match retired elders with young people. In the years that follow, Public/Private Ventures conducts studies of a myriad of mentoring projects and issues, including reviews of campus-based, juvenile justice system, and intergenerational mentoring programs, and an extensive study of the Big Brothers Big Sisters of America programs.

1989   One to One Partnership, Inc., is founded by Ray Chambers (a future board member for the Points of Light Foundation) and Geoffrey Boisi, with the goal of establishing a nonprofit organization dedicated to the expansion of mentoring. One to One seeks to establish local partnerships across the nation. A key strategy is to engage top-level business leadership to commit resources to the promotion of mentoring.

1990 The One to One Partnership becomes the National Mentoring Partnership. The name change reflects the partnership's commitment to a wide variety of mentoring programs, not just those following the one-to-one relationship model.

In May of 1990, the Points of Light Foundation is founded. This organization is dedicated to promoting volunteerism as a means to address social problems. Mentoring is a favored initiative of the Points of Light Foundation.

One to One/The Greater Philadelphia Mentoring Partnership is established by George M. Ross and William H. Gray III. This not-for-profit organization represents a cooperative mentoring effort of businesspeople, educators, social activists, entrepreneurs, and the United Way of Southeastern Pennsylvania.

1992 An amendment to the Juvenile Justice and Delinquency Prevention (JJDP) Act of 1974 (P.L. 93–415: 42 U.S.C. 5667e) establishes the Juvenile Mentoring Program (JUMP) to provide one-to-one mentoring for youth at risk of delinquency, gang involvement, educational failure, or dropping out of school.

1993 The Hospital Youth Mentoring Program (HYMP) begins, administered by the Johns Hopkins Hospital and funded by the Commonwealth Fund. This program supports youth mentoring projects in a variety of hospitals.

1994 A campaign promoting the mentoring initiative concept is launched in California in an attempt to convince the administration of Governor Pete Wilson to support implementation of a statewide mentoring initiative.

The Mentoring Partnership of Minnesota is launched as a community initiative to promote mentoring for Minnesota youth.

The Utah Mentor Network is established, forging a link between existing mentor programs in that state.

1995 Following an executive order signed by Governor Wilson, the California Mentor Initiative (CMI) is formed. The CMI is the first statewide mentoring initiative in the country. This move is accompanied by $10 million in funding to bolster mentoring efforts in the state. A goal of 250,000 mentor matches by the year 2000 is set. Over the next two years, a number of advances are made, including: (a) the establishment of a council of mentor experts and private-sector representatives, (b) development of a Web site, (c) creation of a mentor resource center, and (d) production of quality assurance standards and training guidelines.

Hewlett-Packard's telementoring program begins. The foundation is established when David Neils, a software engineer at Hewlett-Packard, creates an Internet skills class for junior high students in Fort Collins, Colorado. He recruits other professionals to help via e-mail. The success of these ventures leads Neils to organize the International Telementor Program with the backing of Hewlett-Packard. The program currently includes mentors from several large corporations.

Public/Private Ventures publishes an evaluation of Big Brothers Big Sisters. The evaluation studied young people who applied for "Bigs" in 1992 and 1993. (Tierney, J. P., Grossman, J. B., & Resch, N. L. [1995]. *Making a difference: An impact study of Big Brothers/Big Sisters.* Philadelphia: Public/Private Ventures.)

The Virtual Volunteering Project begins. This project seeks to encourage and assist in the development of volunteer activities that can be completed off-site via the Internet.

1997   April 27–29 marks the Presidents' Summit for America's Future, chaired by General Colin Powell. This summit, held in Philadelphia, is attended by Presidents Clinton, Bush, Carter, and Ford, with former First Lady Nancy Reagan representing her husband, as well as a multitude of governors, mayors, community delegations, prominent business leaders and concerned citizens. Co-sponsored by the Points of Light Foundation and the Corporation for National Service, the summit results in the creation of America's Promise, a national effort to make youth a priority. Among the pledges American's Promise makes to youth is the right to an ongoing relationship with caring adults.

The National Mentoring Partnership honors Hewlett-Packard with the 1997 National Corporate Leadership Award for the success of the Hewlett-Packard Telementor Program.

1998 The California Mentor Foundation (CMF) is created as a private-sector partner to the California Mentor Initiative office. Dr. Andrew M. Mecca is appointed the CMF's first director.

The first annual California Mentor Summit takes place at Disneyland. The summit includes speakers General Colin Powell and Governor Pete Wilson.

Big Brothers Big Sisters International is created.

In an effort to reach more students and involve more professionals from a variety of organizations, Hewlett-Packard's International Telementor Program (ITP) moves to a host outside of Hewlett-Packard: the Center for Science, Mathematics, and Technology Education (CSMATE) on the campus of Colorado State University, Fort Collins, Colorado. David Neils leaves HP to become the ITP Director.

2000 At the state capitol in Sacramento, California, on May 31, a bipartisan joint legislative hearing is held. The hearing, "Mentoring: Facing the Challenges, Finding the Opportunities," was convened by state senator Dede Alpert.

Research exploring the mechanisms through which mentoring impacts academic achievement is published. This study, drawn from data on Big Brothers Big Sisters programs, provides preliminary support for the hypothesis that the positive academic gains made by mentees are mediated by the impact mentoring has on mentees' relationships with their parents. (Rhodes, J. E., Grossman, J. B., Resche, N. L. [2000]. Agents of changes: Pathways through which mentoring relationships influence adolescents' academic adjustment. *Child Development, 71,* 1662–1671.)

2001 In January 2001, H.R. 17, The Younger Americans Act, is introduced to Congress. The Act outlines a national youth policy to assure that all youth have access to core resources similar to those promoted by America's Promise. The Act specifically mentions that youth in the United States are entitled to ongoing relationships with caring adults.

2002 In January, the United States Postal Service issues a mentoring stamp to honor the commitment of mentors and to encourage others to participate in mentor-mentee matches.

Working with data derived from Big Brothers Big Sisters programs, Jean Grossman and Jean Rhodes publish a study that examines the impact that mentoring relationship duration has on mentoring outcomes. The study also explores factors that predict how long mentoring relationships will last. (Grossman, J. B., & Rhodes, J. E. [2002]. The test of time: Predictors and effects of duration in youth mentoring relationships. *American Journal of Community Psychology, 30,* 199–219.)

Appendix A: The National Mentoring Partnership Elements of Effective Practice

These *Elements* were developed and published in 1990 by the MENTOR/National Mentoring Partnership and The United Way. (In 2003, the *Elements* were revised and extensively expanded; for a full text copy of the "Elements of Effective Practice, 2nd Edition, see the National Mentoring Partnership's webpage at: http://www.mentoring.org/common/ effective_mentoring_practices/pdf/effectiveprac.pdf or contact the National Mentoring Partnership for a free copy.)

According to the National Mentoring Partnership, responsible mentoring:

- Is a structured, one-to-one relationship or partnership that focuses on the needs of the mentored participants
- Fosters caring and supportive relationships
- Encourages individuals to develop to their fullest potential
- Helps an individual to develop his or her own vision for the future
- Is a strategy to develop active community partnerships

The National Mentoring Partnership's requirements for a responsible mentoring program include:

- A well-defined mission statement and established operating principles

- Regular, consistent contact between the mentor and the mentee
- Support by the family or guardian of the mentee/protégé
- Additional community support services
- An established organization of oversight
- Adherence to general principles of volunteerism
- Paid or volunteer staff with appropriate skills
- Written job descriptions for all staff and volunteer positions
- Adherence to Equal Employment Opportunity (EEO) requirements
- Inclusiveness of racial, economic, and gender representation, as appropriate to the program
- Adequate financial and in-kind resources
- Written administrative and program procedures
- Written eligibility requirements for program participants
- Program evaluation and ongoing assessment
- A long-range plan that has community input
- Risk management and confidentiality policies
- Use of generally accepted accounting procedures
- A prudent and reasonable rationale for staffing requirements that are based on:
  - The organization's statement of purpose and goals
  - The needs of mentors and participants
  - Community resources
  - Staff and other volunteers' skill levels

Appendix B: Academic Volunteer Mentoring Support Program (AVMSP) Quality Standards

(http://www.ose.ca.gov/ose_programs/mentor/qualitystds.html)
California Government Code Section 96102, Statutes of 1992, requires the California Governor's Office of the Secretary for Education to implement 10 state standards for the Academic Volunteer Mentoring Support Program (AVMSP). While mentoring programs using these standards will have a common programmatic core, their approach will vary depending on how the standards are implemented in the overall design of the program.

STANDARD #1: AN EFFECTIVE ACADEMIC MENTORING PROGRAM DEVELOPS CRITERIA TO IDENTIFY STUDENT MENTEES.

There is a process of mentee identification that:

- defines specific criteria for identifying mentees who would most likely benefit from a mentor-mentee relationship,
- includes a procedure for identifying mentees,
- includes the grade levels of students targeted for service, and
- incorporates input from students, staff, and others in the school community.

STANDARD #2: AN EFFECTIVE ACADEMIC MENTORING PROGRAM ASSESSES INDIVIDUAL STUDENT NEEDS AND DEVELOPS STRATEGIES FOR IMPROVING STUDENT PERFORMANCE.

There is a process for assessing individual student need that:

- gathers relevant and specific data to adequately assess individual student need,
- incorporates information from a variety of sources, including students, staff, family, and other stakeholders in the school community,
- identifies specific problem areas with student performance that need improvement, and
- identifies the student's strengths upon which an academic mentoring strategy can be built.

There is a process for developing specific strategies to improve student performance that:

- involves students, family, teachers, and staff,
- targets specific academic areas,
- addresses nonacademic student-performance issues, and
- includes a means to assess the effectiveness of each strategy.

STANDARD #3: AN EFFECTIVE ACADEMIC MENTORING PROGRAM FOLLOWS A WELL-DESIGNED PLAN FOR RECRUITING MENTORS.

There is a well-designed recruitment plan that:

- establishes partnerships with community groups, businesses, and service organizations to provide avenues for mentors to volunteer at school settings,
- implements a year-round marketing and public awareness campaign, and
- identifies a sufficient number of potential mentors to facilitate the process of finding the right match with mentees.

STANDARD #4: AN EFFECTIVE ACADEMIC MENTORING PROGRAM FOLLOWS A DETAILED PLAN FOR SELECTING AND A THOROUGH PROCEDURE FOR SCREENING EVERY MENTOR.

There is a detailed selection plan that:

- develops criteria for selecting mentors that meet the needs of the student population,
- requires an application process that includes a personal interview, and
- selects mentors able to make the minimum commitment of time required by the program.

There is a thorough screening procedure that:

- requires all volunteers and mentors to undergo the same criminal and health checks that school employees are subject to prior to employment.

STANDARD #5: AN EFFECTIVE ACADEMIC MENTORING PROGRAM ESTABLISHES AN ORIENTATION PROGRAM FOR MENTORS, MENTEES, AND OTHER INTERESTED PARTIES.

There is an orientation program that:

- presents an overview of the mentoring program,
- introduces the responsibilities and the level of commitment expected of each participant, and
- provides written program materials explaining program policies and procedures.

STANDARD #6: AN EFFECTIVE ACADEMIC MENTORING PROGRAM DEVELOPS AND INSTITUTES AN ONGOING TRAINING AND SUPPORT PLAN FOR ALL MENTORS.

There is a comprehensive ongoing training plan that:

- provides training in establishing and sustaining a meaningful mentor-mentee relationship,
- helps mentors develop communication skills to understand the students and relate to their circumstances and culture, and
- teaches mentors to identify and build upon the strengths of the student and to support and acknowledge the student's accomplishments.

There is an ongoing support plan that:

- involves school personnel, program staff, and others in supporting mentors and mentees,
- provides ongoing peer support for mentors, and
- supports mentors in addressing mentor-mentee relationship problems.

STANDARD #7: AN EFFECTIVE ACADEMIC MENTORING PROGRAM DEVELOPS AND IMPLEMENTS AN EXPLICIT MATCHING STRATEGY FOR MENTEES AND MENTORS.

There is an explicit matching strategy that:

- articulates a matching rationale,
- employs appropriate criteria that address the needs and preferences of mentees, and
- ensures that both parties understand and agree to the conditions of the match and the mentoring relationship.

STANDARD #8: AN EFFECTIVE ACADEMIC MENTORING PROGRAM ENSURES ONGOING MONITORING AND SUPERVISION OF THE MENTOR-MENTEE RELATIONSHIP.

There is an ongoing monitoring and supervision system that:

- establishes written policies and procedures for the supervision of the mentor-mentee relationship,

- provides periodic checks on the progress of the mentor-mentee relationship and methods for making adjustments to mentoring strategies, and
- ensures appropriate steps to close the mentor-mentee relationship.

STANDARD #9: AN EFFECTIVE ACADEMIC MENTORING PROGRAM RECOGNIZES MENTOR AND MENTEE CONTRIBUTIONS AND ACHIEVEMENT.

There is a recognition program that:

- identifies multiple recognition strategies that validate mentor contributions and mentee achievements,
- promotes public and media awareness of program accomplishments,
- recognizes businesses and community partnerships for their contributions to mentoring, and
- hosts recognition events and social gatherings.

STANDARD #10: AN EFFECTIVE ACADEMIC MENTORING PROGRAM EVALUATES WHETHER THE PROGRAM IS SUCCESSFUL IN IMPROVING INDIVIDUAL STUDENT PERFORMANCE AND ACHIEVEMENT.

There is an evaluation process that:

- tracks the number of students served; the number of mentors serving students; the frequency, duration, and total hours of the mentoring relationship; and the retention of mentors,
- maintains that participant students (mentees) meet with their mentors for a period of not less than 15 hours during one academic quarter to be counted toward annual service goal accomplishments,
- identifies specific student performance and achievement outcomes,

- develops indicators for measuring specific outcomes, including but not limited to demographic data, grade point averages, test scores, attendance (number of days attended divided by number of school days per year), and discipline (referrals and suspensions). Awardees will be required to submit data as specified in the Evaluation Report Format.
- includes data for a comparison group, preferably a random assignment, matched pair, or cut-off criteria design,
- develops attitudinal surveys for mentored students, and
- defines a procedure for collecting data to measure specific outcomes.

Appendix C: Grant Proposal Model

BY MY SIDE

THE PARADISE VALLEY UNIFIED SCHOOL DISTRICT
MENTORING PROGRAM

FOR

GATE STREET ELEMENTARY SCHOOL, DEVON
ELEMENTARY SCHOOL, AND SUNNYSIDE MIDDLE
SCHOOL

Program Design

In June of 1998, Gate Street Elementary School was awarded a three-year mentoring program grant by the Governor's Office of Child Development and Education. The grant proposal, *Project READ*, was developed after an extensive needs assessment and evaluation of the K–5 population at the school. The assessment had revealed an academically underachieving school with clearly identifiable obstacles to student academic achievement, including poor attendance, neighborhood decline, poor study habits, and many busy, stressed families unable to parent properly. The 1998 Gate Street School mentoring grant was written to provide a solution of giving students extra one-on-one help to improve their reading scores while connecting them with a caring adult who, along with family and teachers, would offer underachieving students encouragement, support, and incentives for attending school. This grant pursues the same goals, but seeks to expand the target population in order to give an additional number of students the chance to be successful by being mentored.

The three years (1998–2001) of the mentoring program at Gate Street School have been rewarding academic ones for the students, mentors, staff, and parents, with program results demonstrating that, with mentoring, school attendance can be raised, academic scores can improve, students can feel more connected to schools, mentors will be prized by the students, field trips can happen because mentors chaperone, more community members will come on campus as a result of the mentoring (dispelling an unfounded myth that Gate Street School was an unsafe place), and more! The efficacy of mentoring for students in particular and for schools in general has been proved.

Currently, evaluations of the needs at two nearby Paradise Valley schools have determined that their students also need the benefits of a mentoring program. *This current grant proposal is an extension of the original mentor program at Gate Street School to include two additional school-based sites.* (Additionally, one alternate location for mentoring to take place in the community, during after-school hours, is included.) Such a program expansion would (1) allow older (grades 6–8) students to be mentored at the middle school level, (2) allow younger elementary students already being mentored to continue with their same mentors as they promote to middle school, (3) develop a program at one new elementary site, and (4) expand the locations for mentoring to the Paradise Valley Boys and Girls Club during the hours of 3–6 P.M. weekdays. The program will be called the By My Side Mentor Project, in keeping with the familiar phrase that connotes *support*.

Mentors are asked to provide tutoring, guidance, counsel, reinforcement, friendship, and constructive example to their mentees. Their role is not to be "in front of" the child leading him or her nor "behind" the child pushing him or her. Rather, the mentor's role is to be by a child's side to help that student become the best that he or she can be, both in school and in life.

How the Need for an Academic Mentoring Program Was Determined

Three schools have been selected for the By My Side Mentoring Program, all in close geographic proximity. All three schools are Title I schools. There are profound academic needs at all three sites, especially among English language learners. And, although individual site differences exist, the academic needs at all schools are similar enough that a collective overall program design has been developed. All schools in the By My Side Mentor Program will focus on student performance and achievement in the area of reading or math (elementary grades) and language arts or math (middle school). Limited English proficient students (English language learners) will be particularly monitored for mentoring needs. Profiles of the individual schools are shown in the table below. A school description follows the table.

Gate Street Elementary School is the site of the 1998–2001 mentor program, where 93 mentors currently work with 93 students. Gate Street has shown statistically significant improvement with mentoring in place. (*For example, during the 1998–1999 Gate Street school year, reading levels improved by a factor of 1.54 for mentored children as compared to improvement of 1.04 in a comparison group of nonmentored children; and a 78 percent positive change in the Student Academic Self-Concept Inventory, which reflects such things as being interested in school, caring about grades, completing assignments in a timely manner, and feeling that school is important. Additionally, attendance is up from 1998 and the campus has never looked better, thanks to*

Table A.1
Profile of the Target Schools' Student Population

Profile Data	Devon Elementary	Gate Street Elementary	Sunnyside Middle School
Grade Level	K–5	K–5	6–8
Enrollment	487	472	1211
Ethnicity	White: 49%	Hispanic: 53%	White: 59%
	Hispanic: 39%	White: 36%	Hispanic: 24%
	Black: 9%	Black: 10%	Black: 15%
	Other: 3%	Other: 1%	Other: 2%
Free/Reduce Lunch	297 (61% of students)	354 (75% of students)	357 (31% of students)
LEP	156 (32%)	241 (51%)	194 (16%)
Migrant	26 students	30 students	36 students
Attendance	95%	96%	93%
Discipline Referrals	10% of students referred for behavior discipline	12% of students referred for behavior discipline	30% of students referred (70% of those referred are repeat offenders)

donations from the mentors.) Due in large measure to the mentoring relationships, kids come to school and love it, and mentors have become a part of the students' support systems in ways we had not even imagined: working on sports teams, helping students memorize selections for the oral language fairs, working with the students' families to develop a united parent-mentor front to keep students engaged in school. *This* is the vision we want to replicate in the new program. But Gate Street School is still challenged. Students are still at risk, and the reading gains from the "Success for All" reading program have still not gotten Gate Street students to even the 50th percentile on the SAT9 assessment. Mentoring needs to continue at Gate Street, and this new program will set a target mentor-mentee population of 80 students each year.

Devon Elementary School has similar demographics to Gate Street, and in fact resembles the Gate Street of 1998 with rapidly changing demographics. Those changing socioeconomics and a decline in test scores and in reading proficiency have caused Devon to restructure itself around reading, following the "Success for All" program that has proved successful at Gate Street. Students at Devon are underachieving for reasons similar to those stated in Gate Street's original application: They are coming to school unprepared to learn because they have no homework support, or haven't eaten or slept well, or because of poor hygiene or health habits. Most all of the parents do care about their children, but the parents often need mentoring and support themselves to help their children be successful in school.

The third target school, **Sunnyside Middle School**, is the only middle school in the Paradise Valley. Although it does not have a current mentor program, 16 mentors have "unofficially" followed their Gate Street mentees to the middle school level already and are "unofficially" supervised by the site resource staff. Next year that number will swell to 46 mentors, and the necessity of a formalized, accountable program is obvious. The need for an academic mentoring program at Sunnyside School was determined by data analysis that revealed, among other factors, a marked discrepancy between the 30 percent of the students who get A grades and the 30 percent who get Ds and Fs. Furthermore, at this grade level, the threat of violence has increased, as witnessed by several group attacks on individuals on the campus. Add to the mix more at-risk factors: (1) for boys, the emergence of gangs in Paradise Valley, and (2) for girls, the fact that in this 11- to 14-year-old population, approximately seven girls get pregnant each year at Sunnyside and more than that number engage in risky sexual behavior. Attendance at Sunnyside is on a downswing and more SARTS (Site Attendance Review Teams) took place this year than in years past. Supervision appears spotty in many homes, low academic grades and test scores exist for 30–40 percent of the population, and an alarming rate of drug and alcohol use occurs (overall, on this campus of 11- to 14-year-olds, it is estimated by administration that 30 percent of the students have tried or use alcohol regularly and 45 percent of students have used drugs). This is truly a population in need of mentoring, especially before the students move on to the high school level.

Finally, documentation of academic needs at the three targeted schools is presented in the following tables outlining the most recent SAT9 assessments. The overall scores at the elementary schools are low, but the discrepancy between the limited English proficient and the English proficient students is the most alarming. The discrepancy is even more pronounced at the middle school grades. Limited English

Table A.2
Gate Street School SAT9 National Percentile Rankings (NPR)

Grade	2nd Total	2nd LEP	3rd Total	3rd LEP	4th Total	4th LEP	5th Total	5th LEP
Reading	17	6	23	10	35	15	50	16
Math	29	16	30	13	23	12	37	18

Table A.3
Devon School SAT9 National Percentile Rankings (NPR)

Grade	2nd Total	2nd LEP	3rd Total	3rd LEP	4th Total	4th LEP	5th Total	5th LEP
Reading	39	na	22	7	41	9	41	17
Math	28	na	25	9	26	8	41	19

Table A.4
Sunnyside School SAT9 National Percentile Rankings (NPR)

Grade	6th Total	6th LEP	7th Total	7th LEP	8th Total	8th LEP
Reading	51	17	53	12	53	17
Math	57	32	51	19	57	23

proficient/English language learners will be especially targeted for the mentor program at all three schools.

In summary, the criteria for establishing the academic mentoring focus differed from school to school, but the common thread was that each school (1) was a Title I school with a large percentage of under-achieving students, especially English language learners and a growing migrant education population, (2) had an escalating population of students qualifying for free/reduced lunch (and families qualifying for Family Aid), and (3) had growing concerns about violence, especially at the middle school level.

(Also note that the Paradise Valley Boys and Girls Club is the fourth site where mentoring will take place in the next year. The club, located near the three school-site programs, will be an alternative site for those already-matched mentees from the targeted schools who need mentoring but cannot afford to miss class time. Using the newly built Boys and Girls Clubhouse will also allow the recruitment of new mentors who could not get away from work before 3 P.M. but now have up to 6 P.M. to volunteer. The objectives, goals, and strategies of the mentoring which takes place at the Boys and Girls Club will be identical to the school sites.)

Overall Program Design

The mentoring program at all sites will share common overall service goals:

1. improving student academic achievement,
2. increasing student connectedness* to school, and
3. reaching those achievement and connection goals by the recruitment and retention of 200 mentors serving 80 students at Gate Street, 60 students at Devon, and 60 students at Sunnyside Middle School.

(* NOTE: *"Connectedness" is defined as being committed to, and gaining satisfaction from, that association.*)

Students recruited for the By My Side Mentor Program will be at risk for failure in academics or will have social/emotional/behavioral problems that place them at risk. All such students are at high risk for dropping out of school, often making poor choices (drugs, alcohol, pregnancy, crime, etc.) in the process. Making certain that all students have academic proficiency in reading and math is essential, as research indicates that there is a high correlation between such proficiency and future economic success and emotional stability.

Organizational structure: The program will be structured with a *program director* who will be titled the District School-Community Resource Liaison. This will be a full-time position with responsibility for the overall functioning of the program, including, among other duties, recruitment and training of mentors, public relations, evaluation and report writing, budgeting, coordination of fundraising endeavors, and partial coverage of the Mentor Center at Gate Street School.

The individual mentor sites will be the immediate responsibility of *three part-time site-based school-community resource liaison staff members, at .6 FTE each.* Administrators at each site will have overall administration responsibility for the mentor program and the mentor program staff.

Obviously, to accomplish the mentor program goals, there must be continuous recruitment, training, matching, and support of community mentors to ensure an adequate number for the students who need mentoring.

Program procedures: The program director will recruit potential mentors. The school sites or parents will refer potential mentees. Once recruited, all potential mentors will be interviewed, screened, trained, and matched with a mentee for compatibility and complementarity by the district and site school-community resource staff (*one site person on each campus working part-time, three days a week, six hours per day; the district person will be working full-time*). By My Side mentees will receive mentoring one hour per week (*usually in one-hour blocks, but occasionally in two 30-minute blocks*) at designated mentoring locations, either in the Mentor Centers on each campus or, for some, in the mentor section of the Boys and Girls Club after school.

The mentoring program will be in operation on site three days a week (four days a week at Gate Street, manned on the fourth day by the district school-community resource staff member), staggering days so that mentoring is happening on at least one campus every weekday. Mentors will sign in at the site Mentor Center and meet with their mentees in the Center, supervised at all times by the site mentor staff. Doors are never closed to individual rooms or cubicles. (In the elementary grades the mentor escorts the mentee from the classroom, and in the middle school the mentee comes to the Center after receiving a call slip from the mentor staff.) Mentors will be allowed to mentor only one student, ensuring that each student knows he or she is "the one and only one!" Each mentor will set individualized goals/objectives with the site mentor resource staff regarding "what and how" to work with their mentee. Those individualized goals will be reassessed by staff every eight weeks at the elementary schools, following the "Success For All" reading assessment, and every six weeks at the middle school, following progress reports or the end of the trimester. Initial and ongoing training, materials, coaching, consultation, and more will be available to each mentor. Site staff will monitor the individual goals and objectives for each mentee on site. The general school site objectives are shown in the following tables.

Fiscal accountability: The By My Side program will match 200 students in need of a mentor with 200 mentors. Fiscal accountability will be assured by the maintenance of detailed records of mentoring contact

Table A.5
Gate Street/Devon Schools' By My Side Measurable Objectives

Academic Achievement Objective	Social/Behavioral Objective
90% of the mentees will demonstrate increased academic achievement by: 1. measurable growth in reading and/or math levels based on "Success For All" assessments completed every 8 weeks, 2. academic improvement reflected in SAT9 assessment, and 3. reading at grade level by the third year of being mentored.	90% of the mentees will demonstrate connectiveness to school by: 1. an increase in school attendance, 2. a decrease in behavior referrals, and 3. a measurable positive increase on the Self-Concept Inventory pre- and post-surveys.

Table A.6
Sunnyside Middle School's By My Side Measurable Objectives

Academic Achievement Objective	Social/Behavioral Objective
80% of the mentees will demonstrate increased academic achievement: 1. reflected in positive increase in grade point averages measured annually, comparing first and third trimester grades, 2. supportive documentation of academic improvement reflected in SAT9 scores, and 3. reading at grade level by the third year of being mentored.	80% of the mentees will demonstrate connectiveness to school measured by: 1. an increase in school attendance, 2. a decrease in behavior referrals and suspensions using the prior year's data as a baseline, and 3. a measurable positive increase (aggregated results) on the Resiliency Questionnaire (Section F) of the State Kids' Health Survey, measured annually.

(including the submission of all required reports such as the Academic Volunteer Quarterly and the Annual Reports), the oversight of the budget by the Paradise Valley Unified School District fiscal officer, the reconciliation of expenditures to the number of target mentor/mentee matches, and the amendment of the overall budget in the fourth quarter of each school year if the target quota of mentors is not realized. This district's mentoring program has a proven track record of fiscal accountability as indicated by its compliance with the 1998–2001 mentor program fiscal requirements.

Integration with the School's Total Educational Program and with the Community

The By My Side Mentor Program has been designed to integrate totally with the educational programs at Gate Street, Devon, and Sunnyside schools. At the two elementary schools, the mentoring program has and will supplement and support the "Success For All" (SFA) reading program, a comprehensive schoolwide reading program developed from best practices research by Johns Hopkins University. SFA debuted at Gate Street School the same year (1998) as the initial mentor grant. The two programs (SFA and mentoring) were vital links in the restructuring of Gate Street School's curriculum and bell schedule. Encouraged by the success of SFA and alarmed by its students' own falling reading scores, Devon School has elected to restructure to the SFA program, which will be implemented at that school in the fall of 2001. Mentoring at both schools will not begin until at least 10 A.M. to ensure uninterrupted SFA time each morning. The after-school mentor "satellite" location at the Boys and Girls Club will permit mentoring to continue until 6 P.M., allowing the most academically challenged students to be mentored without losing any instructional time during the regular day program. Mentoring has already provided at Gate Street (and will provide at Devon) the safety net for those students who, despite the schools' restructuring efforts, continue to fall behind academically. That additional one-on-one tutoring and mentoring provided by the adult mentors at Gate Street School has shown that one-on-one does make a difference for the students.

At Sunnyside School, the mentoring program has already been "piloted" (of sorts!): Many of the mentor-mentee relationships which began under the Gate Street School Mentor Program continued on to Sunnyside Middle School as students were promoted from the fifth grade. Several additional mentor-mentee relationships have been established informally during the past two years by members of the Paradise Valley Rotary Club as a result of contacts by the Project READ program director. That director made arrangements for the middle school's community-funded resource coordinator to oversee the 16 mentees who sustained their original mentor relationships as well as to oversee the new Rotarian mentors. (Administrators at Sunnyside Middle School testify that those mentor relationships helped to make the transition a positive one for mentees, *all of whom* are still considered to be at risk of not completing high school.) This current grant proposal, for the By My Side program, will formalize and expand the pilot program established at Sunnyside Middle School. Incoming middle school mentees will be able to continue their relationships begun at the elementary school, and new middle school students (drawn from all six elementary feeder schools and not just from Gate Street and Devon) will be able to be matched with mentors. To minimize core curricular disruptions, mentoring will take place during the student's elective period or during the after-school tutorial period. Some students may elect to meet with their mentors before school begins. Sunnyside School utilizes a family team approach that allows weekly team consultations on meeting individual student needs. This structure easily lends itself to the integration of the mentor as part of the family team's resources for the individual mentee. Teachers at all three sites have been surveyed and expressed a strong commitment to mentoring.

Coordination with community: Lasting partnerships to sustain the practice of mentoring in the community have already been set in place. The By My Side Mentoring Program has been publicly embraced by community service groups, community-based children's services, and the community at large. The current 109 mentors (93 at Gate Street; 16 at Sunnyside) have been recruited from the Paradise Valley. Most mentors are local residents; some are allowed release time by their employer (The Pizza Place, Pompeo Incorporated, Marchi Press, and Office Supply USA are the major business supporters allowing such an arrangement) to mentor students. This release-time arrangement was the result of extensive recruitment on the part of the program director and is a further indication of the integration of the program in the community. Plans have been developed to further expand the base of private businesses that allow time off for mentoring.

Service groups such as the Lions Club (which provides needed eyeglasses for mentees whose families are unable to secure them), the Rotary Club (whose members have begun to mentor at Sunnyside), and the Kiwanis Club (which has provided many mentors for the existing program and has also provided both hours of manpower in developing the mentoring site and materials and furnishings for the Mentor Center) have been community lifelines. Service organizations such as the Boys and Girls Club have already provided resources in the form of consultations and the sharing of ideas and innovations, and will provide a site for mentoring. Additional community agencies and services such as Paradise Valley Youth Guidance Center, the Family Connection, and the Youth and Family Services Collaborative will also continue to be both a resource to and supportive of the expanded Project READ, now titled By My Side.

Program Sustainability/Strategies for Institutionalizing

The original mentor program laid the foundation, in large measure, for eventual self-support. Program effectiveness and mentor-mentee satisfaction have already culminated in broad-based community support of the initial mentor project focus. That breadth of support spawned the recent establishment of a nonprofit corporation (501c3) to raise funds for the sustenance of the program, the Paradise Valley Mentoring Alliance. The three-year plan calls for eventual self-support of a districtwide program which will (when fully implemented) provide a mentor for every school-aged child in Paradise Valley in need of such nurturing. The board of that newly formed nonprofit is currently establishing a base for fundraising activities. These activities, once established as annual fund-raisers, have the capacity to provide the core of the funding base for By My Side. The coordinator, the supporters, the school staff, and the mentors themselves have, by the reaction of the children at Gate Street School, been encouraged in their efforts to continue the mentor program and expand it. It is a privilege to have a mentor at the school. It is seen as a valued norm on the campus. Students eagerly await their assignments and give each other high fives when "matches" are announced. Students not referred for services ask: "Can't I get a mentor, too?" This program will definitely not go away. The value of the relationships that have been formed with the community members is far-reaching and profound. Mentoring has become a part of the culture of the school and is rapidly becoming an established norm in the community as well. Matching grants for this proposal speak also of the program's sustainability and its longevity.

Program Quality Standards

Standard #1: An Effective Academic Mentoring Program
Develops Criteria to Identify Student Mentees

The By My Side Mentor Program will target students in grades K–8, at three school sites, who are performing academically below grade level on reading and/or math indicators (SAT9 or grades of D or F at the middle school; "Success For All" reading assessment, SAT9, or grades of D or F at the elementary level). Students with attendance problems, students needing social mentors because of peer isolation and/or rejection, and students with frequent behavior/discipline referrals may also be eligible candidates, following a recommendation from the student study team. Limited English speakers who meet the academic criteria have high priority for the program. Staff or parents may request a mentor for their child at any time. Students may also request a mentor themselves if they meet the criteria and have the permission of their parents. Students whose behavior indicates that they are at risk for gang involvement, violence, drug/alcohol use, or early sexual experimentation are also eligible for mentor consideration whether or not they currently are showing signs of academic failure.

Any parent, staff member, or student making a referral completes the mentee referral form available in the school office and school staff room. Staff receive in-service training on making referrals at the beginning of each school year in a staff meeting, and parents and students are notified of the service at parent meetings and in parent newsletters (in English and in Spanish). Community child-service organizations such as the Paradise Valley Boys and Girls Club staff and the Youth and Family Services Collaborative have reviewed the mentor application procedure and have suggested ways to make the process user-friendly. Staff, parents, and community members have been involved in the development of the eligibility criteria. Student input has been regularly sought and is seriously considered.

Standard #2: An Effective Academic Mentoring Program
Assesses Individual Student Needs and Develops
Strategies for Improving Student Performance

Once a student has been nominated for mentorship consideration on the mentee referral form, the mentor program site staff member will begin to assess the student's individual needs by analyzing: (1) student profile sheets (strengths, needs, personality traits, and desired outcomes) filled out by parents and students, (2) SAT9, (3) "Success for All" reading assessments at the elementary sites, (4) report cards, and (5) other input, including an individual consultation with the referring party and a personal interview with the student and parent. Student desire to have a mentor will also be determined during that time. If additional information is needed to fully assess student needs, the administrator and/or school counselor will be personally interviewed.

If all stakeholders are ready to move forward toward a "match," the various assessments are essential to obtain a full picture of the student's strengths *and* his or her academic performance problem areas and/or other behavior which might place him or her at risk. Once the assessment is made, the most promising mentor-mentee match can be initiated and effective strategies for the prospective mentor can be suggested.

Student objectives/plans will be individual and based on the student's needs. Identified strategies will require training on the part of the mentor. Examples might be teaching the mentor how to tutor using "Success for All" techniques. Reading specialists, school counselors, school psychologists, resource teachers, and the like have been lined up to provide in-service training sessions to mentors, depending on the needs of their mentees.

The final step here is a consistent assessment of the effectiveness of the strategies. Regular opportunities to meet with the site mentor staff to discuss strategies can be scheduled into any workday. Monthly mentor training meetings provide a forum for those regular discussions. The academic data, such as the "Success For All" reading progress assessments every eight weeks, will be made available to the mentor program and discussed with the mentor and the mentee. Student input will be regularly obtained.

Standard #3: An Effective Academic Mentoring Program Follows a Well-Designed Plan for Recruiting Mentors

The recruitment plan for Project READ was highly successful and will be replicated. By My Side will continue to recruit from the Latino Cultural Center for bilingual, bicultural mentors, as well as from the Kiwanis and Rotary Clubs, from the churches that advertise the mentor program in their bulletins and do active recruitment themselves, and from the business community. The *Paradise Valley Index Tribune* will continue to give liberal space in the twice-weekly local newspaper to recruit mentors and/or contributions to the mentor program. The districtwide program coordinator, Ms. Johnston, has actively recruited at local wellness fairs, town center events, and the local community center and will continue to do so. An interesting brochure and a compelling video of the program have been developed to add to the recruiting efforts. With the addition of two new schools to the mentor program, increased efforts will be made to recruit new mentors and to ensure a significant pool of mentors to find the right match for each student. By My Side will take care not just in making matches, but in making the "right match." Such care may mean that, at times, mentors are waiting for mentees and vice versa. The By My Side Mentor Program will continue the same Project READ philosophy that the matching process is a key element in the future success of the relationship.

Standard #4: An Effective Academic Mentoring Program Follows a Detailed Plan for Selecting and a Thorough Process for Screening Every Mentor

The selection process for By My Side is precise. Mentors need to be role models. They need to have basic academic skills and to be productive members of society. Since a large segment of our target population is non-English-speaking, Spanish-speaking mentors will continue to be actively pursued through recruitment at churches and local organizations. All applicants to the program must complete a mentor profile sheet detailing personal information, language proficiency, background, interests, personality traits, experience working with children, schedules, and preferences for age and gender. They must list references. All potential mentors receive a personal interview. The expectation has been that each mentor must commit to one hour per week for one year. Beginning in the fall of 2001, that commitment will be three years, as the school, parents, mentors, mentees, and mentor staff discussed and decided that a one-year commitment is not enough to meet a child's need for a caring, involved adult.

The By My Side Mentor Program will require all mentor volunteers to be fingerprinted, have a criminal background check, and be fully cleared on both items before they are allowed to meet their mentees. An "expedite fee" will be included with each fingerprint set to ensure that the results are returned in a timely manner. All prospective mentors are made aware of all requirements before they begin the required paperwork.

Standard #5: An Effective Academic Mentoring Program Establishes an Orientation Program for Mentors, Mentees, and Other Interested Parties

The new mentors' orientation session presents an overview of the mentoring program and it lets each participant know the expectations of the program as well as the level of commitment (one hour per week during the school year, three years' duration minimum). Included in the training (and handbook) are suggestions for tutoring students, encouraging students, and redirecting negative behavior. Each new mentor receives the mentor handbook, complete with expectations of mentors, a campus map, a calendar of the school year, class schedules, handouts with tips for tutoring, a behavior management suggestion sheet, and statements explaining the program policies and procedures. Each of the three campuses will have an individualized handbook to reflect the uniqueness of its program and site. Nonmentors are welcome at certain sessions to learn more about mentoring.

Standard #6: An Effective Academic Mentoring Program Develops and Institutes an Ongoing Training and Support Plan for All Mentors

Two six-week evening sessions will be offered for mentors on each campus (spring and fall), with topics focused on enhancing child-adult relationships, on developing communication skills, on behavior management, and on cultural awareness and appreciation. Mentors will learn strategies both for academic tutoring and for appropriate encouragement (rather than "praise").

There is an ongoing plan that involves support for both the mentors and the mentees. Ongoing peer support for mentors includes the monthly roundtable meetings, which will be at each site's mentor center. At such meetings, guest speakers from community mental health and counseling agencies will lead the discussion as an in-kind donation to the program. In the past, roundtable meetings have been held at breakfast time, but for the By My Side Mentor Program, times will be alternated between mornings and early evenings. Role-playing of typical and atypical mentee-mentor situations have been successful in the past and will be further developed for future roundtable discussions. An important component of these trainings will be the development of good communication skills for use in the mentor-mentee relationship. Mentors will receive in-service training using the Cooperative Discipline (1998) method by Linda Albert. The Adlerian-based method is simple to use, gives mentors immediate tools with which to respond to mentee concerns, and is respectful, encouraging, and appropriate for all ethnicities and genders. Cooperative Discipline builds on the strength of the students to appropriately support and acknowledge the students' accomplishments. School staff and others are invited to attend both the initial sessions of the Cooperative Discipline presentation, in which the "goals of student misbehavior" and the "goals of their good behavior" are introduced, as well as subsequent sessions in which ongoing mentor-mentee relationship issues are discussed. School staff (counselors, psychologists, etc.) are available to meet with mentors regarding mentee problems at any time. Voice mail and fax machines are on 24 hours a day at the mentor centers to facilitate mentors leaving messages for the coordinator.

Standard #7: An Effective Academic Mentoring Program Develops and Implements an Explicit Matching Strategy for Mentees and Mentors

Creating matches between mentors and mentees is complicated, and it is one of the most crucial steps in the process. First, the assessment of the strengths and needs of the student is compiled by the program staff (staff will include the site and districtwide resource coordinators, the site administrator, and, if appropriate, the site school counselor). Subsequently, an assessment is completed based on the mentor profile sheet and notes from the personal interview. Considerations include matching mentee needs with mentor strengths, personality profiles, hobbies or interests, and, for some, looking at gender issues (for example, if a male or female role model is needed). The program director uses ingenuity at times to overcome scheduling conflicts when all other criteria lead to a match.

Once the match is envisioned, all parties involved, including the parents of the mentee, are informed regarding the expectations and liabilities of the relationship. A meeting is arranged, with both mentor and mentee knowing they could choose not to continue. By the time of the visit, however, so much has been analyzed about a match that 99 percent of the time it "takes." Only once in the last three years has a match not worked. In that case the procedure for "unmatching" was followed and the situation turned out to be a win-win for all involved.

For the 99 percent of matches that work, each person (student, parent, mentor) signs the expectation agreement (EA). This year, a staff analysis of the EA revealed areas of deficiency that have since been revised for the By My Side program, including an expansion of the time commitment made by both the mentor and the mentee.

Standard #8: An Effective Academic Mentoring Program Ensures Ongoing Monitoring and Supervision of the Mentor-Mentee Relationship

The mentor handbook clearly outlines the expectations for mentors in the program. All mentoring occurs in the Mentor Center on campus. (In the spring of 2002 a satellite site will be established at the Boys and Girls Club for after-school mentor sessions.) Physical supervision of the mentor-mentee meetings is provided for all contact. The doors to mentoring rooms are never closed. All mentors check in at the Mentor Center before commencing the mentoring session. In the rare case that a relationship must be terminated prematurely, the program director will be involved and care will be taken to sensitively end the relationship. No relationship will be ended without advance warning and without allowing for termination and processing of feelings. Care will be taken to ensure a smooth transition, including a "graduation" ritual for the mentee.

Check-ins on the progress of the mentor-mentee relationship occur on a regular basis with both mentor and mentee (separately), and these check-ins are initiated by the site mentor staff.

Standard #9: An Effective Academic Mentoring Program Recognizes Mentor and Mentee Contributions and Achievements

Both mentors and mentees will receive immediate feedback from the program director while on campus for their weekly sessions. Informal feedback will be received from staff, administration, and other students. Every eight weeks, SFA reading results are obtained and will be shared with the mentees, especially when progress is noted. Public "thank-you" notifications will be a regular occurrence. Public awareness will continue to be promoted in the *Paradise Index Tribune* (at cost and/or in-kind). The program director will continue to speak regularly at school board meetings, service club luncheons, and grassroots community gatherings. The Paradise Valley Chamber of Commerce and the Paradise Valley Business and Education Roundtable meeting will be included in the circuit. Supporting businesses and sponsors will be especially honored at an end-of-the-year celebration with appreciations and a plaque. Quarterly gatherings of a festive nature will bring parents, mentors, mentees, and the community together and have already developed an esprit de corps among the mentor-mentee group as a whole at Gate Street. This practice will extend to the other sites.

Standard #10: An Effective Academic Mentoring Program Evaluates Whether the Program Is Successful in Improving Individual Student Performance and Achievement

Data collection for the purpose of assessing the effectiveness of the By My Side Mentor Program will be an ongoing, clearly delineated process. Although the program service objective is to recruit and retain 200 mentors for 200 mentees and have them each meet one hour per week, the most meaningful data will be collected regarding the individual student performance and achievement outcomes. Those objectives are outlined in section "b" of the Overall Program Design of this grant proposal. The site coordinator keeps the data on the program as a whole. This data tracks both the number of students and the number of mentors in the program, and includes the frequency, duration, retention, and total hours involved in mentoring. The By My Side Mentor Program has a multifaceted approach to data collection, beginning with the collection of "Success for All" reading assessments every 8 weeks at Devon and Gate Street Schools. Progress reports or report cards are available every 4 weeks. At the middle school, report cards are available every 12 weeks and progress reports every 6 weeks. For students at risk of failing, such reports can be requested every week. Data will be collected on each individual student's academic performance and achievement. Data will also be gathered on the mentor group as a whole and on a control group of students at each school site.

A corresponding group will be established at each school site to compare changes in grades, attendance and discipline, and improvement in reading and/or math scores on standardized testing such as the SAT9. Comparisons of the "Success for All" assessments will be monitored. The control groups will be selected randomly from each of the three sites.

The program evaluation will use outcome and process components developed by Elizabeth Temple, Ph.D., a consultant from Miller University. Dr. Temple will establish the evaluation plan, collect the data appropriate to the evaluation, analyze all the data collected, and prepare the final report for the Office of the Secretary of Education, according to the reporting guidelines established by the program.

Appendix D: Sample Volunteer Recruitment Letter

Dear (Contact),

My name is Rachel Denton and I am a mentor program coordinator for Paradise Valley Unified School District. I am writing to provide a description of our new mentoring program and to ask for your help.

Paradise Valley recently implemented the By My Side Mentoring Program. This program seeks to provide students extra one-on-one help to improve their reading scores, while connecting them with a caring adult who, along with family and teachers, offers underachieving students encouragement, support, and incentives for attending school.

Research links one-on-one mentor support to improvements in at-risk children and adolescents' psychological, social, academic, and career functioning. Mentoring provides mentors with an opportunity to maintain active roles in their communities while gaining a sense of fulfillment. Successful mentoring programs extend beyond the one-to-one relationship and require the involvement of individuals and organizations in the community.

I am writing to ask your organization to support the By My Side program by helping us recruit volunteer mentors. We believe that there are many individuals in your organization who care about the well-being of at-risk youth and might be motivated to give back to the community by serving as a mentor.

In a few days I will be calling you to schedule a brief meeting to discuss our mentoring program. I hope that you will consider how your organization can partner with By My Side to assist the young people in our community, provide benefit to your employees, and lead to beneficial effects on our society.

Sincerely,
Rachel Denton
Mentor Program Coordinator

Appendix E: Mentor Application

Personal Information

Name: _____

Mailing Address: _____

Home Phone: _____ Work Phone: _____

E-mail Address: _____

Fax: _____

Person to contact in an emergency:

_____

Emergency Phone Number: _____

Date of Birth: _____/_____/_____

Sex: _____M _____F

Marital Status: _____

Ethnicity: _____

How did you hear about the program?

_____

Previous residences during the last five years:

Address: _____ City_____

State_____ Dates_____

Address: _____ City_____

State_____ Dates_____

Address: _____ City_____

State_____ Dates_____

JOB HISTORY

Employment History (past 10 years)
Employer's Name: _____
Supervisor: _____
Address: _____
City/State/Zip: _____
Phone: _____
Your Position/Title: _____
Employer's Name: _____
Supervisor: _____
Address: _____
City/State/Zip: _____
Phone: _____
Your Position/Title: _____
Employer's Name: _____
Supervisor: _____
Address: _____
City/State/Zip: _____
Phone: _____
Your Position/Title: _____

Can we contact your employer/supervisor(s) as a reference? _____
If no, please explain:

_____
_____
_____

EDUCATION

Highest level attained: _____
Name and location of last school attended:

_____

LEGAL HISTORY

Have you ever been investigated for or charged with any offense involving a person under the age of 18? _____ If yes, please explain

_____

_____

_____

Have you been investigated for or charged with any offense in the last 10 years? _____
If yes, please explain

_____

_____

_____

MEDICAL HISTORY

Are you currently a user of illegal drugs? _____ If yes, please explain

_____

_____

Have you had problems with or been treated for alcohol or drug abuse within the last 5 years? ___
If yes, please explain

_____

_____

_____

Do you have any physical or mental condition that would limit your ability to be a mentor?_____
If yes, please explain

_____

_____

_____

REFERENCES

Name   Address   Phone Number

_____

_____

_____

_____

I understand that disclosure of the information that I have provided in this application will be limited to those employees of Paradise Valley Unified School District (PVUSD) and volunteers who participate in the selection and evaluation of mentors for the PVUSD's By My Side Mentoring Program. I further understand that, if my application is denied, I am not entitled to an explanation of the reasons for such denial, nor am I entitled to a review of such action by PVUSD or its Board of Trustees. I represent that all of the information I have provided in this application is true and correct and understand that such information will be relied upon by the By My Side Mentoring Program in considering my application.

_____   _____
Applicant Signature   Date

Appendix F: Mentor Profile Sheet

PERSONAL INFORMATION

Name:
_____

Mailing Address:
_____

Home Phone: _____

Work Phone: _____

E-mail Address: _____

Occupation: _____

Employer: _____

Person to contact in an emergency:
_____

Emergency Phone Number: _____

Date of Birth: _____/_____/_____

Sex: _____M _____F

Ethnicity: _____

How did you hear about the program?
_____

REFERENCES

Name   Phone Number

_____

_____

_____

_____

_____

BACKGROUND INFORMATION:

Hobbies/Interests:

_____

Please list any previous experience working with children:

_____

Please list three traits that best describe you:

_____

_____

PLACEMENT INFORMATION:

Languages spoken:

_____

My primary interest is in helping a child succeed:
( ) Academically   ( ) Socially   ( ) Both
I prefer to work with ( ) Boy   ( ) Girl ( ) Either
Age Preference: ( ) 5–8 years   ( ) 8–12 years   ( ) 13–14 years
Time Availability: Days Available Best Times to Mentor

_____

_____

_____

Appendix G: Mentee Application

Date: _____ / _____ / _____

PARTICIPANT (MENTEE)

Name:_____ Birth Date: _____ / _____ / _____
Age:_____ Grade:_____
Address:_____
Home Phone: _____
School:_____
Teacher:_____

PARENT(S), GUARDIAN, OR RESPONSIBLE ADULT

Name(s): _____
Home Phone: _____
Work Phone: _____
Address:_____
Referred by (or self-referral):_____
Phone: _____
Reason for referral:

_____

PERSONAL SURVEY

1. I have _____ brothers and _____ sisters.

2. I am (circle one) the oldest   the youngest
   in the middle

3. I live with my (circle all that apply)
   Mom   Dad   Stepdad   Stepmom
   Grandmother   Other:_____

4. Complete the following: I would like to have a mentor because . . . (include what you would like your mentor to help you with):_____

5. The first thing I would like to tell my mentor about me is:

6. The kind of job I would like to have when I get out of high school or college is:_____

7. If I could change something about myself, I would change:

   _____

8. The class I like best in school is:

   _____

9. The class I have the most trouble with is:

   _____

10. When I don't do as well as I can in school, it is because:

    _____
    _____

11. I get into trouble with my teacher: _____never _____
    sometimes _____very often
    If "very often," explain why:

    _____
    _____

12. I would like to learn more about:

    _____

13. If I could change one thing about my family, I would change:

    _____
    _____

14. Three things that bug me are:

    _____
    _____
    _____

15. Three things that are exciting:

_____

_____

_____

16. Three things that are very boring:

_____

_____

_____

17. The best thing that has ever happened to me:

_____

_____

_____

18. What makes me angry is:

_____

_____

19. This is what I do when I get angry:

_____

_____

20. The most important person in my life at this time is:

_____

21. If someone asked me how I get along with the other kids at school, I would say:

_____

_____

_____

22. This is what I like to do most in my free time:

_____

_____

_____

23. There are 5 things that I like to do:

_____

_____

_____

_____

_____

_____

24. My favorite TV shows/movies are:

   _____

25. Outdoor activities that I enjoy:

   _____

   _____

26. My favorite sport to watch or play is:

   _____

27. These are my favorite books or magazines:

   _____

28. When I think of a best friend or a parent, this is what I like best about that person (those people):

29. The three words that best describe me are:

   _____

Glossary

Advocate A person who supports and defends another person; someone who is positively and proactively involved in another person's life. "Many young people, especially those living in communities where economic and interpersonal resources are scarce, have been deprived of a network of role models, support persons, and *advocates* that, in yesteryear, helped them to make good decisions and develop healthy plans for the future."

Affective Having to do with emotions and the emotional domain; arising from feelings; emotional. "While the act of mentoring possesses many important *affective* elements common to a friendship, the mentor-protégé relationship is not merely about companionship or camaraderie as is commonly the case between friends."

Age segregation The intentional or unintentional separation of one group from another on the basis of age. "Barriers to such [significant, supportive] relationships [with adults] include *age segregation*, school budget crises, and the changing structure of family and community."

At risk: In danger of becoming involved with drugs, alcohol, teenage pregnancy, gangs, and/or dropping out of school. "Additionally, a variety of mentoring programs focus on young people *at risk* for certain problematic developmental outcomes, such as dropping out of school, school failure, substance abuse, delinquency, pregnancy, or violence."

Classical mentoring The traditional mentoring model of one adult with one student; this model is often found in the business community where a more experienced worker mentors a new worker.

Compensatory relationships Relationships that help support students toward positive development. In a mentoring context, mentors and mentees should be matched in such a way that the mentor helps the mentee compensate for areas of either personal (i.e., skills) or environmental (e.g., lack of role models) deficits, and skills that he or she is lacking. For example, a student who has trouble with math might be matched with a mentor who excels in math, or an angry student might be matched with a mentor with skills in anger management. *"Compensatory relationships* with [people] who care about them allow children to create a new, more positive understanding of their social world, and provide them with resources to draw on to combat developmental challenges."

Confidentiality Privacy or secrecy; for mentors, information regarding a mentee and his or her family is considered "out of bounds" for discussion. The primary goal should always be to protect the mentee. "Protection of *confidentiality* also poses a significant concern, and program directors must decide in advance who will have access to e-mail exchanges."

Cross-age tutoring The involvement of younger students and older students in tutoring or mentoring situations, typically with at least a three-year age difference between the older and younger students. *"Cross-age tutoring* traditionally involves linking students together across at least four grade levels to provide mentoring and academic support to the younger student."

Extrafamilial Refers to significant people who are not blood relatives. "Research on fostering resiliency in at-risk children and adolescents consistently highlights the importance of adult-child relationships, including the important role of nonparent adults and *extrafamilial* sources of support."

Formal mentoring Mentoring is completed under the supervision of a specific mentoring program. "Despite the many benefits of natural mentoring, and the frequency with which this form of mentoring relationship occurs, the popularity of *formal mentoring* programs has grown in recent decades." "Formal mentoring programs operate under the assumption that the benefits of natural mentoring can be replicated in prearranged relationship 'matches.'"

Gifted Having great natural ability or talent. "Mentoring also offers benefits to talented, motivated, and *gifted* youth, an often-overlooked group of students in need of support."

Informal mentoring Mentoring that occurs through the initiation of a mentee who seeks out the support and guidance of someone more experienced. This type of mentoring often occurs in business and academia.

Instrumental mentoring Mentoring characterized by activities such as advising, teaching, coaching, guiding, and advocating. "Sullivan (1996) is concerned that adherence to a model of *instrumental mentoring* may serve to unwittingly perpetuate the male-oriented status quo, much of which she feels is unhealthy for girls."

King Odysseus From Homer's *Odyssey;* King of Ithaca and a Greek leader in the Trojan Wars who wanders 10 years after the war before reaching home. While King Odysseus fights in the Trojan Wars, he leaves his son, Telemachus, in the care of his old and trusted friend, Mentor. "The term 'mentoring' is alleged to have its origin in Homer's *Odyssey*, when an older friend named Mentor cared for King Odysseus' son, Telemachus, while the king fought in the Trojan Wars."

Life skills Basic skills whose acquisition is necessary for healthy adult development. Examples are organization, honesty, responsibility, problem solving, friendship, and caring. "These activities [that a mentor may initiate] include offering advice on concrete career skills such as how to apply for a job, as well as general *life skills* such as budgeting."

Match The selection and linkage or pairing of a mentor and a mentee based on certain criteria. "Formal mentoring programs operate under the assumption that the benefits of natural mentoring can be replicated in prearranged relationship '*matches.*' These *matches* entail a third party, such as an agency, bringing together a young person and an adult who previously did not know each other. It is hoped that, with careful cultivation, meaningful relationships can grow."

Mentee The person who is mentored; nearly synonymous with protégé.

Mentor A trusted counselor, guide, tutor, coach, and friend. From the character Mentor in Homer's *Odyssey*, a friend of King Odysseus who was entrusted with the education of Odysseus' son, Telemachus. "In leaving Telemachus in the care of *Mentor*, the king not only entrusted his child's safety to *Mentor*, but also his son's physical, emotional, and educational development."

Mentoring The process of developing and nurturing a caring, supportive relationship with another person, whereby the mentor serves as a role model.

Muse From Greek mythology; any of the nine sister goddesses presiding over song and poetry and the arts and sciences. A source of inspiration. "A *muse* denotes a mythological character that offers inspiration while recognizing the creative potential of those whom they serve. In this relationship-oriented (*muse*) model, the focus moves to the girls' inner resources and potentials, rather than attempting to instruct girls in areas of a perceived deficit or to direct them toward a specific, concrete goal."

Natural mentoring Mentoring that occurs on its own, not through a formal mentoring program. This often occurs within communities when older members offer support and guidance to youth.

Protective factor/protective influence An influence that helps a person to maintain or develop resilience. "Environmental *protective factors* that help at-risk youth overcome adversity include a secure emotional connection with a caregiver and social support from individuals in the wider community and extended family systems."

Protégé Nearly synonymous with mentee; a person who is trained or whose career is furthered by a person of experience, prominence, or influence. The term is often used when referring to mentoring relationships in business and academia. The mentor usually initiates the relationship, and the mentee is typically selected based on talent. "The classical style encompasses a specific goal or goals-directed relationship in which the mentor directly guides the *protégé* toward a future objective."

Psychosocial Involving both psychological and social aspects. "From a philosophical standpoint, *psychosocial* mentoring encourages overall personal growth."

Resiliency The quality of being able to recover from or adjust easily to adversity or challenge. "Research on fostering *resiliency* in at-risk children and adolescents consistently highlights the importance of adult-child relationships, including the important role of nonparent adults and extrafamilial sources of support."

Role model A person whose behavior in a particular role is imitated by others.

Screening The process of determining which individuals would make appropriate mentors and eliminating those who are not appropriate for any children. This process also involves categorizing potential mentors according to their appropriateness for mentoring particular types or groups of children.

Self-efficacy The sense of feeling empowered or effective; feeling like one has the power or control to accomplish things.

Self-esteem A confidence and satisfaction in oneself; self-respect.

Social skills The ability to relate interpersonally.

Social support Forces or individuals that sustain a person in society.

"In a global sense, mentoring can benefit any young person needing and seeking extra support and guidance, as *social support* is key to human development."

Supervision The process of monitoring the progress and relationships of mentors and mentees.

Telemachus From Homer's *Odyssey;* the son of King Odysseus who is left in the care of Mentor, his father's old, trusted friend, when his father goes away to fight in the Trojan Wars. Telemachus was Mentor's protégé.

Index

About the Authors

MAUREEN A. BUCKLEY is a Licensed Psychologist and an Associate Professor of Counseling at Sonoma State University, Rohnert Park, California. She has published numerous articles regarding youth issues and volunteers as a mentor in various youth programs. Her clinical experience is in the area of family and youth counseling.

SANDRA HUNDLEY ZIMMERMANN is a Licensed Clinical Social Worker and both an Associate Professor of Counseling at Sonoma State University and an Adjunct Professor at Capella University. In addition to published articles, she has written numerous grants in support of mentoring efforts and she mentors youth in a school-based program.